The Political Responsibilities of Everyday Bystanders

The Political Responsibilities
of Everyday Bystanders

STEPHEN L. ESQUITH

The Pennsylvania State University Press
University Park, Pennsylvania

Some of the following material is adapted from
"Toward a Democratic Rule of Law: East and West,"
Political Theory 27, no. 3 (1999): 334–56 (courtesy
of Sage Publications); "War, Political Violence,
and Service Learning," *Teaching Philosophy* 23,
no. 3 (2000): 241–54 (courtesy of the Philosophy
Documentation Center); "Complicity in Mass
Violence," *Philosophy and Public Policy Quarterly* 24
(2004): 28–35; "Reenacting Mass Violence," *Polity* 35
(2003): 513–34; and "An Experiment in Democratic
Political Education," *Polity* 36 (2003): 73–90.

Library of Congress Cataloging-in-Publication Data

Esquith, Stephen L. (Stephen Lawrence), 1949–
The political responsibilities of everyday bystanders /
    Stephen L. Esquith
    p.   cm.
Includes bibliographical references and index.
Summary: "A discussion of how everyday bystanders
can learn to recognize and meet their shared and
institutional political responsibilities for hunger,
poverty, famine, civil war, wars of conquest and
invasion, epidemics and pandemics, and genocide"—
Provided by publisher.
ISBN 978-0-271-03667-0 (cloth : alk. paper)
ISBN 978-0-271-03668-7 (pbk. : alk. paper)
1. Political participation.
2. Democracy.
3. Social participation.
I. Title.

JF799.E78 2010
302'.14—dc22
2010008198

It is the policy of The Pennsylvania State University
Press to use acid-free paper. Publications on uncoated
stock satisfy the minimum requirements of American
National Standard for Information Sciences—
Permanence of Paper for Printed Library Material,
ANSI Z39.48–1992.

For Shirley, Dave, and Amy

The 1994 elections in South Africa brought an end to Apartheid and introduced a period of inquiry and national retribution represented by the Truth and Reconciliation Commission. In this process, amnesty was given by the new government for crimes committed for the sake of the Apartheid government in return for full disclosure of those crimes by their perpetrators. Not by chance, in the years following Apartheid, Kentridge's drawings and films began to express the weight of having been one of the privileged few, exploring the notion and implications of indirect responsibility.

—Carolyn Christov-Bakargiev,
"On Defectibility as a Resource: William Kentridge's Art of Imperfection, Lack, and Falling Short," in *William Kentridge* (2004)

Where grace is concerned, it is impossible for man to come anywhere near a puppet.

—Heinrich von Kleist,
On the Marionette Theatre (1810), trans. Idris Parry

What is our responsibility to the people whose stories we are using as raw fodder for the play? There seemed to be an awkwardness in getting an actor to play the witnesses—the audience being caught halfway between having to believe in the actor for the sake of the story, and also not believe in the actor for the sake of the actual witness who existed out there but was not the actor. Using a puppet made this contradiction palpable. There is no attempt to make the audience think the wooden puppet or its manipulator is the actual witness. The puppet becomes the medium through which the testimony can be heard.

—William Kentridge,
"Director's Note," *Ubu and the Truth Commission* (1998)

So far as we feel sympathy, we feel we are not accomplices to what caused the suffering. Our sympathy proclaims our innocence as well as our impotence. To that extent, it can be (for all good intentions) an impertinent—if not inappropriate—response. To set aside the sympathy we extend to others beset in war and murderous politics for a reflection on how our privileges are located on the same map as their suffering, and may—in ways we might prefer not to imagine—be linked to their suffering, as the wealth of some may imply the destitution of others, is a task for which the painful, stirring images supply only an initial spark.

—Susan Sontag,
Regarding the Pain of Others (2003)

Contents

Illustrations

Fig. 1   A malnourished, dehydrated woman in Gourma-Rharous, Mali, 1985. Photo by Sebastião Salgado. Courtesy Contact Press Images Inc.

Fig. 2   A witness puppet testifies in *Ubu and the Truth Commission*. Jane Taylor, William Kentridge, and the Handspring Puppet Company. Photo by Ruphin Coudyzer.

Fig. 3   Mine workers in the Sierra Pelada gold mine, Brazil, 1986. Photo by Sebastião Salgado. Courtesy Contact Press Images Inc.

Fig. 4   A close-up of mine workers in the Sierra Pelada gold mine, Brazil, 1986. Photo by Sebastião Salgado. Courtesy Contact Press Images Inc.

Fig. 5   A trader puppet in *Ubu and the Truth Commission*. Jane Taylor, William Kentridge, and the Handspring Puppet Company. Photo by Ruphin Coudyzer.

Fig. 6   The climactic moment in *Promethean Fire* by the Paul Taylor Dance Company. Photograph © 2002 Louis Greenfield.

Fig. 7   Simon Srebnik in *Shoah* (1985). Directed by Claude Lanzmann.

Fig. 8   A close-up of Simon Srebnik in *Shoah* (1985). Directed by Claude Lanzmann.

Fig. 9   A "human pyramid" of prisoners at Abu Ghraib. AP Images.

Acknowledgments

....

This book has two related purposes. The first is to map the political responsibilities of a particular set of bystanders, those I call everyday bystanders to severe violence. The second purpose logically presupposes the first but is my primary concern: to describe how teachers, writers, artists, filmmakers, and other intellectuals can contribute to the democratic political education of these everyday bystanders so that they can better recognize and meet these responsibilities.

Political responsibilities, unlike moral duties and legal responsibilities, are not purely individual. Individuals incur political responsibilities by virtue of their membership in groups, institutions, and collectivities. In exploring the political education of everyday bystanders, I will be concerned with the responsibilities of these larger entities as well as the shared responsibilities of their members.

My work has been as a teacher, and most of the individuals who have influenced this project have been in the academy and in an overlapping circle of family and friends. It has been through these institutions and among these groups that I have developed the idea that there are such things as political responsibilities of everyday bystanders. I owe these colleagues, friends, and relatives much more than an acknowledgement, but an acknowledgement is one good place to start.

For almost twenty years my colleagues in the Department of Philosophy and now the Residential College in the Arts and Humanities at Michigan State University have created an atmosphere in which I have been able to pursue my interests in community service-learning, ethics and development, and the scholarship of teaching, learning, and engagement. The arguments in this book are one result of this work. I have had the opportunity regularly to present several parts of the book to faculty and graduate students in our interdisciplinary Ethics and Development Program. I am especially grateful to Fred Gifford, Paul Thompson, and Judy Andre in the Department of Philosophy for their support for this program and their interest in my work. Dick Peterson and Martin Benjamin in the department also have provided valuable advice along the way. Scot Yoder, who traveled with me from Philosophy to the new Residential College, has shared my commitment to practical philosophy and ethics, and I have benefited greatly from our years together. Among the many students who have offered their criticisms and suggestions to me, I am most grateful to Mike Liberato, Steve Wandmacher, John Ouko, Anna Malavisi, Kwangsu Mok, Seth Morton, Nicole Rivera, and Kyle Martin.

My interests in democratic political education also have been sharpened through collaborative work with MSU colleagues in other departments and programs. Two colleagues who have been especially helpful in introducing me to Mali have been agricultural economists John Staatz and Niama Nango Dembélé, both of whom have participated in the Ethics and Development Program. David Cooper, director of the MSU Public Humanities Collaborative; Karen Casey, director of the MSU Community Service-Learning Center; and Cynthia Chalou—who has overseen the Mali study abroad program that Yoby Guindo, my wife, Chris Worland, and I have developed—have been sources of constant encouragement and sound advice. Colleagues in the Offices of the Provost and International Studies and Programs have provided consistent institutional support for various special projects and grants, including the Residential College's Association of American Colleges and Universities Core Commitments Project, its Carnegie Academy for the Scholarship of Teaching and Learning–CASTL Institutional Leadership Program, and a U.S. State Department grant for a cultural exchange program on faith and community between the University of Bamako, Mali, and the Residential College in the Arts and Humanities. I am especially grateful to Karen Klomparens, Rob Glew, Ann Allegra, Jeff Riedinger, Hiram Fitzgerald, Deb DeZure, and Doug Estry for their active support of these programs.

Colleagues at other universities also have played a formative role in my understanding of the opportunities for democratic political education. I am indebted to the U.S. Fulbright Scholar Program for the opportunity to work with colleagues and students at two universities in other countries, Adam Mickiewicz University in Poznan, Poland, in 1990–91 and the University of Bamako in Mali in 2005–6.

I am grateful to several scholars in Poland who introduced me to the challenges that they and their university faced in the first years of the post-communist era, including Leszek Nowak of the Instytut Filozofii, Marek Wilczynski of the Instytut Filologii Angielskiej, Michal Buchowski of the Instytut Etnologii i Antropologii, and Marek Ziolkowski of the Instytut Socjologii at AMU. It was through conversations and scholarly collaborations with them that I began to understand the thin line that separates consolidated democracies from so-called transitional democracies, and how political education can serve a democratic purpose for both.

In Mali, in addition to the indispensable help I have received from Nango Dembélé and Yoby Guindo, I am also indebted to Fafre Samake, Mamadou Moussa Diarra, and Mamoudou Seydou Traoré at the Institut Polytechnique Rural de Formation et de Recherche Appliquée, Ibrahim Traore at the University of Bamako, and Famaka Kyabou at the Centre de Langues at the University of Bamako. They have made it possible for me to teach and learn from both Malian students and students from the United States in Mali about the diverse ethical dilemmas Mali has faced since its turn toward democracy in the 1990s. I also wish to thank Mary Speer and Stephanie Syptak, the public diplomacy officers at the U.S. embassy, and their assistant, Gaoussou Mariko, for their help and encouragement.

David A. Crocker and Verna Gehring at the University of Maryland's Institute for Philosophy and Public Policy have offered valuable editorial encouragement for some of the main ideas of the book that appeared in the *Philosophy and Public Policy Quarterly*. Nicholas Xenos at the University of Massachusetts, Amherst, and former editor of *Polity* published two articles that prefigure arguments in the book; also, as one of the external reviewers of the manuscript for the Pennsylvania State University Press, he has been a source of critical encouragement.

Several other individuals have read parts of the manuscript and offered valuable comments and suggestions. Anita Skeen in the Residential College has helped me begin to understand the importance of voice in poetry. Debra Nails in the Department of Philosophy at MSU and William Levitan of Grand Valley State University regularly have offered sound advice as I have ventured back into the ancient texts they know so well. Eric Gorham, now at Quest University in Canada, has helped me better understand the relationship between civic engagement and academic work. Joan Tronto of the Department of Political Science, University of Minnesota, Twin Cities, has helped me see how my argument intersects with feminist ethics of care. Tom Wartenberg in the Department of Philosophy at Mount Holyoke College provided early critical comments on the project, and his writings on film and contributions to philosophy for younger children are resources on which I continue to rely heavily. John Wallace at the University of Minnesota, and one of the co-founders of the Jane Addams School in the Twin Cities, is responsible for introducing me to Addams's work. His long-standing commitment to civic engagement and the modest, effective way he has conveyed it to others beautifully embody her spirit. It was also through John that I met Wayne Meisel, president of the Bonner Foundation, whose developmental model of service-learning and civic engagement has informed my own practice.

Many people outside the academy also have helped me learn how the work they and other intellectuals do is related to democratic political education. Maria Diarra and Debbie Fredo, co-founders of l'Ecole Ciwara and l'Institut pour l'Education Populaire in Mali, have introduced many of my American students to an inspiring staff of young teachers and students in their community school in Mali. Through my wife, Chris Worland—for more than two decades a teacher of children with special needs, a former member of the political theater company Mass Transit Street Theater, and a fabric artist—I have seen the relationship between art, education, and democratic politics come alive. It also has been through her efforts in Mali that I have learned something about the traditional bogolan artists Nakunte Diarra and her son Bindé Traoré, who play an important role in the concluding section of this book.

Other members of my family have been important in sustaining the project and contributing in substantive ways to the arguments in the book. Our two children, Sam and Sunny, accompanied us to Poland in 1990–91, and through their experiences we were able to understand the strengths as well as the weaknesses of the Polish primary and secondary education system during a time of democratic political transformation. Sunny's experience there as a Korean American schoolgirl at a time when Poland was relatively homogeneous, compared to the home in Michigan that she had known for eight years, allowed us to glimpse briefly what many immigrant families encounter routinely. Sam's later experience as a Peace Corps volunteer in Mali between 2000 and 2002 had an important influence on our decision to work in Mali ourselves, including a full year of teaching and working with artisans in 2005–6. Through his contacts, we also have been able to work during the last six years with the Peace Corps staff in Mali, especially Mamadou ("Sam") Samake, and I have benefited by presenting parts of the arguments in this book to Peace Corps volunteers and staff at their training center in Tubaniso. My brother Dave Esquith, who has devoted his life to the education and training of persons with disabilities, and who also served in the Peace Corps in Tunisia, has read and helped me to clarify the arguments in this book over the years.

Sandy Thatcher at the Pennsylvania State University Press has shown patience and good judgment, reading and rereading drafts, demanding more clarity, and anticipating objections. With help from him and the comments of Nick Xenos, Jim Farr, and another, anonymous reader, I feel that I have managed to make somewhat better sense of the academic trinity of teaching, research, and service through the prism of democratic political education. I am grateful to Carol Cole, whose meticulous review of earlier drafts of the manuscript has made it a much better read than it would have been otherwise, and to Nicholas Taylor, whose final copyediting has sharpened the argument in critical places. I also wish to thank Ian Gray, Michigan State University's vice president for research and graduate study, for his office's generous support for the publication of this volume. I am especially grateful to Nicole Attard for her excellent work constructing the index.

Finally, it has gradually become clearer to me during the past five years, as I have been writing this book and simultaneously working with colleagues and students at Michigan State University to launch the Residential College in the Arts and Humanities, that the two projects have been mutually reinforcing. The ideas and arguments in the book have guided my personal contributions to conversations about new programs and courses in the College, and these same conversations about engaged learning and the value of the arts and humanities have helped me press the ideas and arguments of the book into focus. The College's mission—"to weave together the passion, imagination, humor, and candor of the arts and humanities to promote individual well-being and the common good"—has informed the ideal of teaching as a political vocation I have tried to articulate in the book. I am deeply indebted to Michigan State University, my colleagues in the College, and our students for this opportunity at a time when public higher education in Michigan has been particularly hard-hit. While this is not a debt that I can repay in words alone, I hope that this book provides some support to these colleagues and students who together (in Myles Horton's words) are making this road by walking it. I've come to believe that there really is no other way to get there from here.

INTRODUCTION

There are many questions we could ask about the duties and responsibilities of everyday bystanders. The one I am most interested in is downstream: *how* can everyday bystanders learn to recognize and meet their shared and institutional political responsibilities for severe violence—the hunger, poverty, famine, civil war, wars of conquest and invasion, epidemics and pandemics, and genocide in which more than 1.4 out of 6.7 billion people are trapped?[1]

It is a question about political education, and one that I believe should be answered from a democratic point of view.

While there are no bright lines separating political responsibility and democratic political education from their moral and legal correlates, there are important differences between the former political categories and the growing concern about the need for greater moral literacy and legal accountability.[2]

1. "Trapped" means that even if they could meet their immediate needs, they still would not have the resources to make the small investments that could lift them out of this condition. Paul Collier, in *The Bottom Billion: Why the Poorest Countries Are Failing and What Can Be Done About It* (New York: Oxford University Press, 2007), puts the figure at one billion persons. More recently, the International Comparison Program's *Global Purchasing Power Parities and Real Expenditures* report, published in 2008 by the International Bank for Reconstruction and Development, found that 1.4 billion, or almost one in four people in developing countries who live on less than $1.25 per day, are trapped in this sense. The old poverty measure of $1 per day used by Collier and others was revised to take into consideration the rising cost of living in these countries. See also Chronic Poverty Research Centre, *Chronic Poverty Report, 2008–9: Escaping Poverty Traps* (Manchester, UK: Chronic Poverty Research Centre, University of Manchester, 2009), http://www.chronicpoverty .org/cpra-report-0809.php.

2. For example, see Barbara Herman, *Moral Literacy* (Cambridge: Harvard University Press, 2007); and Gareth Evans, *The Responsibility to Protect: Ending Mass Atrocity Crimes Once and For All* (Washington, D.C.: Brookings Institution Press, 2008). On moral motivation, see Robert E. Goodin, *Motivating Political Morality* (Cambridge, Mass.: Blackwell, 1992).

This distinction between politics on one side and law and morality on the other is not something that can be established a priori. Whether it makes sense to label certain responsibilities for severe violence as political, not just moral or legal, and certain ways of motivating citizens to recognize and meet their political responsibilities as political education, will depend on the coherence and practical worth of the argument as a whole.

Before addressing the question of democratic political education, however, something must be said upstream about *what* everyday bystanders are responsible for doing or neglecting. Without some idea of what they allegedly are responsible for politically, it is impossible to help them recognize and meet their responsibilities for it democratically.

This kind of *what* question is usually about cause and effect.[3] What causes or more generally contributes to severe violence? While much has been said about what perpetrators and collaborators have done to cause harm and what their victims have suffered, relatively little has been said about the political responsibilities of bystanders who stand outside this causal nexus. The political responsibilities of bystanders stem from their roles as beneficiaries not quite as far upstream. The key what question for these bystanders is what benefits they have received, not whether they have caused or otherwise contributed to severe violence.[4]

---

3. The relationship between contribution and responsibility has been explored much more than the relationship between benefit and responsibility, primarily because of the dominance of legal interpretations of responsibility that focus on harm. See, for example, Christian Barry, "Applying the Contribution Principle," in *Global Institutions and Responsibilities: Achieving Global Justice,* ed. Christian Barry and Thomas W. Pogge (Malden, Mass.: Blackwell, 2005), 281–97. Passing references to the responsibilities of beneficiaries of severe violence are less well developed and tend to blend into moral responsibilities of humanity as a whole. See, for example, Ser-Min Shei, "World Poverty and Moral Responsibility," in *Real World Justice: Grounds, Principles, Human Rights, and Social Institutions,* ed. Andreas Follesdal and Thomas Pogge (Dordrecht, the Netherlands: Springer, 2005), 139–56. A notable exception is Daniel Butt, "On Benefiting from Injustice," *Canadian Journal of Philosophy* 57, no. 1 (2007): 129–52.

4. Causal contributions, including indirect contributions such as participation in transnational commerce, have been linked to responsibility in a moral sense by Henry Shue, *Basic Rights: Subsistence, Affluence, and U.S. Foreign Policy,* 2nd ed. (Princeton: Princeton University Press, 1996); Charles R. Beitz, *Political Theory and International Relations,* rev. ed. (Princeton: Princeton University Press, 1999); and Thomas Pogge, *World Poverty and Human Rights: Cosmopolitan Responsibilities and Reforms* (Malden, Mass.: Polity, 2002). Richard W. Miller has called arguments such as these "quest narratives," and according to him they should be replaced by a more empirically grounded set of moral responsibilities to poor countries by individuals, firms, and governments who benefit by taking advantage of the desperate needs of the poor in various unjust ways. This takes many forms, including coercive wage offers, crop subsidies, import quotas, and bullying tactics in international trade negotiations. See Miller's programmatic essay holding rich countries that participate in these unjust practices partially and differentially responsible for the basic needs of the poor in

The practical link between the benefits enjoyed by everyday bystanders (the what in this study) and their recognition of these benefits is the citizen-teacher. It is this figure, I will argue, who can help everyday bystanders see where they stand within a complicated network of moral duties and legal and political responsibilities.[5]

The story of the citizen-teacher is not a story of sacrifice. Tales of heroic individuals who have committed their lives to helping the poor already exist,[6] and they sometimes inspire others to do the same, at least for a short time. This is not that kind of story. There also have been cases of nearly anonymous rescuers working to protect their neighbors despite great odds against them.[7] This is not that kind of story either. Nor is it a story about courageous humanitarian aid workers risking their lives in refugee camps and war zones.[8]

---

developing countries, not just those within their own borders: "Global Power and Economic Justice," in *Global Basic Rights*, ed. Charles R. Beitz and Robert E. Goodin (New York: Oxford University Press, 2009), 156–80. My argument for the political responsibility of corporations in chapter 3 adopts a similar view of the political responsibilities of those who have benefited from forced labor and slavery. For Miller's more detailed arguments, see *Globalizing Justice: The Ethics of Poverty and Power* (New York: Oxford University Press, 2010). See also Butt, "On Benefiting from Injustice."

5. The distinction between moral duties and legal or political responsibilities appears to ignore the important concept of political obligation. I consider some of the political obligations of democratic citizens and officeholders in §9, "Individual Political Responsibility." For a discussion of political obligation based on the fair distribution of benefits and burdens among those "engaged in a joint enterprise," see George Klosko, *Political Obligations* (New York: Oxford University Press, 2005). Klosko distinguishes his account of obligations from those based on natural duties of justice. On the question of whether membership in a political society entails an obligation to uphold the political institutions of that society, see Margaret Gilbert, *A Theory of Political Obligation: Membership, Commitment, and the Bonds of Society* (New York: Oxford University Press, 2006). Gilbert's "joint commitment theory of political obligation" (as distinguished from obligations based on voluntarist consent) bears some resemblance to the account of shared and institutional political responsibilities I propose; however, it is directed at obligations of citizens to obey the laws of their own country, not their responsibilities for severe violence within a wider frame of reference. See also Steven M. DeLue, *Political Obligation in a Liberal State* (Albany: State University of New York Press, 1989).

6. For example, see the story of Paul Farmer's heroic efforts to combat AIDS and tuberculosis in Haiti, as told by Tracy Kidder in *Mountains Beyond Mountains: The Quest of Dr. Paul Farmer, a Man Who Would Cure the World* (New York: Random House, 2003). More recently Kidder has told the story of a similar set of less well-known heroes, one a Burundian refugee named Deogratias who was inspired by Paul Farmer, and others who crossed his path and helped him complete his medical education in the United States and return to Burundi. Tracy Kidder, *Strength in What Remains* (New York: Random House, 2009).

7. For example, see the story of the French Huguenots who helped to rescue the Jews of Le Chambon-sur-Ligne, France, during World War II, as told by Philip Hallie in *Lest Innocent Blood Be Shed* (New York: Harper Colophon, 1980).

8. Many humanitarian aid workers and emergency rescuers who work for organizations such as the International Committee of the Red Cross and Médecins Sans Frontières have written about their personal experiences, and novelists and journalists have told their stories as well. These stories too are often inspiring, although they are not entirely free from the narcissism, despair, and

It is a more commonplace story about mapping the rivers and roads of a new territory. This does not mean that there are no existing landmarks to help citizen-teachers guide everyday bystanders. But it does mean that we must be prepared to look in some unfamiliar places, and then step out onto the road before it has been fully paved. This is how Jane Addams, the 1931 Nobel Peace Prize laureate and founder of Hull-House, characterized the challenge of "social ethics": "We are learning that a standard of social ethics is not attained by traveling a sequestered byway, but by mixing on the thronged and common road where all must turn out for one another, and at least see the size of one another's burdens. To follow the path of social morality results perforce in the term if not the practice of the democratic spirit, for it implies that diversified human experience and resultant sympathy which are the foundation and guarantee of Democracy."[9]

By "mixing on the thronged and common road," Addams argued, we can begin to understand our shared and institutional political responsibilities for the suffering of others and the benefits that come our way. This is a story of how to move people off their familiar "sequestered byways" (the anachronistic liberal map of citizenship) and onto a yet-unfinished common road. It is not a matter of hypothetically projecting ourselves into the place of another, but making their actual acquaintance in a language both parties understand. Only then will we be able accurately to judge the "size of one another's burdens."[10]

Addams's approach to democratic political education is also not a matter of vicariously sharing in the pain of those who endure severe violence by temporarily living among them. This kind of sentimental journey is to be avoided at all costs, and one way to do this is to remember that as we encounter one

---

self-righteousness that understandably accompany this work. For a critical review of this literature, see James Dawes, *That the World May Know: Bearing Witness to Atrocity* (Cambridge: Harvard University Press, 2007). These workers, unlike everyday bystanders, directly contribute to what Fiona Terry has called "the paradox of humanitarian action." At the same time that they provide aid and emergency relief, they also may provide knowingly but unintentionally support to "refugee-warriors" who reside within the camps they serve and to other combatants in so-called safe areas. For a discussion of these and other less visible moral dilemmas that humanitarian aid workers face as actors, not bystanders, in situations of severe violence, see Fiona Terry, *Condemned to Repeat? The Paradox of Humanitarian Action* (Ithaca: Cornell University Press, 2002).

9. Jane Addams, *Democracy and Social Ethics* (1902; repr., Urbana: University of Illinois Press, 2002), 7.

10. I am indebted to James Farr for this distinction. Whether one prefers David Hume's original formulation of sympathy (as Farr does) or a conception of empathy such as the one I develop in chapter 4, the point, as Farr puts it, is that "our sympathizing with others is something we do or engage in, not something which simply happens to us." See James Farr, "Hume, Hermeneutics, and History: A Sympathetic Account," *History and Theory* 17, no. 3 (1978): 296.

another on this common road we bring different skills, orientations, and sensibilities that have to be shared in an atmosphere of mutual respect.[11]

Violence can take many forms, from physical injury and property damage to psychological trauma. Its causes can be direct and intentional, but it also can be the result of unforeseen, unintended, and catastrophic occurrences. Some would prefer that we restrict the definition of violence to injury and damage done by clearly identifiable agents or sources such as a violent individual or storm.[12] Others widen the definition of violence to include both its background conditions (e.g., structural violence, cultural violence) that indirectly can lead to equally harmful consequences over a period of time, as well as its symbolic manifestations in language and art. They argue that the denial of opportunity, the destruction of cultural heritage, the humiliation of minorities (intentional or not), and the manipulation of ideas and symbols can be just as injurious and damaging as a direct assault or a hurricane.[13]

Both the restricted and wide definitions of violence pick out important features of unwanted and harmful suffering. What makes some forms of violence, whether widely or narrowly defined, more severe than others? One answer is the intensity of the pain they cause. Surely, torture is severe violence even though the pain experienced by the victim is not easy to describe.[14] But pain is not the only manifestation of severe violence; the political element alluded to above is more important for my purposes. What do being dispossessed, being disenfranchised, and being "disappeared" have in common that makes them politically severe?

There are actually two senses in which severe violence is political: what we might call its material and its semantic senses. First, severe violence is materially political because of the decisions and actions, sometimes proximate and sometimes remote, that create it. Second, it is semantically political because of the

11. An interesting example of how even survey research on the ways that the poorest citizens make a life for themselves can be informed by this kind of mutual respect is Daryl Collins, Jonathan Morduch, Stuart Rutherford, and Orlanda Ruthven, *Portfolios of the Poor: How the World's Poor Live on $2 a Day* (Princeton: Princeton University Press, 2009).

12. For example, see C. A. J. Coady, "The Idea of Violence," *Journal of Applied Philosophy* 3, no. 1 (1986): 3–19.

13. On structural and cultural violence, see Johan Galtung, "Violence, Peace, and Peace Research," *Journal of Peace Research* 6, no. 3 (1969): 167–91; and John Harris, *Violence and Responsibility* (London: Routledge and Kegan Paul, 1980). On the subject of symbolic violence and related concepts, see Pierre Bourdieu, *Practical Reason: On the Theory of Action,* trans. Randall Johnson (Stanford: Stanford University Press, 1998).

14. Jean Améry, *At the Mind's Limits: Contemplations by a Survivor on Auschwitz and Its Realities,* trans. Sidney Rosenfeld and Stella P. Rosenfeld (Bloomington: Indiana University Press, 1980).

ways in which responsibilities for the benefits and burdens that flow from such violence are shirked, shouldered, or shared; whether violence rises to the level of severe violence depends on a political struggle over the meaning of these responsibilities. These material and semantic political senses of severe violence are clearly visible in the three forms of severe violence I have in mind—famine, civil war, and genocide—when discussing how some everyday bystanders have benefited from displacement, dispossession, disenfranchisement, and disappearance.[15]

Famine is not a chronic food shortage exacerbated by deteriorating climate conditions. In a material sense famine is an economic and political process of exclusion. Segments of the population lose their ability to purchase food for a variety of reasons; falling wages, lack of adequate disposable income, rising food prices due to the policies of other countries, and the intentional destruction of the economic infrastructure can all play a part in this.[16] These are not natural processes. They depend on political choices and political power.

Famine is also political in a semantic sense. While some aid organizations would prefer to define famine solely in terms of mortality rates and malnutrition, it has become clear that defining any particular situation as a famine is politically controversial. For example, to avoid so defining the situation in Niger in 2005, then Nigerian president Mamadou Tandja is reported to have said that there are three signs of a famine: when people are leaving the countryside and going to live in shantytowns; when people are leaving the country; and when beggars are widely prevalent. Those three things, he asserted, did not exist in Niger at the time.[17] As self-serving and politically ineffective as this definition of

15. On the complicated intersection of famine, civil war, and genocide, see Mike Davis, *Late Victorian Holocausts: El Niño Famines and the Making of the Third World* (New York: Verso, 2001); Eric D. Weitz, *A Century of Genocide: Utopias of Race and Nation* (Princeton: Princeton University Press, 2003); Robert Gellately and Ben Kiernan, eds., *The Specter of Genocide: Mass Murder in Historical Perspective* (New York: Cambridge University Press, 2003); Samantha Power, *"A Problem from Hell": America and the Age of Genocide* (New York: Basic Books, 2002); Michael Mann, *The Dark Side of Democracy: Explaining Ethnic Cleansing* (New York: Cambridge University Press, 2005); and Ben Kiernan, *Blood and Soil: A World History of Genocide and Extermination from Sparta to Darfur* (New Haven: Yale University Press, 2007).

16. Amartya Sen, *Poverty and Famines: An Essay on Poverty and Deprivation* (1981), reprinted in Sen and Drèze, *The Amartya Sen and Jean Drèze Omnibus* (New York: Oxford University Press, 1999), 1–257. See also Alex de Waal, *Famine Crimes: Politics and the Disaster Relief Industry in Africa* (Bloomington: Indiana University Press, 1998); and Rhoda Howard-Hassmann, "Genocide and State-Induced Famine: Global Ethics and Western Responsibility for Mass Atrocities in Africa," *Perspectives on Global Development and Technology* 4, nos. 3–5 (2005): 487–516. For a general overview, see Cormac Ó Gráda, *Famine: A Short History* (Princeton: Princeton University Press, 2009); and Roger Thurow and Scott Kilman, *Enough: Why the World's Poorest Starve in an Age of Plenty* (New York: Public Affairs, 2009).

17. "Niger Leader Denies Hunger Claims," BBC News, August 9, 2005, http://news.bbc.co .uk/2/hi/africa/4133374.stm.

famine is, it underlines the fact that where one draws the line semantically and who can draw it will unavoidably be influenced by political considerations. In this case Tandja was no match for the World Food Programme, and he was not able to make those suffering from famine politically invisible.

Similarly, as civil wars became more prevalent than wars of conquest in the twentieth century, civilians have been threatened by violence from one side or the other without recourse to a political system that can provide some buffer. This not only can contribute to famine conditions inside refugee camps but also can lead to a reign of terror (often described metaphorically as an epidemic), sometimes at the hands of peacekeeping authorities themselves.[18] Civil wars invariably cross state boundaries and spread throughout whole regions, weakening economies, corrupting governments, and poisoning large populations. They are political hurricanes, not localized and entrenched blood feuds.[19]

Like the word "famine," the meaning of the term "civil war" is vehemently contested because of the implications it has for political responsibility. For example, the United States refused to intervene in the violence in Liberia in the early 1990s by characterizing it as a civil war. Madeleine Albright, then secretary of state, lectured the Liberians in language that foreshadowed the sophistic distinction the Clinton administration later would make between "acts of genocide" and "genocide" in reference to Rwanda. By misdescribing severe violence as an ethnic conflict contained within one country, Albright was able to understate both the impact of the severe violence emanating from Liberia as well as U.S. responsibility for it.[20]

Critics of the invasion and occupation of Iraq by U.S.-led forces beginning in 2003 have argued that the action triggered a civil war, while defenders of the invasion and occupation have argued until recently that the situation is more accurately described as an unpopular insurgency against the new legitimate Iraqi

18. For example, see Jeffrey Gettleman, "Rape Epidemic Raises Trauma of Congo," *New York Times,* October 7, 2007.

19. Paul Collier, *Breaking the Conflict Trap: Civil War and Development Policy* (Washington, D.C.: Oxford University Press and the World Bank, 2003). For an argument that civil wars are actually declining in the poorest parts of the world, see the Human Security Report Project's *Human Security Brief, 2006* (Vancouver: Human Security Centre, University of British Columbia, 2006), http://www.humansecuritybrief.info/2006/index.html.

20. "I can confirm to you that the president and his advisors are deeply committed to the future of this country and its people. The United States should take a risk for peace when we have the means to make a difference. This civil war is your war. The peace of Abuja is your peace. Either you take the courageous steps needed to secure it now or Liberia will again experience tragedy. The future is yours alone to determine." Albright quoted in Howard W. French, *A Continent for the Taking: The Tragedy and Hope of Africa* (New York: Vintage Books, 2005), 176.

government and its supporters. A similar debate occurred during the U.S. war in Vietnam: some critics of the war argued for withdrawal because it was an internal affair that ought to be left to the opposing parties, while defenders of the war characterized it as a defensive action on behalf of South Vietnam against North Vietnamese aggression.

Even more than famine and civil war, the definition of genocide indicates just how political a phenomenon severe violence is. In cases of genocide, according to international humanitarian law, groups are intentionally targeted for extinction and humiliation because of who they are. Recent attempts, such as the 2007 Genocide Prevention Task Force co-chaired by Madeleine Albright and former U.S. secretary of defense William S. Cohen, have attempted to define genocide as "large-scale and deliberate attacks on civilians" instead of as directed against the identity of the targeted population. The hope has been that this would make it less political and thus more preventable by multilateral forces, including the United States.[21]

What makes genocide especially cruel and humiliating to a people is not so much the vicious intentions of the génocidaires as the fact that it is condoned by the very political authorities responsible for protecting them: the victims have no recourse to the political body to which they belong,[22] and often they must struggle to peel away state-sanctioned euphemisms such as "ethnic cleansing."[23]

In many cases, famine, civil war, and genocide converge. The current situation in Darfur illustrates how civil war can escalate into famine and charges of genocide.[24] The violence that dominated the former Yugoslavia in the 1990s and the violence that continues to spread from Rwanda throughout the Democratic Republic of Congo and neighboring countries in central Africa also illustrate how famine, civil war, and genocide can feed on one another.[25] That does

21. See Sarah Sewall, "Do the Right Thing: A Genocide Policy That Works," *Boston Review* 34, no. 5 (2009): 33–35. Avoiding group identity, however, does not address the political root of the problem.

22. Richard Vernon, "What Is Crime Against Humanity?" *Journal of Political Philosophy* 10, no. 3 (2002): 231–49.

23. Michael A. Sells, *The Bridge Betrayed: Religion and Genocide in Bosnia* (Berkeley and Los Angeles: University of California Press, 1998).

24. Mahmood Mamdani disputes the claim that Darfur represents a case of genocide. In *Saviors and Survivors: Darfur, Politics, and the War on Terror* (New York: Pantheon Books, 2009), he argues that while the problems in Sudan can be described in terms of civil war and famine, the argument that this is a case of genocide has been used to "racialize" the conflict to serve the interests of the United States and its allies, who advocate waging a global war on terror. Cf. Nicholas D. Kristof, "What to Do About Darfur," *New York Review of Books*, July 2, 2009, http://www.nybooks .com/articles/22771.

25. Gérard Prunier, *Africa's World War: Congo, the Rwandan Genocide, and the Making of a Continental Catastrophe* (New York: Oxford University Press, 2009). Prunier is perhaps overly critical

not mean that they always occur together; not all famines result from or lead to civil war and then genocide. But there are enough cases in which they do appear together to warrant asking questions about what they have in common as forms of severe violence.[26]

In short, severe violence is political violence perpetrated against groups of persons who are sometimes exiles or immigrants, sometimes powerless, displaced minorities within an oppressive state, and sometimes groups left in political limbo to fend for themselves when their state has failed. What groups like these have in common is the cruel way they have lost their political voice and have no legitimate political way to regain it.[27] They have been geographically displaced, legally dispossessed, politically disenfranchised, or militarily "disappeared."[28] Those individuals and institutions that have *caused and contributed* to this radical depoliticization certainly bear a wide range of moral duties and legal

---

of the Rwandan government's military policies since the 1994 genocide. For a more sympathetic view by a journalist who covered the immediate aftermath of the genocide and then returned in 2008, see Philip Gourevitch, "The Life After: Fifteen Years After the Genocide in Rwanda, the Reconciliation Defies Expectations," *New Yorker*, May 4, 2009, 36–49.

26. One might argue that the debate over the political responsibilities of everyday bystanders began with Peter Singer's article "Famine, Affluence, and Morality," in *Philosophy and Public Affairs* 1, no. 3 (1972): 229–43. Singer referred to the "poverty, cyclone, and civil war" in East Bengal at that time, recognizing just how intimately connected famine and civil war are. By characterizing this conjunction as "just the latest and most acute of a series of major emergencies in various parts of the world," however, he understated the long-term political processes at work (230). On the limitations of this characterization, see Jennifer Rubenstein, "Distribution and Emergency," *Journal of Political Philosophy* 15, no. 3 (2007): 296–320. I return to Singer's allegory of emergency rescue in chapter 5, §16.

27. Philip Hallie, following Frederick Douglass, describes cruelty as an act or practice that erodes the capacity for political membership. Severe violence does not disenfranchise; it weakens the will to participate in political society. "The opposite of cruelty is not kindness," Hallie observes. "The opposite of cruelty is freedom" in a positive participatory sense. See *The Paradox of Cruelty* (Middleton: Wesleyan University Press, 1969), 159. The same is true of the word "severe." Leif Wenar uses the term "severe poverty" to describe poverty that reaches the level of deprivation of human rights. While avoiding the model of clinical intervention and the metaphor of traps of severe suffering, Wenar suggests that we generalize from nonpolitical cases. He starts with ordinary cases such as car accidents and the like, hoping to defend what he calls a "least cost" principle of responsibility that can be applied at the global level. Responsibility should be allocated with the least overall cost to society. See Wenar, "Responsibility and Severe Poverty," in *Freedom from Poverty as a Human Right: Who Owes What to the Very Poor?* ed. Thomas Pogge (New York: Oxford University Press, 2007), 255–74.

28. This term "disappeared" (*los desaparecidos*) refers to the kidnappings, killings, and other human rights abuses perpetrated by the military junta in Argentina between 1976 and 1983 (the so-called Dirty War). See *Nunca Mas: The Report of the Argentine National Commission on the Disappeared* (New York: Farrar, Straus and Giroux, 1986). On the adoption of orphaned children during the Dirty War in Argentina, see Laura E. Oren, "Righting Child Custody Wrongs: The Children of the 'Disappeared' in Argentina," *Harvard Human Rights Journal* 14 (Spring 2001): 123–200.

and political responsibilities. They are the perpetrators of severe violence and their collaborators. Those bystanders who have *benefited* from severe violence bear a different kind of responsibility, which I describe as shared and institutional political responsibility.

The examples of severe violence that I use are not controversial: the Nazi Holocaust, apartheid in South Africa, legalized segregation and forced labor in the United States, the civil war and genocide in the former Yugoslavia, and the Rwandan genocide of the Tutsis. My purpose is not to prove that these are forms of severe violence as I define it; I assume that they are. My purpose is to explore how those of us who accept this description of these events can learn to broaden our understanding of political responsibility for severe violence and teach others to do the same.

It would be irresponsible to place anyone, and especially students, in a situation of severe violence in order to teach them about political responsibility. That is the obvious reason why the community service-learning and study abroad programs I use to illustrate the work of a citizen-teacher are not held in refugee camps or war zones. But there are ways students and teachers can become better acquainted with those who have lived in conditions of severe violence without necessarily experiencing it themselves. Simulations provide one way of doing this, but I argue that these representations of severe violence usually do not encourage empathy and self-understanding. Alternatively, refugee resettlement and support programs exist throughout the developed world, not just in war zones. Deep pockets of suffering exist within relatively rich countries as well as in very poor countries that have managed to avoid outbreaks of severe violence. There are ways of representing these sites of severe violence, both through critical reenactments and interpretations of these reenactments that encourage empathy and greater awareness of political responsibility.[29]

Reenactment can refer to a wide range of performances, dramatic renditions, and other symbolic representations that replay key events and moments in history. In the United States, the most well-known form is the make-believe Civil War reenactment performed by volunteers, not professional actors. Reenactments of this type have a celebratory if not always patriotic purpose.[30] In contrast, a

29. Becoming acquainted, in Addams's sense, is a process of civic engagement on difficult, sometimes divisive issues. There is no guarantee that coming into contact with severe violence will lead to what I call empathy (and what Addams calls sympathy). It may be just as likely that contact will lead to greater callous acceptance of violence and suffering, or worse.

30. See Tony Horwitz, *Confederates in the Attic: Dispatches from the Unfinished Civil War* (New York: Pantheon, 1998).

critical reenactment, as I will be using this term, can be an embodied performance, an abstract representation, or some combination of the two. For example, modern dance can abstractly reenact a violent event in a critical fashion, and so can a poetry reading. The most defining characteristic of a critical reenactment is its purpose: to raise difficult questions about the shared political responsibilities of bystanders who are neither perpetrators nor victims of severe violence, and to raise these questions in a voice that can motivate these bystanders to reconsider their institutional roles, not just their personal moral duties.

Critical reenactors can be stand-ins for the original subjects or they can be the original subjects retracing their steps literally or figuratively. Plato's *Apology* is a critical reenactment of the trial of the historical Socrates. Claude Lanzmann's *Shoah* is a critical reenactment of one chapter of the Nazi Holocaust. Jane Taylor's and William Kentridge's *Ubu and the Truth Commission* (pictured at the front of this book) is a critical reenactment of one aspect of life in South Africa in the early 1990s. In Kentridge's case, he chooses to use puppets to reenact the brutal exploitation that connects apartheid and postapartheid South Africa to avoid further complicity on his own part. White South Africans, whether they actively opposed or tacitly supported apartheid, may have still been indirectly responsible for the violence done to street peddlers like the one represented by this trader puppet. This abstract reenactment allows Kentridge to raise the question of his own complicity and the possible indirect responsibility of others without forcing victims of apartheid to repeat their experience in a literal sense. The trader puppet bears witness to his own past suffering and demands that the audience, the actors, and the director ask who these two handlers represent. The purpose of critical reenactment is to help us see for ourselves the expanding boundaries of severe violence, the hand we may have in this process, and the voice we may have in its democratic reconstitution.

There are certainly other forms of violence besides famine, civil war, and genocide, and other political ways of responding to them. I do not mean to depreciate the importance of these other forms of violence or the importance of other responses by not including them in this discussion. For example, some have argued that terror, including state terror, will be the most serious threat to political societies in the twenty-first century.[31] I do not address this threat or the more abstract notion of terrorism, but not because I believe that its importance is overstated; its relationship to famine, civil war, and genocide indeed may prove to be a very close one.

---

31. Philip Bobbitt, *Terror and Consent: The Wars for the Twenty-first Century* (New York: Knopf, 2008).

Recognizing and accepting shared and institutional political responsibilities as beneficiaries of severe violence will require a process very different from moral argument or legal prosecution. It must begin with something like what South African Breyten Breytenbach has called spiking the self and pickling the heart.[32]

Writers, poets, filmmakers, and artists such as Breytenbach, Claude Lanzmann, William Kentridge, Mandy Jacobson, Alfredo Jaar, Antjie Krog, Carolyn Forché, Wisława Szymborska, and W. G. Sebald have tried to do just that: prompt us to recognize our shared and institutional political responsibilities as everyday bystanders to severe violence. I describe their work as critical reenactment, a term I explain in more detail below. But these sharp reminders by themselves are not enough: They reach only a small audience able to decipher their complex messages. Another layer of interpretation is needed if these reenactments are to move a larger audience. I refer to the secondary interpreters of critical reenactments as citizen-teachers, and I call this two-staged practice of critical reenactment and interpretation democratic political education.

The argument for this particular conception of democratic political education is divided into four sections. Part 1 contrasts the vocation of citizen-teachers with liberal and neoliberal conceptions of citizenship in order to understand one particular set of institutional political responsibilities for the severe violence of forced labor and slavery. Part 2 describes why everyday bystanders to severe violence have difficulty recognizing their shared and institutional political responsibilities, and how this can be changed through critical reenactments. Part 3 presents several examples from my own experience of how citizen-teachers as interpreters of critical reenactments can help everyday bystanders recognize and meet these political responsibilities for severe violence. The conclusion locates the work of citizen-teachers as interpreters of critical reenactments within the context of contemporary theories of development and democracy.

I do not mean to suggest that intellectuals and educators should not be strong advocates for political causes. The vocation of the citizen-teacher is not the only role that intellectuals can or should play to heighten awareness of and lessen severe violence. Some intellectuals have spoken in a prophetic voice from within their own community of suffering and oppression for just these reasons.[33] The vocation of the citizen-teacher, however, is not a prophetic one in the sense of

---

32. Breyten Breytenbach, "Fumbling Reflections on the Freedom of the Word and the Responsibility of the Author," in *End Papers: Essays, Letters, Articles of Faith, Workbook Notes* (New York: Farrar, Straus and Giroux, 1986), 144.

33. Cornel West, *Prophesy Deliverance! An Afro-American Revolutionary Christianity* (Louisville, Ky.: Westminster John Knox Press, 2002).

calling back those who have strayed from the path of righteousness. The challenge for the citizen-teacher is to help those who do not belong to communities of suffering and oppression to recognize how they have benefited unjustly from the suffering and oppression of others.

The goal of this book is to help citizen-teachers—and through them, everyday bystanders to severe violence—see themselves within a more democratic frame of reference. This is why suggestive figures of speech, visual images, and poetic voices occupy a central place in the stories I tell.[34] I already have distinguished upstream contributions, causes, effects, and benefits from downstream recognition, and this mapping metaphor will be expanded. The political responsibilities of everyday bystanders will be presented in terms of contrasting allegories and stories that influence (not merely illustrate) how recognition may be blocked or enhanced. Political education's reliance on language and innovation is hardly new. What may be new are the global challenges that recognition faces and the speed at which citizens are losing their ability to respond democratically to them.[35]

Riparian metaphors of upstream causes, contributions, effects, and benefits and downstream political education and recognition can be complicated. Unlike products in the "flow of commerce,"[36] responsibilities are not always either in or out of the stream of harm and suffering. Some bystanders feel morally obligated to save an innocent victim (e.g., the proverbial drowning child; more on this in chapter 5), and in some of these cases they are criminally negligent if they don't. Sometimes their mere marginal presence, even downstream, makes the harm worse; and if they try to mitigate that harm, they may exacerbate it and increase their responsibilities.

Consider the complicated case of Specialist Sabrina Harman, a member of the 372nd Military Police reserve unit of the U.S. Army, a bystander in 2003 during the torture and humiliation of prisoners in the Abu Ghraib prison in Iraq. I will return to the way that allegories of rescue and more unusual stories

---

34. See Egbert J. Bakker, "Mimesis as Performance: Rereading Auerbach's First Chapter," *Poetics Today* 20, no. 1 (2001): 11–26.

35. Sheldon S. Wolin, *Politics and Vision: Continuity and Innovation in Western Political Thought,* exp. ed. (Princeton: Princeton University Press, 2004); and Wolin, *Democracy Incorporated: Managed Democracy and the Specter of Inverted Totalitarianism* (Princeton: Princeton University Press, 2008).

36. Article 1, section 8 of the U.S. Constitution gives Congress the power "to regulate commerce with foreign nations, and among the several states, and with the Indian tribes." One interpretation of this power is that Congress has the power to regulate commercial activity, including manufacturing, so long as the commercial products are part of a flow of commerce that crosses these jurisdictional lines.

like Abu Ghraib are photographed, filmed, reenacted, and interpreted downstream to hinder or help bystanders recognize and meet their responsibilities. For the moment, I want to use Harman's case as a counterexample to underscore how the political responsibilities that everyday bystanders incur as beneficiaries differ from the political responsibilities of Harman's superiors and her own extraordinary but apolitical responsibilities in this case.

The following description, based on interviews with Harman and other military and civilian personnel serving in the Iraq war, comes from the book *Standard Operating Procedure* by Philip Gourevitch and Errol Morris:

> The MPs knew very little about their prisoners or the culture they came from, and they understood less. But at Fort Lee, before they deployed, they were given a session of "cultural awareness training," from which they'd taken away the understanding—constantly reinforced by MI [Military Intelligence] handlers—that Arab men were sexual prudes, with a particular hang-up about being seen naked in public, especially by women. . . . Harman understood. She didn't like being naked in public herself. To the prisoners, being photographed may have seemed an added dash of mortification, but to Harman, taking pictures was a way of deflecting her own humiliation in the transaction—by taking ownership of her position as spectator.[37]

As Gourevitch and Morris suggest, Sabrina Harman played an unusual role in a situation in which torture had become a standard operating procedure: "She did not pretend to be a whistle-blower-in-waiting; rather, she wished to unburden herself of complicity in conduct that she considered wrong, and in its cover-up, without ascribing blame or making trouble for anyone in particular."[38] By photographing these scenes of torture, she hoped to partially exculpate herself. She was willing to document human rights abuses at the same time that she realized her presence as a woman documenting the abuses added to the suffering of the victims. Harman was extraordinary in what she hoped to accomplish as a

---

37. Philip Gourevitch and Errol Morris, *Standard Operating Procedure* (New York: Penguin, 2008), 113. Gourevitch wrote this volume based on the coeval film by the same name directed by Morris. For an illuminating discussion between the two in which they describe their complementary contributions to the project, see the video recording of their *New Yorker* 2007 Film Festival session, http://www.newyorker.com/online/video/festival/2007/MorrisGourevitch.

38. Gourevitch and Morris, *Standard Operating Procedure*, 112.

bystander, not because the torture was extraordinary. In fact, at Abu Ghraib events like those she participated in were not at all out of the ordinary.[39] One might say she contributed to the harm but didn't plan or instigate it.

Harman's role as a "spectator," however, was not political. She and other low-ranking soldiers were convenient scapegoats for their superiors and politicians precisely because she had one foot in the stream of harm and suffering.[40] The responsibilities of the politicians and officers who encouraged and then lied about these practices are political because of the decisions they made and the orders they gave, and therefore they ought to be held accountable politically.[41] Harman's responsibility was not political in this causal sense: She took orders; she didn't give them. She made bad moral judgments, but she did not make any political decisions.

Everyday bystanders are not involved in harm and suffering in the extraordinary way that Harman was. Their responsibilities as beneficiaries are political, but not in the same sense that Harman's superiors' responsibilities were. Unlike Harman, who had one foot in the causal stream of violence, and her superiors, who were firmly anchored farther upstream giving orders, everyday bystanders stand on the banks, not as silent witnesses or frightened rescuers but as beneficiaries

39. Another related form of extraordinary behavior is what the George W. Bush administration called "extraordinary rendition," the clandestine transportation of prisoners by the United States to sites in other countries where torture is condoned. Those who transport alleged "enemy combatants" in this way are not bystanders at all, but collaborators in an illegal form of imprisonment and interrogation. See Stephen Grey, *Ghost Plane: The True Story of the CIA Torture Program* (New York: St. Martin's Press, 2006).

40. Reports of human rights abuses at Abu Ghraib, Guantánamo, and detention centers in Afghanistan—most notably by Seymour M. Hersh, *Chain of Command: The Road from 9/11 to Abu Ghraib* (New York: HarperCollins, 2004); and Mark Danner, *Torture and Truth: America, Abu Ghraib, and the War on Terror* (New York: New York Review of Books, 2004)—initially were followed reluctantly by official government reports confirming the knowing participation of military officers and responsible politicians. See, for example, *A Review of the FBI's Involvement in and Observations of Detainee Interrogations in Guantanamo Bay, Afghanistan, and Iraq* (Washington, D.C.: Oversight and Review Division, Office of the Inspector General, U.S. Department of Justice, 2008), http://graphics8.nytimes.com/packages/pdf/washington/20080521_DETAIN_report.pdf. The Obama administration has declassified additional documents, and the International Committee of the Red Cross has issued a detailed report. For discussion of these documents, see Mark Danner, "U.S. Torture: Voices from the Black Sites," *New York Review of Books*, April 9, 2009, http://www.nybooks.com/articles/22530; and Danner, "The Red Cross Torture Report: What It Means," *New York Review of Books*, April 30, 2009, http://www.nybooks.com/articles/22614.

41. At this writing, there is still a chance they will be. See United States Senate Armed Services Committee, *Report of the U.S. Senate Armed Services Committee Inquiry into the Treatment of Detainees in U.S. Custody* (Washington, D.C.: United States Senate Armed Services Committee, 2009), http://armed-services.senate.gov/Publications/Detainee%20Report%20Final_April%2022%202009.pdf.

of the deposits and changing landscape left in the wake of this stream of harm and suffering.

Initially, unlike Harman, everyday bystanders fill the once-filled jobs, hold the once-held offices, occupy the once-occupied homes, farm the once-farmed land, and even parent the once-parented orphans of the disappeared. None of these benefits came Harman's way. Later, everyday bystanders and their offspring attend the schools, cultivate the land, buy the products, and inherit the property made available to them by earlier displacements, disappearances, and less overt acts of ethnic cleansing. Everyday bystanders benefit from continuing harm and suffering through the decisions they make about property, parentage, and labor, even if they are not instigators or unapologetic profiteers. Sometimes these are shared decisions made by members of families or ethnic groups; sometimes they are decisions made by the governing bodies of institutions such as private corporations, public universities, or other international nongovernmental organizations. These decisions, whether they are made tacitly or explicitly, are political because they ratify the violence done to the displaced, the dispossessed, the disenfranchised, and the disappeared.

It would be a serious mistake to assume that all everyday bystanders are wealthy or powerful, or that they all benefit greatly from the severe violence endured by others. The corporations that opportunistically take advantage of the suffering of others certainly are often well-off and do profit. But the neighbors and small shopkeepers who step in to take over the homes, farms, and stores left behind by those who have fled or disappeared may be no more well-off than the victims themselves were beforehand. It would also be wrong to assume that everyday bystanders do not feel remorse for the way they and their descendants benefit from severe violence, any more than there is a simple way for them to make amends.[42]

I was reminded of this recently when I received an e-mail from a former student who had taken a philosophy course of mine in spring 2007 dealing with the material in this book. As an undergraduate she was active in the Latino community on and off the Michigan State University campus, and she became disillusioned with the university's commitment to its minority students. To her, the university was standing by as other students baited and harassed international and minority students under the banner of national identity and security.

---

42. For a discussion of the ethical dilemmas facing attempts to remedy the severe violence of geographical displacement, see Jay Drydyk, "Unequal Benefits: The Ethics of Development-Induced Displacement," *Georgetown Journal of International Affairs* 8, no. 1 (2007): 105–13.

When the university acted, she believed, it did so to support the freedom of speech of those calling for anti-immigrant legislation.[43]

She spent her last semester in fall 2007 on a study abroad program in Quito, Ecuador, and decided to stay on to teach English for another year. Her experience in Ecuador, she wrote, helped her to rethink her college education and the problems of injustice in the Latino communities in Michigan and her hometown, Los Angeles. In the e-mail, she reflected on the philosophy course and on an incident that had occurred the summer before she left for Quito in fall 2007:

> Actually, some of the ideas that were harder for me to grasp—ideas of citizenship and moral responsibility—helped me confront truths I learned later that same year. My grandfather—who took care of me my whole life—died during the last year of college, and so I spent the summer after spring 2007 mourning with my family in LA and learning more about his life. And I actually found out something that was very hard for me to accept. I learned that my grandparents, who had been very poor and struggling immigrants themselves, had actually lived in the house of Japanese immigrants who were taken to internment camps. I've always considered my family to be hardworking survivors, and people who were victims of so many inequalities. So learning this fact was VERY unsettling . . . and I just could not believe that MY family had benefited from other people's injustice. But, I worked through it . . . and accepted it . . . but I really think that the themes we discussed in your class gave me the means to process and understand why my grandparents had done that, but also to recognize that it was not ok.[44]

I have no reason to doubt this student's sincerity and gratitude, and I am pleased that the course gave her "the means to process and understand" the complexity of her family's relationship to the Japanese internment in the United States. But there is a general message here that is more significant. Discovering that her family had benefited from racist, anti-immigrant policies not only changed her

43. One particularly acrimonious incident was prompted by a speech sponsored by the local university chapter of Young Americans for Freedom given by Chris Simcox, of the militant anti-immigration group the Minuteman Civil Defense Corps. For the MCDC's own description of themselves and this incident, see "Chris Simcox Under Attack at Universities," MinutemanHQ .com, April 13, 2007, http://www.minutemanhq.com/hq/article.php?sid=253.

44. E-mail message to author, October 9, 2008.

view of her family, it affected how she understood her own education and the different groups she had encountered during that time.

A democratic political education that addresses the political responsibilities of everyday bystanders is not primarily about justifying official apologies or reparations. For some cases, such as the internment of Japanese American citizens in World War II, these may be appropriate,[45] but by themselves they cannot sustain democratic dialogues between beneficiaries and victims, especially when some parties have both benefited and suffered from severe violence. Families and communities like those of this student, whether they inherit the property of the displaced and disenfranchised or earn their wages at a firm that historically has benefited from severe violence, must be included in these dialogues. Because we cannot be sure who is an everyday bystander, including ourselves (see §11), citizen-teachers ought to presume that some of us someday are. It is not such a remote possibility, and it may be the best way to help everyday bystanders recognize that they are not simply guilty (or innocent), and that they are not alone in their political responsibility for severe violence.

45. See the discussion of reparations and responsibility in chapter 3. On the political value and limitations of official apologies, see Melissa Nobles, *The Politics of Official Apologies* (New York: Cambridge University Press, 2008). On the case of Japanese American internment in particular, see U.S. Congress, *Civil Liberties Act of 1988,* August 10, 1988, Civics Online, http://www.civics-online.org/library/formatted/texts/civilact1988.html. See also Commission on Wartime Relocation and Internment of Civilians, *Personal Justice Denied: Report of the Commission on Wartime Relocation and Internment of Civilians* (Washington, D.C.: National Park Service, 1982), http://www.nps.gov/history/history/online_books/personal_justice_denied/.

PART 1

Grounding Responsibility

1 TEACHING AS A POLITICAL VOCATION

Teaching as a political vocation can occur within a classroom, but it also can occur through a theatrical performance, an interactive Web site, a film, or the imaginary world created within the pages of a novel or the lines of a poem. Its practitioners are citizen-teachers. Their vocation is not civic education in the liberal sense of teaching tolerance and respect for individual freedom,[1] but rather helping everyday bystanders recognize how they have benefited from severe violence.[2] In this chapter I describe teaching as a political vocation from three convergent angles: teaching critically, teaching responsibly, and teaching democratically. Together they define the virtues of citizen-teachers, one part of a conception of democratic citizenship that I describe more fully and contrast with competing conceptions of liberal and neoliberal citizenship in the next two chapters.

Important practical work has already been done to teach primary and secondary school students and their teachers about the causes of, consequences of, and possible responses to severe violence, perhaps most notably by the organization Facing History and Ourselves.[3] By no means do I think of myself as a

1. Eamonn Callan, *Creating Citizens: Political Education and Liberal Democracy* (New York: Oxford University Press, 1997); and Rob Reich, *Bridging Liberalism and Multiculturalism in American Education* (Chicago: University of Chicago Press, 2002). See also Stephen Macedo and Iris Marion Young, eds., *Moral and Political Education,* Nomos 43 (New York: New York University Press, 2001).

2. I have discussed elsewhere the weaknesses of extending the Weberian conceptions of politics and science as vocation to teaching. See Stephen L. Esquith, *Intimacy and Spectacle: Liberal Theory as Political Education* (Ithaca: Cornell University Press, 1994), 75–82.

3. Facing History and Ourselves: Helping Classrooms and Communities Worldwide Link the Past to Moral Choices Today, Brookline, Mass., http://www.facinghistory.org/.

pioneer; the rough experiments I describe in part 3 of this book have been inspired by the work of this organization and many others like it. There is also considerable research on the debilitating effects of famine, civil war, and genocide on survivors, especially young people; and practical research on what can be done to help them come to terms with these experiences.[4] Experiments like the ones I present need to be developed carefully and examined in the context of this growing body of theory and practice.

1. Teaching Critically

To begin, the citizen-teachers I have in mind are critics of a certain type. They understand that they have benefited from severe violence, or may in the foreseeable future, even if they cannot tell the whole story in detail. They have seen simulations, representations, and reenactments of severe violence, even if they have not witnessed the events themselves; and as beneficiaries of severe violence, they feel the bonds of complicity that tie them to other bystanders. They are capable of thinking about their own past and future critically and of teaching other bystanders to do the same.

I include myself and other academics among this group of citizen-teachers, but also journalists, writers, clergy, and curators. We are critics, but not what Michael Walzer calls "connected social critics," because our primary vocation is that of teacher, even though we are not all classroom teachers. Unlike Walzer's paradigmatic social critics (from Randolph Bourne to Simone de Beauvoir), who also have worked as journalists, writers, and professors, citizen-teachers are connected to other everyday bystanders in a different pedagogical way. We operate within a smaller circle, and our goal is to locate ourselves and other bystanders within this frame of reference so that our connections to severe violence are more visible to one another. Unlike the social critic, who operates on the main stage and whose primary job is to point out the hypocrisy of perpetrators and collaborators,[5] the citizen-teacher's audience consists of fellow everyday

---

4. For example, see Marcelo M. Suarez-Orozco, ed., *Learning in the Global Era: International Perspectives on Globalization and Education* (Berkeley and Los Angeles: University of California Press, 2007); Veena Das and others, *Remaking a World: Violence, Social Suffering, and Recovery* (Berkeley and Los Angeles: University of California Press, 2001); and Antonius C. G. M. Robben and Marcelo M. Suarez-Orozco, eds., *Cultures Under Siege: Collective Violence and Trauma* (New York: Cambridge University Press, 2000).

5. For a more theoretical discussion of this conception of social criticism, see Michael Walzer, *Interpretation and Social Criticism* (Cambridge: Harvard University Press, 1987); and Ian Shapiro, *Political Criticism* (Berkeley and Los Angeles: University of California Press, 1990).

bystanders who have yet to recognize their institutionally based complicity in severe violence.[6] Complicity is not the same as collaboration. It is not a matter of guilt or liability for purely individual actions or inactions. Complicity refers to the role-specific benefits that individuals enjoy as participants in institutionalized social practices. Teaching is one such social practice, but there are many others.[7]

A contemporary example of a Walzerian social critic of severe violence is the Croatian journalist Slavenka Drakulić. In *They Would Never Hurt a Fly: War Criminals on Trial in The Hague,* she criticizes the conduct and attitudes of the defendants appearing before the International Criminal Tribunal for the former Yugoslavia. In this series of portraits, Drakulić takes us inside the courtroom at The Hague to see how defendants respond to the charges against them. Some slip quickly into a state of near-clinical denial. Others lower down in the chain of command recognize what they have done but have no way of making sense of it. Yet, she concludes, "once you get closer to the real people who committed those crimes," you realize that they are not "monsters." They are "ordinary," and they would not have succeeded without the acquiescence of other ordinary people, including herself.[8]

Contrast Drakulić's interpretation of these trials with a critical reenactment of one of these proceedings in the 1997 film *Calling the Ghosts,* which I discuss in detail in §24. By reenacting parts of their ordeal, director Mandy Jacobson helps her main characters, two Muslim victims of the Serbian campaign of ethnic cleansing in Bosnia-Herzegovina, recognize the ways in which even as victims

6. Brooke A. Ackerly offers another model of Walzerian social criticism, "feminist social criticism," which is closer to my own view. For Ackerly, the social critic is an "everyday critic" who can help those who have been heretofore silenced by oppressive social practices and institutions articulate their interests through imperfect local and informal deliberative democratic structures. She objects to the idealism of contemporary theories of democratic deliberation and grounds her version of "connected social criticism" in the work of grassroots activists and organizers. As I have, she relies on John Dewey's theory of democratic education, although she does not explicitly invoke the concept of acquaintanceship. Where we differ is that she is concerned with how "everyday critics" can help those who have been silenced find their voices in democratic politics, while I am concerned with the complicity of everyday bystanders who have benefited from severe violence. See Brooke A. Ackerly, *Political Theory and Feminist Social Criticism* (New York: Cambridge University Press, 2000).

7. The report of the South African Truth and Reconciliation Commission identified institutional, not just individual, accomplices after the fact, including religious denominations and parts of the legal profession. Beyond that, the report criticized the commission itself for focusing on exceptional perpetrators while ignoring the "little perpetrator" in each of us: "It is only by recognizing the potential for evil in each one of us that we can take full responsibility for ensuring that such evil will never be repeated." Mark Sanders, *Complicities: The Intellectual and Apartheid* (Durham: Duke University Press, 2002), 2–4.

8. Slavenka Drakulić, *They Would Never Hurt a Fly: War Criminals on Trial in The Hague* (New York: Penguin, 2004), 186–91.

they also have been bystanders in the violence done to women during times of civil war. These two women, Jadranka Cigelj and Nusreta Sivac, become citizen-teachers over the course of their work with Jacobson. Drakulić tells us she feels like one of the collaborators who made criminals like Tudjman and Milošević possible, and that we should feel the same way about ourselves.[9] Citizen-teachers like Cigelj and Sivac avoid this irrationality[10] by using the reenactment of their own experience in *Calling the Ghosts* to help other everyday bystanders see themselves within a frame of reference in which even dramatic spectacles such as the trial of Slobodan Milošević have meaning in their own lives.

Citizen-teachers may not always have the full impact they want in order to turn the tide of severe violence. But through their sometimes enduring association with others (i.e., their students, readers, congregants, visitors, and neighbors), they can play an educational role as interpreters of critical reenactments of severe violence (e.g., Jacobson's reenactment of crimes against humanity being tried at The Hague) to foster new empathetic relationships among fellow bystanders and those who suffer from severe violence. The egregious collaboration of intellectuals can be contagious, but so can our ability to recognize and transform sometimes subtle and pervasive forms of complicity in severe violence.[11]

2. Teaching Responsibly

As a visiting faculty member at the University of Bamako, Mali, in 2005–6, I caught a fleeting glimpse of what it might mean to be a more responsible citizen-teacher. While Mali has managed to avoid protracted civil war (and genocide) since independence from the French in 1960 and then the overthrow of the dictator Moussa Traoré in 1991,[12] it continues to live in the shadow of two major famines in the 1970s and 1980s and a standard of living that places it regularly among the poorest nations in the world.[13] Minor periodic violence has also erupted in the

9. Ibid., 195.

10. See Jon Elster, *Closing the Books: Transitional Justice in Historical Perspective* (New York: Cambridge University Press, 2004), 243.

11. Two other citizen-teachers whose work, while not as philosophically developed as Jane Addams's, has helped me think through this argument are Myles Horton, *The Long Haul: An Autobiography* (New York: Teachers College Press, 1998); and Earl Shorris, *Riches for the Poor: The Clemente Course in the Humanities* (New York: Norton, 2000).

12. Robin-Edward Poulton and Ibrahim ag Youssouf, *A Peace of Timbuktu: Democratic Governance, Development, and African Peacemaking* (New York: United Nations, 1998).

13. Mali ranks 173rd out of 177 countries on the United Nations Human Development Index. The HDI measures life expectancy at birth, adult literacy rate, school enrollment, and gross domestic

North between government forces and Tuaregs seeking greater independence, but since 1996 not on a scale that has threatened severe violence.

During 2005–6 I was supported by the U.S. Fulbright Foundation, my own Michigan State University, the University of Bamako, and the U.S. embassy in Mali. While I was there, several of the University of Bamako's academic programs were closed for the entire fall semester when faculty refused to teach because of poor working conditions and low salaries. The year before, students had been on strike after several were killed by the police during a demonstration protesting faculty grading practices. While the situation throughout the university was tense in 2005–6, my graduate courses did not seem to be particularly affected. My students came to class regularly and did their work competently and conscientiously.

One of my responsibilities was to introduce these Malian graduate students in the university's agriculture program—l'Institut Polytechnic Rural de Formation et de Recherche Appliquée—and in the social science and humanities program—l'Institut Supérieur de Formation et de Recherche Appliquée—to ethical theories of development that could be of use to them in their own disciplines. This entailed raising their expectations of themselves as original thinkers who could contribute to academic and practical debates in their fields with an appropriate degree of ethical sophistication.

In the process I created several practical dilemmas for these students and for their institutions. How were they to continue to stay abreast of the ethical debates in their own field when they did not have affordable access to the literature? Very few classic texts and scholarly journals were available to them in Mali, and Internet access was expensive and unreliable. How were they to improve their English language skills in a francophone educational system whose students and faculty are not native French speakers? How could their institutions provide opportunities for exchange programs for faculty and students without tempting Malian professors and students to stay abroad after their studies, and when they barely had enough money to pay regular faculty salaries and virtually no money for graduate student stipends? In short, at the same time that I benefited from this opportunity to present my own ideas about ethics and development to an audience with firsthand experience, I created new professional and scholarly expectations in my students that could not be met by their own institutions without further outside assistance. I felt that I had benefited from the relationship

---

product per capita. See United Nations, *Human Development Report, 2007/2008: Fighting Climate Change: Human Solidarity in a Divided World* (New York: Palgrave Macmillan, United Nations Development Programme, 2007), http://hdr.undp.org/en/reports/global/hdr2007-2008/.

and consequently shared some responsibility with the institutions that supported me in Mali not to leave my students more frustrated or demoralized than they had been before I arrived.

Gestures such as leaving behind copies of used books or writing letters of recommendation, while appreciated, are not enough to meet these responsibilities. Without institutional support to match these one-time gifts, including strong linkages between universities in less and more developed countries, these gestures will not substantially improve the lot of these students or their instructors.

One might argue that the frustrated expectations of my students and colleagues in Mali, no matter how real, are not symptoms of severe violence. This is true, but there is more to it than frustrated expectations. Responsibilities in situations like these are never purely individual, and their consequences are rarely restricted to the feelings of individuals. We normally work in groups, and so our personal and social responsibilities are normally shared with other members of the group. We depend on institutional support, and so our personal and social responsibilities are inextricably bound up with the responsibilities we have for these institutions. The claims we make against one another based on individual rights cannot be settled without an understanding of the responsibilities we have to one another. The consequences of meeting or failing to meet this complex network of responsibilities are cumulative. Like small land mines, the aftermath of acting or failing to act on these responsibilities can be less visible and more profound than the immediate impact of our individual actions or inactions.

The considerable benefits that I derived from my relationships with my Malian students would not have been possible without the help and sometimes considerable sacrifice of Malian colleagues. We shared in the production of my courses and research, but we have not shared equally in the rewards and benefits. Further, this unequal sharing was made possible by larger political institutions (our public universities and our governments). Without the U.S. Department of State, the Council for the International Exchange of Scholars, and Michigan State University I would not have been able to participate in this project, and as a U.S. citizen I share some of the responsibility for both the creation and the consequences of programs like these.

3. Teaching Democratically

From the perspectives of most philosophers, social and political theorists, and cultural critics, the problem of recognition is the failure of dominant groups to recognize the full humanity of the poor and disenfranchised, sometimes referred to as "the subaltern Other."[14] This is not the problem of recognition with which I am concerned, although the two are related. I am primarily interested in correcting the myopic self-understanding of those of us who have benefited from the suffering of heterogeneous subaltern populations at the hands of severe violence. Too often as bystanders to severe violence we do not recognize our roles within the institutions that sustain it.[15]

Even where benefits follow quickly on the heels of the most brutal violence, there seems to be unwillingness, especially on the part of beneficiaries, to see the connection. For example, only recently have historians filled in this part of the story of complicity in the Nazi Holocaust against the Jews in Germany.[16] In the United States, only recently have the beneficiaries of twentieth-century legal segregation, along with the federal housing and lending policies that perpetuated it, been scrutinized.[17] As I shall argue in §11, despite this burgeoning scholarship, the responsibilities of the beneficiaries of chattel slavery in the United States are still not taken seriously.

Rather than search for the sources of our shared political responsibilities for severe violence on metaphysical ground,[18] I propose to think about how they can be constructed democratically through a process of critical reenactment. Among the contemporary critical reenactments that I will consider, in addition to *Shoah* and *Ubu and the Truth Commission*, are Hannah Arendt's book-length report *Eichmann in Jerusalem* and W. G. Sebald's novel *Austerlitz*.[19] The purpose

14. For example, see Charles Taylor, "The Politics of Recognition," in *Multiculturalism,* ed. Amy Gutmann, exp. ed. (Princeton: Princeton University Press, 1994), 25–73; and Gayatri Chakravorty Spivak, "Can the Subaltern Speak?" in *Marxism and the Interpretation of Culture,* ed. Cary Nelson and Larry Grossberg (Urbana: University of Illinois Press, 1988), 66–111.

15. One could argue that bystander responsibility is still a kind of causal responsibility, but it is not one that can be adequately described as a linear causal sequence or chain of events. See Peg O'Connor, *Oppression and Responsibility: A Wittgensteinian Approach to Social Practices and Moral Theory* (University Park: Pennsylvania State University Press, 2002).

16. Götz Aly, *Hitler's Beneficiaries: Plunder, Racial War, and the Nazi Welfare State,* trans. Jefferson Chase (New York: Henry Holt, 2005); but more accurately, Adam Tooze, *The Wages of Destruction: The Making and Breaking of the Nazi Economy* (New York: Viking, 2007). See also Victoria J. Barnett, *Bystanders: Conscience and Complicity During the Holocaust* (Westport, Conn.: Greenwood, 1999).

17. Matthew D. Lassiter, *The Silent Majority: Suburban Politics in the Sunbelt South* (Princeton: Princeton University Press, 2006).

18. See Karl Jaspers, *The Question of German Guilt,* trans. E. B. Ashton (1947; repr., New York: Fordham University Press, 2000).

19. As this short list illustrates, while some are critical reenactments of particular trials or hearings (beginning with Plato's *Apology of Socrates*), these official proceedings also can be the backdrop for reenacting other surrounding events. The work of the Tricycle Theater in North London illustrates how varied critical reenactments can be. On the one hand, in *Justifying War: Scenes from the Hutton*

of reenactments such as these, I shall argue in chapter 6, is not to adjudicate wrongdoing or vindicate the innocent; it is to create a public space in which the responsibilities of bystanders who are neither perpetrators nor victims can be democratically discussed and met. Critical reenactments like these are the first step in a process of democratic political education. They are hardly above criticism; on the contrary, they provoke and sometimes demand criticism of themselves as much as of the world they represent. With further interpretive help from citizen-teachers, these reenactments can serve as the basis for what John Dewey and Jane Addams called democratic acquaintanceship.[20] Lecturing on Addams in 1902, Dewey appears to have agreed with her that "democracy means certain types of experiences, an interest in experience in its various forms and types. It is not an interest any longer in philanthropy, in other words. You do not set out with the interest to do good to other people because it is your duty to do it. You set out with an interest in life, in experience; in life because it is the experience of people. Hence the demand for becoming acquainted, for making that a part of your experience." Continuing in his own words, Dewey stressed the gradual and indirect way in which ethical solutions occur: "You cannot decide that you are going to be good to the laboring man or be just to him, and then go to work and do this or that particular thing. You must get back to this idea of the acquaintanceship that comes about through actual interaction."[21] It is through democratic acquaintanceship that we can know who shares political responsibility for severe violence.

Addams's own service at Hull-House in Chicago is exemplary in this regard. In her work with prostitutes and her writings on this "social evil" (which she compared to slavery), she was guided by the belief that "sympathetic knowledge is the only way of approach to any human problem, and the line of least

---

Inquiry (2003) their texts are the official hearings on military interventions like the war in Iraq, and the reenactment is set in a courtroom. Then, in *Guantánamo: Honor Bound to Defend Freedom* (2004), they investigate the plight of British citizens imprisoned at Guantánamo using the words of their relatives, some freed prisoners, and British and American officials. A more recent work, *Called to Account: The Indictment of Anthony Charles Lynton Blair for the Crime of Aggression Against Iraq—A Hearing,* is also based on actual documents, speeches, and reports. As the title indicates, it anticipates a preliminary hearing investigating Prime Minister Tony Blair's statements leading up to British participation in the war in Iraq. See the Tricycle Theater Web site, http://www.tricycle.co.uk/.

20. Clarissa Rile Hayward, "Binding Problems, Boundary Problems: The Trouble with 'Democratic Citizenship,'" in *Identities, Affiliations, and Allegiances,* ed. Seyla Benhabib, Ian Shapiro, and Danilo Petranović (New York: Cambridge University Press, 2007), 181–205.

21. John Dewey, *Lectures on the Sociology of Ethics,* Lecture 22, November 19, 1902, Center for Dewey Studies, Southern Illinois University, Carbondale, Ill. I am indebted to John Wallace for the original reference and to Donald Koch for this citation.

resistance into the jungle of human wretchedness must always be through that region which is most thoroughly explored, not only by the information of the statistician, but by sympathetic understanding."[22] Anticipating contemporary feminist ethics of care, what Addams called a "sympathetic understanding" of working-class women and men was "garnered through her physical involvement in the Hull-House community."[23] This involvement included the arts and theater. She believed that the performing arts in particular could be a form of democratic education. That is, they could teach citizens how to challenge "current moral instruction": "I have come to believe, however, that the stage may do more than teach, that much of our current moral instruction will not endure the test of being cast into a lifelike mold, and when presented in dramatic form will reveal itself as platitudinous and effete. That which may have sounded like righteous teaching when it was remote and wordy will be challenged afresh when it is obliged to simulate life itself."[24] As one Dewey scholar has said, democratic education requires dramatic rehearsal and improvisation, not didactic assertions.[25] Addams neither lectured the poor nor pretended to be one of them; she worked hard to avoid "righteous teaching" on the one hand and "Tolstoyism" on the other.[26]

It would be much easier, of course, if we could begin with a list of fixed political responsibilities. But this is not how political responsibilities, shared or otherwise, are created in a democratic society. They are neither handed down to us from some moral high ground nor deduced from a deeper foundational principle.[27] If it is to be democratic, the process of recognizing our shared political

22. Jane Addams, *A New Conscience and an Ancient Evil* (New York: Macmillan, 1912), 11.

23. Maurice Hamington, *Embodied Care: Jane Addams, Maurice Merleau-Ponty, and Feminist Ethics* (Urbana: University of Illinois Press, 2004), 101. See also Judy D. Whipps, "Jane Addams's Social Thought as a Model for a Pragmatist-Feminist Communitarianism," *Hypatia* 19, no. 2 (2004): 118–33.

24. Jane Addams, *Twenty Years at Hull-House* (1910; repr., New York: New American Library, 1981), 270.

25. Steven Fesmire, *John Dewey and Moral Imagination: Pragmatism in Ethics* (Bloomington: Indiana University Press, 2003).

26. Her account of her visit to Tolstoy's farm is one of the most interesting self-reflective passages in *Twenty Years at Hull-House*. Chided by the Russian novelist for the clothes she was wearing, Addams began to reflect on how she might spend her time baking bread every day at Hull-House the way he labored with the peasants. She recognized that if she did this, she would not have time for the many other things necessary to keep Hull-House afloat. She also recognized that she would be putting her own salvation above the lives of others: "The half dozen people invariably waiting to see me after breakfast, the piles of letters to be opened and answered, the demand of actual and pressing human wants—were these all to be pushed aside and asked to wait while I saved my soul by two hours' work at baking bread?" *Twenty Years at Hull-House*, 197.

27. For example, Michael Dummett begins with a principle of egalitarian justice founded on the value of common humanity. From this principle, he derives a policy of open borders with citizenship

responsibilities for severe violence will be gradual, contested, and imperfect, not a matter of instantaneous sympathetic projection, which is what major writers on severe violence such as Peter Singer and Jeffrey Sachs seem to assume is possible (see §16). This kind of activity was common at Hull-House, especially in what Addams called its "social clubs": "The social clubs form a basis of acquaintanceship for many people living in other parts of the city. Through friendly relations with individuals, which is perhaps the sanest method of approach, they are thus brought into contact, many of them for the first time, with industrial and social problems challenging the moral resources of our contemporary life."[28]

Teaching democratically is not teaching a catechism of democratic rights and duties. It is teaching "through friendly relations with individuals," a kind of structured companionship with a particular focus on the burdens and benefits that society as a whole generates and for which individuals must learn to bear a shared responsibility. Dewey and Addams believed that citizen education should be conducted democratically in order to prepare citizens for the highest aspirations of democracy, not inoculate them against its temptations. But the democracy they had in mind was national, not global.[29] Teaching democratically today means teaching ourselves how to share responsibilities in a much more interconnected world—in other words, what it means to be citizens when the conventional language of political rights and duties falls short.

---

rights for immigrants and refugees. This is not an absolute principle, but it is only weakly limited by countervailing principles of state security and national cultural identity. See his *On Immigration and Refugees* (New York: Routledge, 2001).

28. Addams, *Twenty Years at Hull-House,* 254.

29. See Katharyne Mitchell, "Education for Democratic Citizenship: Transnationalism, Multiculturalism, and the Limits of Liberalism," *Harvard Educational Review* 71, no. 1 (2001): 51–78; and Ian Davies, Mark Evans, and Alan Reid, "Globalising Citizenship Education? A Critique of 'Global Education' and 'Citizenship Education,'" *British Journal of Educational Studies* 53, no. 1 (2005): 66–89.

2 CITIZENSHIP

Individual rights and duties have been the defining terms of citizenship in capitalist democracies since the nineteenth century. With the fall of the Soviet Union and most of its client states in the late twentieth century, coupled with antiauthoritarian movements in other parts of the world, these terms have achieved greater global currency. They include, most notably, political rights to vote and run for office, civil rights such as freedom of religion, and social and economic rights to basic healthcare, education, and welfare.[1] The duties of citizens have been less extensive, focusing primarily on the duty to honor the outcomes of free and fair elections, and in some cases to serve in the military and pay taxes. The rights that citizens enjoy are guaranteed by the state, and the duties they are expected to meet are owed to the state. There are many other rights and duties, some more firmly established in social custom and others more provisionally in law, but they have not been considered the exclusive rights and responsibilities of citizens, at least not until recently.

As other institutions have challenged the state's monopoly over coercive power, the meaning of citizenship has become problematic. "We are like travelers navigating an unknown terrain with the help of old maps," Seyla Benhabib observes, "drawn at a different time and in response to different needs." According to the old maps, social, economic, civil, and political rights are neatly nested in ascending priority within the closed borders of single nation-states. In practice, however, "one can have political membership rights without sharing the com-

---

1. Thomas H. Marshall, *Class, Citizenship, and Social Development* (New York: Doubleday, 1965).

mon identity of the majority; one can have access to social rights and benefits without sharing in self-governance and without being a national."² In other words, we have to understand how the old boundaries dividing citizens and noncitizens are giving way to a more fluid movement of entrepreneurs, refugees, exiles, and internally displaced persons. Only then will it be possible to imagine a more democratic alternative populated by responsible citizen-teachers and everyday bystanders.

4. Changing Maps

Citizenship is not just a legal status; it is also a process of becoming a certain kind of political agent. This process is most obvious for refugees seeking asylum, undocumented workers searching for assistance, prisoners clandestinely remanded for interrogation outside the jurisdiction of the prosecuting state, stateless adults and children quarantined in political limbo, or immigrants from one state applying for naturalization in another, but it is equally true for individuals who enjoy certain advantages at birth. They too must learn how to obtain legal counsel, interpret local customs, stay healthy, succeed in school, hold their families together, and fit into a global society in which the ties of traditional communities are being tested and often superseded by the demands for mobility, entrepreneurship, and general flexibility.³ In capitalist democracies of the twentieth and twenty-first centuries, these are the ways in which we become citizens.

Developing one's citizenship in this dynamic sense while using the old maps Benhabib refers to can be costly. For skilled Polish workers seeking employment in Germany, for Malian day laborers paying high fees to wire remittances from France back to their villages in West Africa, and for undocumented workers in the United States from Central and South America demonstrating for equal educational opportunities, basic healthcare, and other citizenship rights for their children, this means frustration, detention, and often tragic suffering. Conversely, for western European, British Commonwealth, and North American citizens facing new waves of immigrants, refugees, and exiles from eastern Europe, Africa,

2. Seyla Benhabib, "Democratic Citizens and the Crisis of Territoriality," *PS: Political Science and Politics* 38, no. 4 (2005): 674–75. More extensively, see Benhabib, *The Rights of Others: Aliens, Residents, and Citizens* (New York: Cambridge University Press, 2004).

3. Aihwa Ong, *Buddha Is Hiding: Refugees, Citizenship, the New America* (Berkeley and Los Angeles: University of California Press, 2003).

Asia, and the Middle East, the lines on the old maps seem virtually porous, leading to fear and resentment.[4]

If we turn to academia for help, we find sharp disagreements over alternative conceptions of citizenship. Some commentators have argued that citizens often have to balance their national citizenship with the special rights and duties they have as members of national minorities or immigrant groups (illegal as well as legal). Their goal is not so much to replace state citizenship as to make it more hospitable and accommodating so that they and others like them will be at home within the nation-state.[5]

In contrast to this multicultural conception of citizenship within states is an equally strong communitarian conception that transcends state boundaries. These transnational communities can be based on membership in particular religious, ethnic, racial, and language groups. They can be indigenous and concentrated in a particular region, or they can be spread over a wider diaspora. They can be cosmopolitan in the sense that their membership is based on belief in a universalistic ethic or program such as conserving the natural environment or protecting young children, or they can be parochial. The goal of these transnational communities is to perforate the boundaries between states and create new (even virtual) spaces where state citizenship is not the only legitimate political status a person can have.[6]

Both multicultural and communitarian conceptions of citizenship begin with a complex conception of identity and then infer a corresponding political ideal from it. In contrast, there are also conceptions of flexible citizenship that do not seek to stabilize the borders of territorial states. One such conception of flexible citizenship that comes out of public choice theory in economics suggests that citizens be allowed to choose from a large menu of citizenship rights across state boundaries. For example, citizens should be able to enjoy certain local rights and duties of one state while retaining their national citizenship rights within another. This is only the beginning, of course. Political membership in clubs, private organizations, universities, and other nongovernmental and quasi-

4. Office of the United Nations High Commissioner for Refugees, *The State of the World's Refugees: Human Displacement in the New Millennium* (New York: Oxford University Press, 2006). See also Wang Gungwu, ed., *Global History and Migrations* (Boulder, Colo.: Westview, 1997).

5. Will Kymlicka, *Multicultural Citizenship: A Liberal Theory of Minority Rights* (New York: Oxford University Press, 1996). See also David Miller, "Immigrants, Nations, and Citizenship," *Journal of Political Philosophy* 16, no. 4 (2008): 371–90; and Melissa S. Williams, "Nonterritorial Boundaries of Citizenship," in *Identities, Affiliations, and Allegiances*, ed. Seyla Benhabib, Ian Shapiro, and Danilo Petranović (New York: Cambridge University Press, 2007), 226–56.

6. Jana Evans Braziel and Anita Mannur, eds., *Theorizing Diaspora: A Reader* (Oxford: Blackwell, 2003).

governmental international organizations should also be possible. Just what political membership would entail and how the state's monopoly over various functions would be shared by these other bodies is vague. For the public choice theorist, however, the promise of a more efficient mix of citizenships is worth exploring.[7]

A very different conception of flexible citizenship is more constrained than the public choice variety and less utopian than communitarian citizenship. In Aihwa Ong's formulation, flexible citizenship comes in two colors. The first, call it green (for go), is market-oriented and self-centered. In certain "zones of hypergrowth" that neoliberal globalization has favored, immigration laws are adjusted and citizenship is conferred quickly and selectively on those individuals who can make growth happen. In emerging areas, these are enterprising "knowledge workers." In established areas, "elite actors exploit the possibility of capital accumulation through the astute deployment of multiple passports." In contrast, in the red "zones of exclusion," refugees, illegal immigrants, and other unwanted citizens are admonished to be more self-governing by the state and granted "biological citizenship" rights by NGOs, pharmaceutical companies, and multilateral organizations concerned with protecting their basic human rights. Survival outside (not participation inside) the neoliberal market defines citizenship in these red zones.[8]

Ong is clear that this does not mean individuals have no choices, but the choices they do have are limited and strategic. Suppose, for example, you live in a politically fragile society and it is not clear which way things are going (she uses the example of Hong Kong just before the British turnover to the People's Republic of China): "Many Hong Kongers opted to work in China while seeking citizenship elsewhere. Caught between British disciplinary racism and China's opportunistic claims of racial loyalty, between declining economic power in Britain and surging capitalism in Asia, they sought a flexible position among the myriad possibilities (and problems) found in the global economy."[9]

Flexible citizenship in Ong's sense is not a matter of celebrating one's hybrid identity by defying state power any more than it is a matter of choosing from a public choice menu. As capital and labor flow across state borders, citizens may have some political choices between shades of green and red, but hardly the ones that most academic intellectuals have and project on a romanticized "subaltern Other."

7. Bruno S. Frey, "Flexible Citizenship for a Global Society," *Politics, Philosophy, and Economics* 2, no. 1 (2003): 93–114.

8. Aihwa Ong, "(Re)articulations of Citizenship," *PS: Political Science and Politics* 38, no. 4 (2005): 697–99.

9. Aihwa Ong, *Flexible Citizenship: The Cultural Logics of Transnationality* (Durham: Duke University Press, 1999), 123.

Yet another conception of citizenship that academics have promoted is global citizenship. On the one hand, global citizenship can be very job-specific. Capitalists who preside over multinational corporations and operate within many countries and across many national borders are global citizens in one sense. So are their critics who seek international laws and sanctions against them. On this understanding, global citizenship is not so much a function of your identity as it is what you do. If you organize around the world to protect a resource or a cultural good, or if you extract natural resources globally, then you are a global citizen. But there is a stronger sense of global or cosmopolitan citizenship: if you enjoy the human rights of a citizen of the world, regardless of your country of origin or national citizenship, then you are arguably a global citizen as well. The defining characteristic here is not so much individual identity or behavior but rather the existence of an effective, legitimate political authority that can ensure protection of these universal human rights.[10]

This academic debate over the meaning of citizenship is not surprising, since these new conceptions have been incubated in educational and research institutions that are part of the same changing world in which new patterns of work, travel, and migration have occurred. Academic disciplinary boundaries are stressed to the breaking point, and academic attempts to redraw their own maps, depending on the type of institution and its mission, have been imperfect at best.

For example, at large public universities, relatively higher tuition rates for international students are used to offset the fall in other revenues, especially state appropriations, thereby driving a deeper wedge between international students and others. In many liberal arts colleges, the study of literature and foreign languages has been challenged by proponents of global cultural studies and world languages, creating further tension between postmodernist faculty members and the old guard. In departments of history, anthropology, and sociology at research universities, new interdisciplinary fields such as migration studies, diaspora studies, and transcultural studies are competing successfully for scarce resources for graduate education, scholarly journals, and office space. Academia has become a microcosm of mixed patterns of migration, globalization, and local resistance.

Like many others who have benefited from their membership in institutions that occasionally have sustained or failed to correct severe violence, I have relied on the old liberal map of citizenship to make sense of my role in the world.

---

10. Darren O'Byrne, "Citizenship," in *Cultural Geography: A Critical Dictionary of Concepts,* ed. David Atkinson and others (New York: I. B. Tauris, 2005), 135–40; and more thoroughly, Daniele Archibugi, *The Global Commonwealth of Citizens: Toward Cosmopolitan Democracy* (Princeton: Princeton University Press, 2008).

Over the past fifteen years I have tried to use it to navigate from the liberal, capitalist United States through post-communist Poland and post-socialist Mali, as the latter two countries have aspired to meet the membership requirements of the neoliberal world. I have tried to use the old map to understand my responsibilities toward those fellow citizens in the United States whose life expectancies are no higher than citizens of much poorer countries. I have even tried to use the old map when confronted by nameless children hawking cell phone cards and boxes of tissues in the blazing heat on street corners in rush-hour traffic in overcrowded cities in these poorer countries. I have used it to accept, without much hesitation, U.S. immigration, trade, and military policies that protect the high levels of consumption in my own country that I enjoy at home and sometimes even abroad.

To be sure, in the relative comfort of my university classroom I sometimes have criticized the distortions and assumptions of the liberal map—its individualism, its depreciation of politics as interest group bargaining, and its spoken and unspoken gender and racial hierarchies. But when I have been faced with severe poverty and the casualties of war, not just on paper, and my own health and security have been involved, I have found it much more difficult not to fall back on this detailed liberal map of the world and the privileges in healthcare, transportation, and education it affords to some.

This liberal map has two levels. The first is a moral topography centered on the individual private citizen and the values of liberty, equality, and justice he or she holds dear. The larger areas of this layer of the map—zoned residential and commercial—are where private citizens make a life for themselves and their families. This is where we believe we are free to exercise our social, economic, and civil rights. This is where the moral virtues of kindness, friendship, and care are supposed to take hold. The smaller, shadowy areas on this level of the map are public spaces. They are reserved for elections, public administration, and extraordinary events such as the waging of war and the declaration of peace. This is where our political rights are exercised and the public virtues of tolerance and loyalty to the state and to the political process are inscribed, if not practiced. There are disputed territories: for example, public parks and forests exist as an endangered species, government welfare programs minister to only the very neediest, big business takes its subsidies, and social movements contest the law. The mass media works both sides of the street, denouncing private corruption and embedding itself in public ministries and departments. But there remains a basic moral lay of the land on this surface level of the liberal map; the lives of private citizens occupy the high ground, and the functions of government are left the rest.[11]

There is a second, more subterranean level on the old liberal map that I call its cultural geography. On this level liberalism refers to a way of being and acting in the world, what Tocqueville called manners (*les moeurs*), not just a set of rules. But these are no longer the moderate habits of the heart that Tocqueville and his admirers have argued lead liberal citizens to take an interest in the interests of others. Liberalism's methods of reasoning elevate individual role models (John Stuart Mill's *Autobiography* is a good example) that obscure their historical prejudices behind what John Rawls called a "veil of ignorance." These habits of the mind have reinforced two contradictory orientations toward power and violence. The methods of practical reasoning and the metaphors that have developed gradually within the liberal tradition to cloak them have bred a tendency to defer to professional expertise and a voracious appetite for the spectacular show of force and its rewards. They constitute a second level of liberal citizenship: a mix of clientelism and consumerism. Again, these are not formal legal statuses but processes for becoming certain types of political agents.

As I was finishing *Intimacy and Spectacle: Liberal Theory as Political Education* in 1992–93, I began to explore how so-called transitional democracies in the early 1990s (the term has since fallen out of favor[12]) viewed the relationship between intellectual work, including political theory, and political education. I was looking for more democratic alternatives to liberal citizenship, and what I found surprised me. What turned out to be missing in the liberal and neoliberal conceptions of citizenship—the traditional surface idealization of private rights and public duties and the deeper processes of clientelism and consumerism—was a conception of political responsibility.

5. Responsibility

In 1990–91 Polish state employees (including academics) and pensioners on fixed incomes were reeling from two years of free-market "shock therapy" and high inflation. In this tumultuous situation I found that intellectuals in the Solidarity

11. John Kenneth Galbraith's *The Affluent Society* (1958; repr., New York: Houghton Mifflin, 1998) remains an insightful description of private wealth and public want in the United States.

12. Thomas Carothers, "The End of the Transition Paradigm," *Journal of Democracy* 13, no. 1 (2002): 5–21.

labor movement, such as Adam Michnik, were most interested in three political theorists: Alexis de Tocqueville for his emphasis on rights and democratic civil society, their compatriot Leszek Kołakowski for his uncompromising stand against Soviet Marxism, and Hannah Arendt for her erudite condemnation of Soviet as well as Nazi totalitarianism. Poles knew that Michnik had his differences with Arendt, whose analysis of totalitarianism did not quite fit the Polish experience, and with Kołakowski, whose early interpretation of the Catholic Church's role in politics he thought was one-sided.[13] But many Poles shared with Michnik a deep respect for the latter two theorists as courageous advocates for democratization, even if they agreed with Michnik on these finer critical points. In Tocqueville's *Democracy in America* they believed they had found a vision of American democracy that would help them limit the excesses of capitalism (inequality) and democracy (majority tyranny).

Before 1990, none of these three theorists had been of much interest to me as defenders of democracy. I had been put off by Tocqueville's aristocratic airs, Arendt's conception of the "banality of evil," and Kołakowski's uncharitable rejection of Marx. Once in Poland, however, I was struck by the way that their work had contributed to a democratic social movement that cut across some class and social lines. What was it, I asked myself, that the Polish intellectuals and professionals found in the work of these three theorists that I had overlooked? The answer, I believe, had more to do more with the complexity of the Poles' views about responsibility than their considerable personal courage to stand up to antidemocratic regimes.

After Solidarity's 1989 political victory, the Poles, like many other eastern Europeans in the post-communist era, were facing some difficult historical questions. In particular, they were trying to come to terms with the divisive role of the bystander that they had too readily accepted during World War II and then found so difficult to repudiate during the Cold War. The bystander had not been an abstraction during the second half of the twentieth century. In Poland, bystanders included young scholars who chose, out of expedience, self-interest, or fear, to quietly join the Party (a necessity for a university appointment) and then tried to maintain an ambiguous relationship to the government.

---

13. Adam Michnik, *Letters from Prison, and Other Essays,* trans. Maya Latynski (Berkeley and Los Angeles: University of California Press, 1985), 2; Michnik, *Letters from Freedom: Post–Cold War Realities and Perspectives,* trans. Jane Cave (Berkeley and Los Angeles: University of California Press, 1998), 104; and Michnik, *The Church and the Left,* trans. David Ost (Chicago: University of Chicago Press, 1993), 247–52.

This question of who had been an innocent bystander to the crimes of Nazism and then Soviet communism, and who had collaborated with, cooperated with, or merely lent their name to these regimes, was resurfacing in debates in the early 1990s over proposed plans for "lustration" (de-communization). In Poland, unlike in Czechoslovakia where Vaclav Havel had made lustration a moral imperative at the time, politicians were trying to postpone judgment day.[14]

In a revealing 1992 interview Michnik, who spent several years in prison and then became the editor of the leading liberal newspaper in Poland, *Gazeta Wyborcza*, posed the following question to Kołakowski: "Each system that emerges from dictatorship, from despotism, faces the question: how to deal with the past, with its own historical memory? What do you think are the dilemmas of post-communist countries in this respect?" Kołakowski first responded sarcastically: "How to deal with the past? I think that the way to do it was invented long ago: make it colorful so that it will look nice. This is already being done, and I suppose the process will go on. After all, we can see what's happening. It turns out that all have bravely struggled against communism for half a century, right? With no exceptions, all have shed blood for all those decades, all but a handful of renegades. This is necessary to feel good. Still, we do know the truth."[15]

There is some wisdom in this gibe. All tribunals—whether they are for prosecution or reconciliation—single out a few famous cases, and then those who are not prosecuted can assure themselves that they did the right thing. Kołakowski knew that there is very little consistency in who is called to account, who is quietly passed over, and who is allowed to prosper in the aftermath (e.g., at that moment some former high-ranking Communist Party members were rumored to be cashing in on the new free-market ideology by purchasing foreign car dealerships and other profitable enterprises). Nevertheless, there were clear cases; some people did collaborate (even if they did not join the Party) and some, despite their youth, did not:

> Well, I've read about some crazy plans to introduce a kind of apartheid according to the criterion of former party membership or party position.

14. The Czech and Slovak Federal Republic, before it split apart, passed its first lustration law in 1991; the Poles waited until 1998. For a discussion of the Czech rationale and Polish response, see Adam Michnik and Vaclav Havel, "Confronting the Past: Justice or Revenge," *Journal of Democracy* 4, no. 1 (1993), reprinted in *Transitional Justice*, ed. Neil J. Kritz (Washington, D.C.: U.S. Institute of Peace, 1995), 2:539–40.

15. Adam Michnik, "Communism, the Church, and Witches: An Interview with Leszek Kołakowski," originally published in *Gazeta Wyborcza*, November 21–22, 1992, and translated by Marek Wilczyński in *Centennial Review* 37, no. 2 (1993): 25.

And so, people who for years performed the role of *claquers* in the consecutive mute parliaments of the Polish People's Republic (PPR), but who were not party members, would be considered good. They were taking advantage of all communist privileges, but now they'll be good because they weren't members. And was PAX [a licensed Catholic organization—tr.] better than the party? And an individual like Jacek Kuron, who was perhaps the most hated and persecuted oppositionist of the PPR, who spent many years in prisons, who was arrested an infinite number of times—would he be made responsible for the atrocities of communism because as a young man he was a party member?[16]

The idea that Kuron could be prosecuted for his party membership as a youth indeed would have been absurd to any Pole in 1992. Party membership (much like PAX membership by itself) could not be a criterion for collaboration. Yet in Czechoslovakia, the 1992 case of Jan Kavan, who was accused of having spoken with the secret police while he was a young leader of the opposition in exile, was not at all clear-cut to many Czech citizens.[17]

Political responsibility, it seemed to me at the time, was neither a matter of legal guilt or innocence (under which laws should Kuron or Kavan be prosecuted?) nor a matter of moral praise or blame (according to which moral principles should they be judged?). The problem seemed both more complicated and more urgent.[18] Were people like Kuron and Kavan responsible in some indirect way for the violence committed by the party they belonged to or the secret police with which they may have been (naively) in contact? Were they to be denied public office twenty-five years later and no longer to be trusted as full citizens so that others would not make the same mistake?

I encountered several graduate students and faculty members caught in this dilemma during 1990–91 when I was a Fulbright scholar in the Institute of Political Science and Journalism at Adam Mickiewicz University in Poznan, Poland. The institute had the reputation of being one of the most orthodox Marxist programs at the university, and had enjoyed close ties with the Communist Party and the official state media. Faculty in the Institute of Sociology—such as Marek Ziołkowski—and in Philosophy—such as Leszek Nowak—who

16. Ibid.
17. Lawrence Weschler, "The Velvet Purge: The Trials of Jan Kavan," *New Yorker*, October 19, 1992, 68–94.
18. Giorgio Agamben overstates the problem as the "irremediable contamination" of responsibility by the law. *Remnants of Auschwitz: The Witness and the Archive*, trans. Daniel Heller-Roazen (New York: Zone Books, 2002), 20.

had been more critical of the old regime, were disdainful of elder members of the Institute of Political Science and Journalism, who appeared to me to be relatively unproductive and unrepentant for the blacklisting they had supported during the 1980s.

The doctoral graduate students in Political Science and Journalism seemed to be split between those eager to talk with me about research opportunities in the United States and those fearful of being labeled opportunists. The latter were not ready to drop their previous research projects simply because they would not be able to obtain U.S. funding. The students in my classes actually were advanced undergraduates from all these programs, but I seemed to have more from Philosophy than any other single institute. These Polish undergraduates were more erudite than the students I was used to in the United States, eager to improve their English language skills and wary of the conservative (what the Poles called "liberal") factions at the university, especially those in the English Language and English Literature programs who seemed to be most uncritical of American foreign policy and American culture. In addition to these Polish undergraduates, I had several African students who had come to Poland with Polish state funding, but since the fall of the Soviet Union they were without support. Civil wars in their home countries made it dangerous for them to return there, and as a result some had apprenticed themselves to older faculty in Political Science and Journalism, although it was not clear what they were doing beyond providing companionship and clerical services. Others were less fortunate and seemed to be slipping deeper into Ong's "zone of exclusion." For them, I appeared an unexpected lifeline, and they would call our apartment regularly hoping to arrange a trip with me back to the United States as a research assistant. I would explain that this was impossible, but they were not easily discouraged. Long after our return from abroad I continued to receive phone calls and e-mail messages from them.

Just as I have found more recently in Mali, my sheer presence in Poland created expectations among my faculty colleagues similar to those of the African students. The outcome in one case was far from happy. The Institute of Political Science and Journalism had its own academic journal. Most of the scholarly research done by the tenured members of the institute was published in this journal, and from my cursory inspection it did not appear to be rigorously refereed. In effect, it was a way for the university and especially the institute to keep up academic appearances while faculty members did more well-paid work for the Party and the official media. Now, however, there was no income to be earned in this way, and if faculty and graduate students were to win external grants, they would have to publish in more respectable venues. Two members of the institute, a junior faculty member and an advanced Polish graduate student, had shown particularly strong interest in my research, and I shared with them an article of mine recently accepted for publication. Several months after I returned to the United States, another graduate student from the institute sent me a copy of a newly published article in Polish by this pair in the institute's journal, *Edukacja Polityczna*. It was a translation of the now-published article I had shared with them but under their names only. The footnotes remained in English, mostly references to journals not available in Poland as far as I could tell.

I was angry, of course, but also felt somewhat responsible. I probably should not have tempted them with this unpublished article. A greater disappointment came when I informed the Council for International Exchange of Scholars (CIES), which was overseeing this new eastern European Fulbright Program. I told them that I did not think this particular institute in Poznan was ready to work with U.S. scholars, and I wanted CIES to bring this case of plagiarism to the attention of the university rector. I provided them with the relevant documents but never received a response, despite a follow-up e-mail. Perhaps some action was taken; I was never informed one way or the other. If an institution like CIES takes the initiative to create a new program like this one and then something goes wrong, as it well may the first time around, is there an institutional responsibility to pursue the matter and prevent it from happening again? Is CIES responsible to the students at the university, not just visiting faculty members like myself, to help them create alternatives to this kind of desperate attempt to escape the zone of exclusion?

The issue of institutional responsibility is nothing new in Poland. Polish intellectuals had been wrestling with it for decades before I arrived in Poznan in 1990. In fact, an important collection of essays, *The Political Responsibility of Intellectuals*, written by Polish and British scholars, was published in 1990 based on conference papers presented a few years prior to the events of 1989.[19] While most of the essays dealt with individual responsibility, one in particular—by Jerzy Jedlicki, professor of history in the Polish Academy of Sciences in Warsaw—addressed the subject of collective ("inherited") responsibility for the past deeds of the state, the Party, and the Catholic Church.[20]

---

19. Ian MacLean, Alan Montefiore, and Peter Winch, eds., *The Political Responsibility of Intellectuals* (New York: Cambridge University Press, 1990).

20. Jerzy Jedlicki, "Heritage and Collective Responsibility," in MacLean, Montefiore, and Winch, *Political Responsibility of Intellectuals*, 56.

Jedlicki recasts the history of events in Claude Lanzmann's 1985 documentary film *Shoah* and the films of Polish filmmaker Andrzej Wajda in order to help his fellow citizens "overcome a suppressed fear" that they may have to accept responsibility for their institutional past. Making that fear conscious is the first step in a process that Jedlicki hopes will break the vicious circle of violence: "Collective responsibility—I wish to repeat with emphasis—I understand here as the obligation of symbolic compensation for wrongs once committed and not as anyone's right to retaliation. Symbolic compensation in human society has purifying properties, properties of catharsis: it prevents the breeding of hateful emotions and extinguishes the right to retaliation."[21] By symbolic compensation Jedlicki means teaching. The Poles themselves must teach the history of their complicity if they are to reform their institutions and "extinguish the right to retaliation."

6. Bystanders

Can individuals inherit the responsibilities of their predecessors? (Jedlicki thinks so: if we collectively take patriotic pride in the past, then we also have an obligation to accept responsibility for other elements of our past of which we are not at all proud.) How should responsibilities be distributed among individual members of responsible groups? How should responsibilities be shared among individuals, groups, and the institutions they have created or benefited from? What should happen to those who default on their responsibilities? These questions are difficult, even when considering the responsibilities of everyday bystanders in close proximity to severe violence. They are especially difficult when we realize that there is a much wider circle of everyday bystanders that extends beyond state and regional boundaries.

Let's begin at home with the disturbing series of photographs and documents of lynchings *Without Sanctuary,* collected in 2000 by James Allen and John Littlefield. One photo shows the lynching of Lige Daniels on August 3, 1920, in Center, Texas. Daniels was accused of killing an elderly white woman. Captain W. A. Bridges of the Seventh Cavalry was wired orders from Austin to protect Daniels from the threat of mob violence; his excuse for failing to follow those orders was the inability to "find any members of his company in time for mobilization."[22]

---

21. Ibid., 72.

22. James Allen and John Littlefield, *Without Sanctuary: Lynching Photography in America* (Santa Fe, N.Mex.: Twin Palms, 2000). See also http://www.withoutsanctuary.org/.

One thousand men stormed the Center jail, battered down the steel doors, wrecked the cell, chose a courthouse yard oak, and lynched Daniels. Afterward they posed for pictures with the body. The perpetrators of this crime were not bystanders, and arguably neither was Captain Bridges, who failed in his official duty to protect Daniels.

There may have been onlookers in the crowd who did not participate in the lynching, possibly some of the youngest boys in the front of the photo. But there is another circle of bystanders whose responsibility comes into question. The photograph was made into a postcard, one copy of which was sent shortly after the lynching with the following handwritten message: "He killed Earl's grandma. She was Florence's mother. Give this to Burt."[23] What were the responsibilities of those who sent or made postcards of lynchings? Did they benefit improperly from this egregious crime? Did they contribute indirectly to future acts of violence? In what sense were they members of an institution, not just a loosely structured group of opportunistic individuals? It is hard to answer these questions without knowing more about them.

David Lyons argues that if a government fails to correct the injustices that result from the cumulative history of legalized slavery and racial discrimination, then that government is responsible.[24] I would describe the government in this case as an institutional bystander to the harmful legacy of slavery. Further, citizens who have had the chance to change these laws and policies but have not acted are complicit, regardless of whether they have personally benefited from this legacy. If they could have done something, even if it was only to call attention to this legacy, and they chose not to, they too are responsible—they have a share in the government's institutional responsibility.

What about noncitizens and citizens of other countries who do not have the same opportunities to affect current laws and policies? Are these bystanders also complicit everyday bystanders? That depends on what counts as an opportunity to affect current laws and policies. In some cases, especially where the bystander is a multinational corporation, a humanitarian nongovernmental

23. Photographs such as these and more recent ones of torture victims in the Iraq war, Sharon Sliwinski has observed, create an "immediate anguish" in the spectator: "The almost automatic judgment that 'this is wrong,' is the very stroke which opens the possibility for the recognition of the other *as* human and so deserving of dignity. Indeed, it is perhaps only those of us whose flesh has not been wounded directly—but whose imagination has been aroused by such images—who can afford to face and to judge these horrors. Photographs are undoubtedly part of the arsenal of modern war, but they are also conduits of justice." Sharon Sliwinski, "Camera War, Again," *Journal of Visual Culture* 5, no. 1 (2006): 92.

24. David Lyons, "Corrective Justice, Equal Opportunity, and the Legacy of Slavery and Jim Crow," *Boston University Law Review* 84 (December 2004): 1375–1404.

organization, or a consortium of universities and research institutes whose power cuts across state boundaries, they and those who work for and benefit from them also may be responsible. It depends on their role within the institution and, in cases such as these, how much they have benefited.

Sometimes institutional everyday bystanders and their members are based in poor countries. They live side by side with those who suffer, and it is not hard for them to see how their lives are connected to the lives of these victims.[25] More often they operate out of richer countries, where their shareholders, owners, managers, donors, vendors, and staff are occasionally disturbed by the poverty and violence they hear about in the media, but are only dimly aware of how the lives they lead depend on this suffering and how their acquiescence to state and other institutions legitimates it. These connections are not clearly visible or keenly felt along the coordinates of rights and duties that structure liberal maps of citizenship. Another set of axes—what I call bonds of complicity and acquaintance—will have to be developed through a process of democratic political education before everyday bystanders are able to understand their complicity in severe violence across national boundaries and their political responsibility for addressing it. This is the first obstacle facing the recognition of shared and institutional responsibilities.

When I refer to the existing bonds of citizenship as bonds of complicity, I do not mean exactly what Primo Levi did when he coined this term to describe the complicity of prisoners forced to labor in Nazi concentration camps.[26] The bonds of complicity that link everyday bystanders to one another and to those

25. David H. Jones examines the moral responsibility of bystanders to the Nazi Holocaust in situations like this. He concentrates on different types of bystander responsibility and mentions in passing accomplices who were more involved in atrocities than mere bystanders. The most morally egregious accomplices were those who added insult to the injuries inflicted by others. My use of the term "complicity" does not comprise the responsibility of the accomplices that Jones describes. See *Moral Responsibility in the Holocaust: A Study in the Ethics of Character* (Lanham, Md.: Rowman and Littlefield, 1999), 217.

26. Levi used this phrase to describe how Nazi concentration camp officials treated collaborator prisoners (who had done so prior to their internment so that they could be "trusted") with horrific low-level tasks inside the camps: "Collaborators, who originate in the adversary camp, ex-enemies, are untrustworthy by definition: they betrayed once and they can betray again. It is not enough to relegate them to marginal tasks; the best way to bind them is to burden them with guilt, cover them with blood, compromise them as much as possible, thus establishing a *bond of complicity* so that they can no longer turn back. This way of proceeding has been well known to criminal associations of all times and places" (emphasis added). Levi, *The Drowned and the Saved,* trans. Raymond Rosenthal (1988; repr., New York: Vintage, 1989), 43. I should also distinguish my use of the term "complicity" from Christopher Kutz's careful treatment of its legal meaning in *Complicity: Ethics and Law for a Collective Age* (New York: Cambridge University Press, 2000). I am grateful to Martin Benjamin for first suggesting that I consider the term.

who suffer are not tightened by new feelings of guilt, as Levi says they are. Institutions do not feel guilty, and typically the members of these particular institutions do not feel guilty for what their institutions have done (nor is it important for my argument that they should). Institutions may apologize and their members may sympathize with those who suffer, and sometimes they may feel remorse for not having donated more time or money to alleviate suffering. What makes everyday bystanders complicit, more than their failure to change their behavior toward severe violence, is the benefit they derive after the fact from severe violence.

Democratic acquaintanceship is one way for bystanders to help one another work through difficult memories of complicity and suffering in order to replace these bonds with a greater recognition of their interdependence and common fate. This relationship is neither cathartic nor therapeutic. It involves retrieving painful, sometimes repressed memories and even retracing one's steps alongside others. It is like walking through a museum that one gradually discovers is dedicated to a people whose suffering one did not know beforehand and with whom one did not realize one had a relationship. This is what W. G. Sebald has called an "alternative Holocaust museum."[27] It is not a museum of horrors, but rather a museum of abandoned and confiscated property, sometimes of significant personal value, sometimes trivial. It is a museum of untitled images, assembled without the help of a trained curator, that trace the unspoken connections between past and present.

Why do everyday bystanders so often fail to recognize how they benefit from famine, civil war, and genocide? Both the passivity of clients dependent on professional experts and the low attention span of consumers of mass political spectacles (which I described in *Intimacy and Spectacle*) continue to operate. Liberal theory as a cultural factor that distracts many citizens in liberal societies from severe violence continues to play an important role in our political life. To jettison this political attitude, one must have a clearer understanding of how globalization's place on the old liberal map obscures the complicity of everyday bystanders and impedes their recognition of new opportunities for acting on their shared and institutional political responsibilities.

27. In *Austerlitz*, Sebald uses photomontage, dialogue, architectural criticism, and other interview techniques to gradually excavate and reassemble the life of Jacques Austerlitz, a Czech émigré sent by his parents to Wales in 1939 and tormented by fleeting memories and a vague sense of despair: "Six months before his death in December 2001, in an interview with the Spanish newspaper *El País*, Sebald reflected on his work. Speaking of his great novel, *Austerlitz*, he said that he had intended to 'create an alternative Holocaust museum.'" Philip Schlesinger, "W. G. Sebald and the Condition of Exile," *Theory, Culture, and Society* 21, no. 2 (2004): 44. I return to *Austerlitz* in the book's conclusion.

Globalization is an incomplete characterization of the current global structures of power and patterns of violence that have evolved over the past three
decades. Global changes in communications, transportation, and production
technologies have been shaped by particular neoliberal policies and practices.
That is, globalization has occurred according to neoliberal rules of trade liberalization, military intervention, and selective financing.[28] Neoliberal globalization
(like its liberal colonial and imperial predecessors) has exacerbated the tendency
to turn a blind eye toward severe violence at the same time that it sheds a sympathetic tear for the world's poor and hungry. The structure of neoliberal globalization has made informed empathy for the chronically poor and those who suffer
from other forms of severe violence more difficult.

Neoliberal ethical theories of development (or development ethics), like
their classical and modern precursors, have played an important role in the
creation of this landscape—what I have called its moral topography. They too
have been forms of political education. Just as there are important themes that
connect the work of Hobbes, Locke, Kant, Mill, and Rawls as forms of political
education, we can discern a common method of reasoning in the work of contemporary development ethicists. I will call this the allegory of individual responsibility, and in §16 I will consider several examples of it in the work of Peter Singer,
Jeffrey Sachs, and Amartya Sen.

At the level of cultural geography, neoliberalism is defined by a culture of
simulation, described in more detail in §13. Our moral perceptions of development, severe violence, and responsibility are refracted through this new culture
of simulation as well as large traces of the older culture of professional authority
and clientelism that classical liberal theory enshrined. The difficulty that everyday
bystanders have in recognizing how they benefit from severe violence on a global
scale is the product of this conjunction of the longer liberal tradition and the
more recent culture of simulation, not only its allegorical methods of discerning
individual responsibility.

It takes time to establish the moral and cultural grounds that support this kind
of bystander complicity in severe violence. It is a process of making small daily
choices to accept certain benefits and privileges, rather than one characterized

28. Jan Nederveen Pieterse, *Globalization or Empire?* (New York: Routledge, 2004), 1–16. Where
poorer countries have resisted neoliberal globalization because of its adverse effects, different economic, military, and political patterns have emerged. For example, see John M. Staatz and others,
"Agricultural Globalization in Reverse: The Impact of the Food Crisis in West Africa" (paper presented at the Geneva Trade and Development Forum, Crans-Monana, Switzerland, September
17–20, 2008).

by inertia or rudderless indifference.[29] Similarly, a long process of democratic political education will be required to forge a new, more inclusive sense of political responsibility. This notion of the everyday bystander and what it will take to break these habits is expressed elegantly by the poet Carolyn Forché: "We are responsible for the quality of our vision; we have a say in the shaping of our sensibility. In the many thousand daily choices we make, we create ourselves and the voice with which we speak and work."[30]

An important element in this process of democratic political education is the reenactment by writers, filmmakers, and other artists of the many tribunals, commissions, and official proceedings that have been created to assess responsibility for severe violence. Through embodied and sustained reenactments, not sympathetic imagination or religious conversion, everyday bystanders to severe violence can become more aware of how they have benefited from severe violence and how they could become more capable of democratically reforming the neoliberal structures of power they reproduce daily.

7. Citizen-Teachers

Democratic political education requires more than a series of televised tribunals and truth commissions. Counter-simulations that attempt to shock and scold bystanders into greater self-consciousness and action—like a tour of a virtual refugee camp or a performance of a slave auction—also will not do. At worst they are video games that suggest that with a click such tragedies can be removed; at best they are momentarily cathartic. The ideal of democratic citizenship that I am recommending depends crucially on the figure of the citizen-teacher. The reenactments of complex events such as war crimes tribunals and truth commissions that I have in mind are not going to be immediately accessible to everyday bystanders. Their poetic diction and literary allusions are not designed for direct popular consumption. They will have to be interpreted with the help of allegorical stories like the two I offer about Jim and Ousmane. Citizen-teachers can play this mediating role between everyday bystanders and the writers, filmmakers, and artists who create complex reenactments. They are interpreters and storytellers, not heroic rescuers.

29. Norman Geras, *The Contract of Mutual Indifference: Political Philosophy After the Holocaust* (New York: Verso, 1998).

30. Carolyn Forché, "Sensibility and Responsibility," in *The Writer and Human Rights,* ed. Toronto Arts Group for Human Rights (Garden City, N.Y.: Anchor Press, 1983), 25.

Unlike the classical liberal ideal of the citizen-soldier who is willing to suspend private life in a public emergency, or the contemporary client-consumer for whom the privatization of public life is the ideal, the citizen-teacher strives to promote public values that he or she believes are important as a regular part of everyone's private life. There is a difference between the duty to act on one's own values and the responsibility to promote those values more broadly.[31] The citizen-teacher is specifically responsible for promoting appropriate opportunities for democratic discussion and participation, and explaining when those opportunities do and do not present themselves. It is in this sense that citizen-teachers strive to teach greater critical self-awareness of the origins, effects, and benefits of severe violence.

It is, of course, easy to caricature this ideal of the citizen-teacher as a busybody who is forever trying to pull bystanders aside, speak in allegories, and declare every mishap a teachable moment. Teachers who do this are prone, I believe, to inflating their own importance and exaggerating their effectiveness. They believe unreservedly in the truth of their message and the individual courage required to deliver it.[32] This self-confidence may be reassuring to some, but it safely ignores how teachers themselves become implicated in the unfolding history of the institutions on which they depend.

To make the ideal of the citizen-teacher more appealing and more plausible, I will offer two allegories of political responsibility that, like the ruling allegories of individual responsibility, focus on themes that have become more acute under neoliberal globalization: rescue and hostage-taking. The inspiration for these two stories comes from my own encounters with the critical reenactments of artists such as Lanzmann and Kentridge, and my face-to-face experience as a teacher with students, some of whom have been much closer to severe violence than I have.

"Ousmane at the Crossroads" and "Jim in the Grand Marché," discussed in chapter 6, illustrate what it means to think about political responsibilities in terms of our everyday participation in institutions that exercise enormous power in our lives and lead to violence in the lives of others. They also illustrate how fluid the roles of bystanders are and how development as an ongoing project of democratic political education (rather than development as technology transfer, economic

---

31. I borrow this distinction between the duty to act in accordance with values and the responsibility to promote them from Nigel Dower, *An Introduction to Global Citizenship* (Edinburgh: Edinburgh University Press, 2003).

32. For example, see Parker J. Palmer, *The Courage to Teach: Exploring the Inner Landscape of a Teacher's Life* (San Francisco: Jossey-Bass, 1998).

growth, or political security) can help us critically monitor these changing roles.[33] Whereas neoliberalism recommends that we limit rescue efforts until corrupt regimes are eliminated and that we treat hostage-taking as an act of war, these two allegories stress the importance of empathy on the part of citizen-teachers. Citizen-teachers must recognize that they and the bystanders they work with are beneficiaries of severe violence. One way to do this, I argue, is through close acquaintanceships between teachers and students.

The acquaintanceships I have in mind are democratic, not Platonic. They are carefully structured, not casual or intimate. Their goals are not joy or some kind of ecstatic experience. In order to build this kind of practical, empathic acquaintanceship, the citizen-teacher needs two other political virtues besides empathy.

The first is the capacity to translate between bystanders and the displaced persons, deportees, and refugees with whom they share their worlds. Citizen-teachers must be able to show bystanders how the seemingly innocuous language they use to describe neoliberal globalization is heard by others. To do this effectively, citizen-teachers must become acquainted with the ways of life of both the bystanders and those who suffer silently in the shadows, on the pavement, and in the pages of reports on severe violence. Only then will the inflections in and resonances of their political conversations carry. This means that citizen-teachers must learn how to hear the sounds of severe violence in their own words and translate the repressed language of those who suffer from severe violence into public speech. These acts of translation take time and patience. Translation is hidden by myths of instantaneous and simultaneous globalization. Without translators, however, neither neoliberal policies nor alternatives to them are possible. The citizen-teacher, then, makes these acts of translation explicit.[34]

Second, citizen-teachers striving for empathy must also show poise under fire. They must expect the political ground to shift under their feet (as Emerson was fond of saying) and the terms of every argument to change when it is most inconvenient for their cause. They must be able to listen for the merits of opposing positions, despite the hyperbole and ad hominem attacks. They must

---

33. The need to supplement ethical theories of development like Sen's capability approach with institutional and role analyses is discussed in William A. Jackson, "Capabilities, Culture, and Social Structure," *Review of Social Economy* 63, no. 1 (2005): 101–24.

34. "The network underpinned by information technologies brings Anglophone messages and images from all over the globe in minutes and seconds, leading to a reticular cosmopolitanism of near-instantaneity. This cosmopolitanism is partly generated by translators themselves who work to make information available in the dominant language of the market. However, what is devalued or ignored in the cyberhype of global communities is the effort, the difficulty, and above all else, the time required to establish and maintain linguistic (and by definition, cultural) connections." Michael Cronin, *Translation and Globalization* (New York: Routledge, 2003), 49.

remember that there is no final "at the end of the day" in democratic politics, only provisional stopping points: all issues can be revisited, all questions can be reopened. Most of all, they must be able to maintain political respect for those who suffer most. They cannot allow sympathy to substitute for empathy (see §8).

A fictional example of the citizen-teacher is Paul Bereyter, one of four main characters in W. G. Sebald's 1996 novel *The Emigrants*. While not a completely successful citizen-teacher, Bereyter illustrates the quiet intensity and self-reflectiveness that democratic political education requires of its practitioners.

Paul, as his primary school students called him, left an indelible impression on the narrator. He was a "free thinker," which in early 1950s Germany meant he refused to participate in religious instruction in his classroom. He loved to whistle but was also inclined to become extremely pensive, often staring off into the distance, while still intensely engaged in his students' learning. He covered the required curriculum, but he also did much more: "Indeed, Paul's teaching was altogether the most lucid, in general, that one could imagine. On principle he placed the greatest value on taking us out of the school building whenever the opportunity arose and observing as much as we could around the town—the electric power station with the transformer plant, the smelting furnaces and the steam-powered forge at the iron foundry, the basketware workshops, and the cheese dairy. We visited the mash room at the brewery, and the malt house."[35]

Only later in the narrator's adult life (after reading Paul's obituary) did he set out to discover the source of his teacher's equally intense melancholy. As a young teacher Paul had been expelled by the Third Reich because his father was half Jewish, and his family's business had been confiscated. Paul did not have a clear memory of these events, which took place between 1934 and 1936, until he began to go back through old family albums and piece the story together with the help of others. In the words of one such informant:

> What horrified Paul was not only the coarse offences and the violence of those Palm Sunday incidents in Gunzenhausen, not only the death of seventy-five-year-old Ahron Rosenfeld, who was stabbed, or thirty-year-old Siegfried Rosenau, who was hanged from a railing; it was not only those things, said Mme Landau, that horrified Paul, but also, nearly as

35. W. G. Sebald, *The Emigrants,* trans. Michael Hulse (New York: New Directions Books, 1996), 38.

deeply, a newspaper article he came across, reporting with *Schadenfreude* that the schoolchildren of Gunzenhausen had helped themselves to a free bazaar in the town the following morning, taking several weeks' supply of hair slides, chocolate cigarettes, coloured pencils, fizz powder and many other things from the wrecked shops.[36]

After spending some unhappy time as a family tutor in France, Paul returned to Germany in early 1939, took several nonteaching jobs, and ended up serving for six years in the "motorized artillery, variously stationed in the Greater German homeland and in the several countries that were occupied." After the war he took up gardening, and his sight gradually failed him. He committed suicide by lying down in front of an oncoming train, something not mentioned in his obituary, which bore the headline "Grief at the Loss of a Popular Teacher."

We only have a snapshot of Paul Bereyter, but in it we can glimpse the virtues of the citizen-teacher and also some of the dangers that an interpreter of severe violence in everyday life will face. Paul was reserved, almost distant, with those he taught, but he was able to bring students of varying abilities together in cooperative exercises, sometimes inspiring the weaker student and enabling the stronger to see how, through collaborative learning, he or she too would profit. For many of his students he could muster considerable empathy. He could also be harsh toward students whose posturing and conceit annoyed him. He was hardly a saint, and ultimately he could not resist returning to his own native land, regardless of the consequences. Citizen-teachers are not intimate confessors or paragons of virtue. Cut off from their work, they will grasp for straws. In Paul's case, perhaps, this explains his return to Germany in 1939. Perhaps as his eyesight failed his sense of hearing became more acute, as often happens. Perhaps he no longer could live with the newly assembled memories of those transported by rail to their death or, as he was, exiled.

As narrators and translators of critical reenactments of severe violence, citizen-teachers can reach a wider audience of everyday bystanders. Then, when it comes time to choose the rules of citizenship, those who choose will have the benefit of a democratic political education. They will choose with greater awareness of their own feelings and complicity in severe violence. This is no guarantee that they will choose wisely, but their choices will be better informed and they will know what they mean for others, not just for themselves. In some cases, their choices may still be unbearable, as Paul Bereyter's proved to be for him.

36. Ibid., 54–55.

8. Empathy and Care

If citizen-teachers are to help everyday bystanders see themselves as citizens who both share a common life with those who suffer severe violence and do not blithely benefit at their expense, what exactly do we mean by empathy? Unlike sympathy, which is a kind of monotonic compassion, empathy requires that we understand others cognitively, affectively, and emotionally.[37] Empathy is not an overwhelming feeling of sympathy for the innocent victim; it may often be joined with sympathy, but it need not be. For example, one can empathize with a very unsavory character and understand how the institutional roles he occupies drive him to do what he does, without feeling much sympathy for him. It is this danger that leads Martha Nussbaum to warn us that empathy is not sufficient for compassion for others, and in some cases it may not even be necessary. The torturer, she reminds us, may have a very acute feeling of empathy for his victim—the better to torture him.[38]

But Nussbaum also recognizes that the absence of empathy may be an invitation to or symptom of a greater evil, not unlike what I have termed severe violence. With Nazism in mind, she writes:

> In short, empathy does count for something, standing between us and a type of especially terrible evil—at least with regard to those for whom we have it. The habits of mind involved in this exercise of imagination make it difficult to turn around and deny humanity to the very people with whose experiences one has been encouraged to have empathy. . . . Thus many Germans constructed for themselves, in effect, a double life. Brought up to have empathy for those they recognized as human, they led lives of cultivated imagination with those people; toward those whom they killed and tortured, they denied the very recognition of humanity.[39]

I do not mean to suggest that Nussbaum believes that empathy is a moral sentiment; she does not. She does acknowledge, however, its special connection to severe violence, if only in a negative rather than a curative way.

What empathy promises beyond an immediate sympathetic response is a sustained interest in and concern for others and an understanding of one's connections

---

37. Alex Neill, "Empathy and (Film) Fiction," in *Post-theory: Reconstructing Film Studies,* ed. David Bordwell and Noël Carroll (Madison: University of Wisconsin Press, 1996), 179–80.

38. Martha C. Nussbaum, *Upheavals of Thought: The Intelligence of Emotions* (New York: Cambridge University Press, 2001), 329.

39. Ibid., 334–35.

to their suffering. Fiction is perhaps the most familiar vehicle for prompting and sustaining empathy. The novelist Barbara Kingsolver puts it this way:

> The power of fiction is to create empathy. It lifts you away from your chair and stuffs you gently down inside someone else's point of view. . . . A newspaper could tell you that one hundred people, say, in an airplane, or in Israel, or in Iraq, have died today. And you can think to yourself, "How very sad," then turn the page and see how the Wildcats fared. But a novel could take just one of those hundred lives and show you exactly how it felt to be that person rising from bed in the morning, watching the desert light on the tile of her doorway and on the curve of her daughter's cheek. You could taste that person's breakfast, and love her family, and sort through her worries as your own, and know that a death in that household will be the end of the only life that someone will ever have. As important as yours. As important as mine.[40]

Yet Kingsolver conflates empathy as an active engagement with others, which reveals what Jane Addams called "the size of one another's burdens," and sympathy as a vicarious projection of oneself into the other's place. Susan Sontag, in her ambivalent meditation on the dangers of photographing violence, worries that there is a dangerous illusion in images and passages that "show you exactly how it felt to be that person" suffering at the hands of others:

> So far as we feel sympathy, we feel we are not accomplices to what caused the suffering. Our sympathy proclaims our innocence as well as our impotence. To that extent, it can be (for all good intentions) an impertinent—if not inappropriate—response. To set aside the sympathy we extend to others beset in war and murderous politics for a reflection on how our privileges are located on the same map as their suffering, and may—in ways we might prefer not to imagine—be linked to their suffering, as the wealth of some may imply the destitution of others, is a task for which the painful, stirring images supply only an initial spark.[41]

Again, whether one calls it sympathy or empathy, the important thing is that the desired social sentiment and moral feeling is one that allows us to see "how

---

40. Barbara Kingsolver, *High Tide in Tucson: Essays from Now and Never* (New York: Harper Perennial, 1996), 231.
41. Susan Sontag, *Regarding the Pain of Others* (New York: Picador, 2003), 102–3.

our privileges are located on the same map as their suffering"—indeed, how "the wealth of some may imply the destitution of others."

Feminist writers and activists have been saying similar things about the importance of care and empathy for several decades,[42] and in many cases creating new institutions that reflect these values.[43] I have already indicated the importance of Jane Addams's conception of "sympathetic understanding" based on democratic acquaintanceship for this conception of social care. At this juncture I want to make more explicit where my own argument intersects with work that I will subsequently call feminist ethics of care. The conceptions of empathy and care I favor do not "stuff you gently down inside someone else's point of view," but they do draw on other insights of feminist ethics of care akin to Addams's more practical conception of "sympathetic understanding."

Let me restate the general argument explicitly in terms of empathy and care. If everyday bystanders are to see their complicity as beneficiaries of severe violence more clearly, they must be able to empathize, not just sympathize, with the victims of severe violence. Further, if citizen-teachers are to facilitate this change and encourage the kind of acquaintanceships that I say may be needed to sustain it, then they must do this with care. What does it mean to interpret critical reenactments of severe violence carefully so that everyday bystanders may understand their place as beneficiaries of such actions with greater and lasting empathy?

In literary theory, empathy and its cognates refer to the capacity of the reader to enter the text and see the world from the point of view of another. This is sometimes described as *verstehen,* but others prefer the Aristotelian notion of hermeneutic interpretation.[44] The role of the citizen-teacher, for example, involves a certain set of skills in textual interpretation. Whether it is a play, a poem, or a painting, the citizen-teacher must be able to render this critical reenactment accessible to a larger audience of everyday bystanders. The audience then must be able to see themselves in the text without losing sight of their actual place in society.

Empathy also has been explored by academic psychologists and professional psychotherapists. According to Robert L. Katz, "When we empathize, we lose

---

42. Much has been written by feminist philosophers about empathy as a way of knowing and about care as an individual moral virtue. See, for example, Rosemarie Tong, "Feminist Perspectives on Empathy as an Epistemic Skill and Caring as a Moral Virtue," *Journal of Medical Humanities* 18, no. 3 (1997): 153–68. For a more recent comprehensive view, see Virginia Held, *The Ethics of Care: Personal, Political, and Global* (New York: Oxford University Press, 2006). From a nonfeminist perspective, see Michael Slote, *The Ethics of Care and Empathy* (New York: Routledge, 2007).

43. See the United Nations Development Programme Web site devoted to women's empowerment, http://www.undp.org/women/.

44. For example, Karl F. Morrison, *"I Am You": The Hermeneutics of Empathy in Western Literature, Theology, and Art* (Princeton: Princeton University Press, 1988).

ourselves in the new identity we have temporarily assumed"; in contrast, "when we sympathize, we remain more conscious of our separate identity." Here too there is a connection with the conception of empathy I have in mind. The empathetic psychotherapist, like the empathetic bystander, does not become sympathetically self-absorbed. Sympathy, unlike empathy, "turns our attention back on ourselves."[45] It is this limitation of sympathy that I think citizen-teachers must guard against and avoid inculcating.

More recently, psychologists and cognitive scientists have begun to explore empathy on another level, which has prompted a debate between them and philosophers about just what may be going on inside our heads when we empathize with another. One school of thought holds that we must have some kind of theory of other minds in order to know what other people are thinking. In this view autism is the inability to feel empathy because for the autistic person other people are merely objects, not subjects with their own mind. The other school of thought, called simulation theory, holds that we do not need a theory of other minds to empathize. All that is needed is the ability to imaginatively put oneself in the other's place step-by-step and then rationally deliberate from that point of view. We do what we would do as if we were in their place, not as if we somehow were that other person. We do not have to believe that the other has a mind like our own.[46] Some simulation theories of empathy take for granted that empathy can be reduced to a matter of simulating the behavior of another, and that it does not involve any critical self-reflection on one's relationship to the other, which is what interests me.

Empathy also has been of great interest to moral psychologists studying early childhood development. One model allows us to distinguish between several stages, from empathic arousal to distress to anger. The existence of an "empathic affect" may be the functional equivalent of stepping behind Rawls's "veil of ignorance."[47] For other psychologists, this affect may be the natural moral grammar of our species.[48] These claims, which often focus on the behavior

45. Robert L. Katz, *Empathy: Its Nature and Uses* (New York: Free Press of Glencoe, 1963), 9.

46. Hans Herbert Kögler and Karsten R. Stueber, eds., *Empathy and Agency: The Problem of Understanding in the Human Sciences* (Boulder, Colo.: Westview, 2000); Karsten R. Stueber, *Rediscovering Empathy: Agency, Folk Psychology, and the Human Sciences* (Cambridge, Mass.: MIT Press, 2006); and Alvin I. Goldman, *Simulating Minds: The Philosophy, Psychology, and Neuroscience of Mindreading* (New York: Oxford University Press, 2006).

47. Martin L. Hoffman, *Empathy and Moral Development: Implications for Caring and Justice* (New York: Cambridge University Press, 2000).

48. Marc Hauser, *Moral Minds: The Unconscious Voice of Right and Wrong* (New York: HarperCollins, 2007); and Greg Bock and Jamie Good, eds., *Empathy and Fairness,* Novartis Foundation Symposium 278 (Hoboken, N.J.: John Wiley, 2006).

of "innocent bystanders" to unanticipated emergencies, still do not address the problem faced by bystanders who are already complicit in severe violence. In §16 I review the allegories of innocent bystanders that frame the arguments of moral psychologists but misrepresent the situations of everyday bystanders to severe violence.

One common theme among feminist theories of care is the place of empathy as a virtue, not merely an attitude, disposition, or some other psychological trait. Along with some feminist theorists, I am particularly interested in empathy as a political virtue of citizens—that is, a normative concept that describes the resilience and motivational basis of good citizenship. While I do not offer a general theory of democratic political education for caring citizen-teachers who can teach everyday bystanders to empathize with victims of severe violence, my view of care is indebted to several strands in feminist ethics of care.

One strand, beginning with the work of Joan Tronto, has sought to extend the feminist ethics of care in a political direction. Tronto argues that while responsibilities to care for, not just care about, others are not reducible to political and legal obligations, they are still responsibilities that citizens ought to have for one another. Tronto emphasizes that this responsibility to care for others does not convert society into "one big family." Rather, it "makes citizens more thoughtful, more attentive to the needs of others, and therefore better democratic citizens."[49] The result of this change in perspective is that feminist theorists of care can provide us with a more resourceful view of the provision of social services, health-care, and education.[50] They argue that care need not be built on a conception of moral identity in which mothering symbolizes the virtues of a good citizen. According to Selma Sevenhuijsen, a political ethics of care replaces questions of individual duty to care for another with "situated questions concerning responsibility." This avoids reducing responsibility to self-sacrifice.[51] In chapter 4 I criticize the narrowness of the dominant allegories of bystander responsibility for reducing complex, shared responsibilities to categorical duties of self-sacrifice.

Another strand in recent feminist ethics of care is a concern with globalization and the ways that a focus on women and gender has improved both our

49. Joan C. Tronto, *Moral Boundaries: A Political Argument for an Ethic of Care* (New York: Routledge, 1993), 131, 169.

50. For example, see Maurice Hamington and Dorothy C. Miller, eds., *Socializing Care: Feminist Ethics and Public Issues* (Lanham, Md.: Rowman and Littlefield, 2006).

51. Selma Sevenhuijsen, *Citizenship and the Ethics of Care: Feminist Considerations on Justice, Morality, and Politics* (New York: Routledge, 1998), 56.

understanding of this process and the concomitant neoliberal policies that have shaped it.[52] A feminist study of international relations, Gillian Youngs has argued, highlights the "transnationalization of production; the feminization of labour; restructuring in postsocialist societies; growth in services, including domestic and sexualized work; migration, including that of qualified workers to take strategic jobs . . . or more menial work that is nevertheless more highly paid than what they can do at home; human trafficking, including enforced prostitution; women and development; the decline of the welfare state and its impact on women; and women's rights as human rights."[53]

Against this fuller understanding of neoliberal and "masculinist" globalization, the feminist emphasis on care has stressed the limitations of both cosmopolitan and communitarian theories of citizenship and justice. According to Fiona Robinson, a "critical ethics of care" should promote "healthy, caring relations among individuals and groups, not through the application of some minimal, abstract principles of what justice demands, but according to the demands of the given situation, where real social relations among concrete persons need to be created and restored."[54] This emphasis on particular social relations, or what I am calling acquaintanceships, is perhaps the most important and most challenging element that my view of democratic political education shares with feminist ethics of care. Creating (not restoring) relations among everyday bystanders and those who suffer severe violence cannot be legislated according to "abstract principles" of justice or of care. In chapter 9 I offer some imperfect examples of this kind of creative work, consistent with these two strands in the feminist ethics of care literature, which illustrate what it means to describe empathy as a discursive practice rather than a vicarious thought experiment.

52. Ofelia Schutte, "Dependency Work, Women, and the Global Economy," in *The Subject of Care: Feminist Perspectives on Dependency,* ed. Eva Feder Kittay and Ellen K. Feder (Lanham, Md.: Rowman and Littlefield, 2002), 138–58.

53. Gillian Youngs, "Feminist International Relations: A Contradiction in Terms? Or: Why Women and Gender Are Essential to Understanding the World 'We' Live In," *International Affairs* 80, no. 1 (2004): 86.

54. Fiona Robinson, *Globalizing Care: Ethics, Feminist Theory, and International Relations* (Boulder, Colo.: Westview, 1999), 132. This is not a precious utopian model for social reform that cannot be extended to global concerns; Robinson has discussed more recently the application of the critical ethics of care to global human rights discourse. See Robinson, "Human Rights and the Global Politics of Resistance: Feminist Perspectives," *Review of International Studies* 29 (December 2003): 161–80; and Robinson, "NGOs and the Advancement of Economic and Social Rights: Philosophical and Practical Controversies," *International Relations* 17, no. 1 (2003): 79–96; also Allison Weir, "The Global Universal Caregiver: Imagining Women's Liberation in the New Millennium," *Constellations* 12, no. 3 (2005): 308–30.

3 POLITICAL RESPONSIBILITY

In a July 2001 article in the *Wall Street Journal* reporting on the entanglement of major U.S. corporations with slave labor, Douglas A. Blackmon described the following case.

> On March 30, 1908, Green Cottenham was arrested by the Shelby County, Ala., sheriff and charged with vagrancy. After three days in the county jail, the 22-year-old African-American was sentenced to an unspecified term of hard labor. The next day, he was handed over to a unit of U.S. Steel Corp. and put to work with hundreds of other convicts in the notorious Pratt Mines complex on the outskirts of Birmingham. Four months later, he was still at the coal mines when tuberculosis killed him.
>
> Born two decades after the end of slavery in America, Green Cottenham died a slave in all but name.[1]

When contacted by Blackmon, U.S. Steel officials denied that such practices had occurred and then suggested that there is no reason to revisit these matters. For corporations that believe they are being responsible citizens now, historical injustices are not an issue. I will argue that such corporations (including their employees and stockholders) are complicit everyday bystanders to severe violence. Because they continue to enjoy benefits from these past unjust practices, they have shared and institutional responsibilities to bring these benefits to light and create appropriate political methods for addressing them fairly.

---

1. Douglas A. Blackmon, "From Alabama's Past, Capitalism and Racism in a Cruel Partnership," *Wall Street Journal,* July 16, 2001. See also Matthew J. Mancini, *One Dies, Get Another: Convict Leasing in the American South, 1866–1928* (Columbia: University of South Carolina Press, 1996).

This web of complicity and political responsibility can extend in surprising directions. In his subsequent book-length study of "industrial slavery" from the mid-nineteenth century until 1945, Blackmon locates the Cottenham case alongside many other similar stories, including his own family's use of forced labor: "I had no hand in the horrors perpetrated by John Pace or any of the other twentieth-century slave masters who terrorized American blacks for four generations. But it is nonetheless true that hundreds of millions of us spring from or benefit as a result of the lines of descent that abided those crimes and benefited from them."[2] While the beneficiaries of severe violence are often large corporations and other institutions, sometimes small business owners like Blackmon's family and even other immigrants, refugees, and displaced persons can be the reluctant beneficiaries of the unjust actions of others.

Responsibility, as David Miller has reminded us, is one of the most important yet unclear terms in our political vocabulary.[3] This is true despite the many efforts to distinguish between perfect and imperfect, special and general, and positive and negative responsibilities.[4] This is particularly true of political responsibility. Within liberal theories of justice, political responsibility tends to occupy a relatively small space between prior but optional moral duties and mandatory legal responsibilities. Where individual political responsibilities are not reducible to moral duties or legal responsibilities, they tend to be either indeterminate—such as the obligation to play the role of the loyal opposition—or extraordinary— such as the obligation to perform national service.

In addition to the political responsibilities of individual citizens, there are also collective political responsibilities of states, multilateral organizations, and nongovernmental organizations, including transnational corporations and more informal groups or associations of citizens.[5] Many liberal philosophers, including David Miller, have done a careful job comparing the responsibilities of wealthy nation-states for the suffering of poor and powerless peoples, on the

2. Douglas A. Blackmon, *Slavery by Another Name: The Re-enslavement of Black Americans from the Civil War to World War II* (New York: Doubleday, 2008), 396.

3. David Miller, *National Responsibility and Global Justice* (New York: Oxford University Press, 2007), 82.

4. For example, see Henry Shue, "Mediating Duties," *Ethics* 98, no. 4 (1988): 687–704; and Elizabeth Ashford, "The Alleged Dichotomy Between Positive and Negative Rights and Duties" in *Global Basic Rights*, ed. Charles R. Beitz and Robert E. Goodin (New York: Oxford University Press, 2009), 92–112.

5. For opposing views, see Virginia Held, "Group Responsibility for Ethnic Violence," *Journal of Ethics* 6, no. 2 (2002): 157–78; and Joel Feinberg, "Collective Responsibility," *Journal of Philosophy* 65, no. 21 (1968): 674–88.

one hand, with their responsibilities for the suffering of their own citizens.[6] It is less clear how we can think about the institutional political responsibilities of corporations within this liberal framework and the political responsibilities of individuals who occupy roles within these institutions.[7] This is not only true for companies like U.S. Steel and other industrial and manufacturing corporations; it is also true for universities and humanitarian organizations. I use the term "shared responsibility" (as opposed to "collective responsibility" or "group responsibility") to refer to the political responsibilities of individuals who occupy positions of authority in institutions that are themselves politically responsible for severe violence.[8]

9. Individual Political Responsibility

According to many liberal theorists, moral individual duty is less stringent than legal responsibility in the sense that so long as coming to the aid of those in need is not too risky, then regardless of who is at fault moral persons have a duty of beneficence to intervene and help. If it is too risky for them, regardless of who is at fault, they are not bound to act on this duty. In contrast, legal responsibility normally depends on who is at fault, and in cases of severe violence those who have contributed causally, either through their actions or omissions, ought to be held legally liable.

From this liberal perspective, we think of duties of beneficence or justice in terms of the responsibility that an individual has for his or her actions. In this case, responsibility depends on whether the individual was free enough to make his or her own decisions and act on them. Varying degrees of freedom lead to varying degrees of responsibility. In philosophical terms, this concept of responsibility

6. See Deen K. Chatterjee, ed., *The Ethics of Assistance: Morality and the Distant Needy* (New York: Cambridge University Press, 2004).

7. For one attempt to address institutional responsibilities from a moral, not a political, point of view, see Michael Green, "Institutional Responsibility for Moral Problems," in *Global Responsibilities: Who Must Deliver on Human Rights?* ed. Andrew Kuper (New York: Routledge, 2005), 117–34.

8. Larry May has offered an existentialist interpretation of the shared individual responsibilities of members of these groups that he calls "liberationist communitarianism." He acutely distinguishes between the guilt feelings associated with individual moral responsibilities and the ways that shame and feelings of "taintedness" arise when individuals fail to meet their shared group responsibilities. Primarily concerned with what he calls moral responsibilities, he does address the special political responsibilities of philosophers and philosophical associations. Though I have benefited greatly from his careful analysis, my use of the term "shared responsibility" is narrower than his. Larry May, *Sharing Responsibility* (Chicago: University of Chicago Press, 1992).

depends on how one resolves the metaphysical problem of free will and determinism—that is, how responsible one is as a freely choosing self within the institutional roles that constrain us.[9]

Individual moral duty and legal responsibility can certainly overlap in some cases. What is morally wrong can also be legally punishable, and certainly what is legally punishable is often considered morally wrong. These responsibilities also can become shared responsibilities in cases where no one is individually at fault. Joel Feinberg, among others, has described situations in which despite the absence of any individual wrongdoing, there may be a shared responsibility among a group of bystanders. In his own hypothetical case of a drowning swimmer, where none of the bystanders has a special relationship to the victim or a special capacity to rescue safely, the bystanders as a group may be held accountable.[10] Nation-states, even when they do not have obligations based on past colonial relationships or present special capacities, may have similar responsibilities to suffering peoples outside their borders.[11]

From a democratic perspective we can distinguish between two types of individual political responsibilities. *First-order* political responsibilities include obligations to respect the political rights of others, such as freedom of speech, association, and assembly, or the obligation to vote or respect the rights of due process of others. They also include public or military service and other forms of mutual political support during emergencies and natural disasters, such as obligations to evacuate dangerous areas. Some of these duties and obligations will be legally binding, such as those governed both by constitutional protections of speech and by administrative and executive orders restricting freedom of movement and residence during civil emergencies, but not all first-order political responsibilities have to be. For example, at certain times and in certain democratic countries the political obligation to serve in the military or to vote in elections is voluntary.

---

9. See, for example, the essays by A. John Simmons, *Justification and Legitimacy: Essays on Rights and Obligations* (New York: Cambridge University Press, 2001). For a critical discussion of the ontological presuppositions of the liberal conception of responsibility that draws on the writings of Hegel, Marx, and Judith Butler, see Chad Lavin, *The Politics of Responsibility* (Urbana: University of Illinois Press, 2008).

10. Joel Feinberg, *Doing and Deserving* (Princeton: Princeton University Press, 1970), 244.

11. Kok-Chor Tan, "The Duty to Protect," in *Humanitarian Intervention*, ed. Terry Nardin and Melissa S. Williams, Nomos 47 (New York: New York University Press, 2006), 84–116. See also J. L. Holzgrefe and Robert O. Keohane, eds., *Humanitarian Intervention: Ethical, Legal, and Political Dilemmas* (New York: Cambridge University Press, 2003); and Gareth Evans, *The Responsibility to Protect: Ending Mass Atrocity Crimes Once and For All* (Washington, D.C.: Brookings Institution Press, 2008).

In contrast to these first-order political responsibilities, *second-order* individual political responsibilities are obligations that persons accept rather than responsibilities that others hold them to. For example, the political responsibility to take an interest in the integrity of the political process by studying the issues, listening to opposing views, and formulating an informed view of one's own is a second-order political responsibility. It presupposes the value of certain first-order political responsibilities, but one can still be politically responsible in this second-order sense even if one's right to vote has been suspended, say, during martial law or some other civil emergency.

The second-order political responsibility to prepare oneself (and one's children) to be informed and tolerant participants in the democratic political process is what I will call a *general* second-order political responsibility. It is not limited to particular elections or political controversies, nor is it limited to individual human beings. In a society committed to becoming more democratic, I would argue, there is a general responsibility for individual persons and groups to participate in good faith on an appropriate footing with other persons in the periodic assessment of the effects of the distribution and exercise of power and wealth on the quality of democratic life. Call it taking stock of the body politic. Jefferson's belief that a constitutional convention should be held once every nineteen years— so that each generation can write its own constitution—has some kinship to this idea. Those who are engaged in the production of wealth and power and who will be responsible for using it well, he believed, periodically should revise the political rules under which they live.[12]

There is a different kind of second-order political responsibility, the *specific* second-order political responsibility of persons to participate in the design of fair procedures for organizing the benefits that continue to accrue in a democratic society from past undemocratic practices and thereby obstruct the democratic transition. This is an obligation to correct the legacy of tainted benefits by participating in the creation of a special charter or treaty, not a general constitutional convention.

Not all persons should take the same responsibility for designing fair procedures for redirecting this flow of tainted benefits. Injured parties and neutral mediators will play certain roles, and persons who have enjoyed these tainted benefits but who cannot be ignored in the design of new procedures will play other roles. For example, take the problem of including members of former

---

12. Thomas Jefferson to Samuel Kercheval, July 12, 1816, in *The Portable Jefferson,* ed. Merrill D. Peterson (New York: Penguin, 1979), 560.

communist regimes in particular phases of the post-1989 democratic transitions in eastern Europe; there are certainly different degrees of complicity among them. Before examining cases such as this in §11, however, we must confront the more general question of what constitutes corporate identity: should corporations be treated as if they are individuals, or do they have a more sui generis institutional political responsibility?

10. Institutional Political Responsibility

Corporate responsibility is not usually thought of in either a first-order or a second-order political sense. Typically corporate responsibility is divided into three asymmetrical and overlapping categories: legal, moral, and social. The legal responsibility not to mislead customers, the moral responsibility to support charitable causes, and the social responsibility not to pollute the environment illustrate how these three categories may overlap. Charitable corporate giving is encouraged through tax laws that reward corporations; consumer protection laws protect the consumer's freedom of choice; and environmental protection laws sometimes rest on the moral status of nonhuman entities.[13] But given the major roles corporations play in almost every aspect of life in capitalist democracies today, there is a need to understand the general and specific second-order political responsibilities of corporations beyond the moral responsibilities of individuals implicated in corporate misdeeds and their limited legal liabilities.

This raises a prior question: should corporations be involved as agents in any aspect of the democratic political process, or are they simply forms of property with no moral or political standing?[14] My view is that while they do not have any moral standing and should not have any first-order political responsibilities, given their current influence on the distribution of power and wealth in democratic societies, they do have some specific second-order political responsibilities.[15]

13. See Kurt Baier, "Moral, Legal, and Social Responsibility," in *Shame, Responsibility, and the Corporation,* ed. Hugh Cutler (New York: Haven, 1986), 183–95.

14. I am indebted to John Ladd for raising this question. See Ladd, "Morality and the Ideal of Rationality in Formal Organizations," *Monist* 54, no. 4 (1970): 507–8; and Ladd, "Corporate Mythology and Individual Responsibility," *International Journal of Applied Philosophy* 2, no. 1 (1984): 1–21.

15. This does not mean that corporate persons and other group persons cannot legitimately have political rights, such as a limited right to political speech in the form of advertising their views about particular public issues. But this is not the same as having a political responsibility to participate

Let me begin by criticizing the view that corporations are moral persons. According to Peter French, corporate actions, intentions, and responsibilities cannot be reduced to the actions, intentions, and responsibilities of their constituent members.[16] A corporation's moral "personhood" should guide our views about its legal and political status, not the other way around.[17] French believes that a corporation's moral responsibility extends backward in time to cover some of its prior acts. According to his Principle of Responsive Adjustment (PRA), even though a corporation may have acted unintentionally in committing a morally untoward act, it may be held responsible for that act if, in the future, it does not make adjustments in its policies and procedures to ensure that the act does not reoccur. The failure to make adequate adjustments, when it is in the power of the corporation to do so, is an intentional act ("from practiced indifference to blatant repetition") that makes the earlier unintentional act something the corporation should be held responsible for, even though the earlier act is not reassessed and found to be intentional after all.[18] That which the failure to comply with the PRA tells us about the character of the person—in this case a corporate person—is what warrants holding such a person responsible retroactively.[19]

One reason for rejecting the PRA's strong personification of the corporation, beyond any support it gives to the doctrine of limited liability,[20] is that it presupposes a misleading hierarchical model of the corporation in which general policy goals are annunciated at the top and then filter down as specific tasks.

---

in legislative debates on these issues. The lack of connection between first- and second-order political responsibilities in the case of corporations underlines the difference between this distinction and Harry Frankfurt's famous distinction between first-order and second-order desires in his analysis of free will. One must have first-order desires in order to have a second-order desire to want to be moved by first-order desires. A corporation need not have first-order political responsibilities in order to have a second-order political responsibility in the sense described here.

16. Peter A. French, ed., *Individual and Collective Responsibility: The My Lai Massacre* (Cambridge, Mass.: Schenkman, 1972); French, *Collective and Corporate Responsibility* (New York: Columbia University Press, 1984); and French, *Responsibility Matters* (Lawrence: University Press of Kansas, 1992).

17. For a review of the literature on holism and individualism as these concepts are applied to the corporation, see Michael J. Phillips, "Reappraising the Real Entity Theory of the Corporation," *Florida State University Law Review* 21, no. 4 (1994): 1061–1123; and James J. Brummer, *Corporate Responsibility and Legitimacy: An Interdisciplinary Analysis* (New York: Greenwood, 1991).

18. French, *Collective and Corporate Responsibility*, 15.

19. Ibid., 160.

20. For a criticism of French along this line, see Manuel Velasquez, "Why Corporations Are Not Morally Responsible for Anything They Do" (1983), reprinted in *Collective Responsibility: Five Decades of Debate in Theoretical and Applied Ethics,* ed. Larry May and Stacey Hoffman (Savage, Md.: Rowman and Littlefield, 1991), 111–32.

The structure of large-scale organizations now is a "coalition of groups of divergent claims and interests, engaged in a continuous process of bargaining with one another."[21] Policy goals and procedural rules are contested as various groups bargain and position themselves to influence decisions that may or may not satisfy their conceptions of the corporation's first-order responsibilities and their own personal interests. There is not one corporate internal decision structure, as French assumes, but rather several interconnected and contested ones.

Larry May has argued that treating the corporation as a single person with a moral responsibility to reexamine and adjust its behavior in light of the consequences of past unintentional wrongdoing obscures this complexity.[22] French's retroactive PRA, premised on the possibility of a monolithic corporate character, should be replaced by a more democratic procedure for determining the extent of corporate political responsibility. Such a procedure should include representatives of all of the corporation's stakeholders. This does not mean that corporations deserve all the political rights, duties, and first-order responsibilities of other political persons, any more than they should enjoy the legal rights, duties, and responsibilities of other moral persons. In other words, is it possible and desirable for corporations to have second-order political responsibilities even if they do not have any of the first-order political responsibilities of full moral persons?

One way to answer this question is to examine the relationship between individuals, groups, and artificial persons. I contend that corporations are artificial group persons that can act as accomplices and take a specific kind of political responsibility for these actions, even though they are neither full moral persons nor mere instruments. As Annette Baier has said, doing things with others is more basic than doing things alone.[23] Philosophers who have sought to analyze doing things in groups, however, have not paid adequate attention to institutional or artificial groups. They prefer to analyze two friends deciding to go on a walk together, a married couple deciding to paint a room together, or as Hume did, two oarsmen rowing together in the same boat. They argue that we ought to treat these small groups with the same kind of rational respect that we treat rational individuals. For example, if groups, like individuals,

21. Meir Dan-Cohen, *Rights, Persons, and Organizations* (Berkeley and Los Angeles: University of California Press, 1986), 19. For a detailed discussion of the implications of this model of the corporation for criminal liability, including comments on French's theory, see Jennifer A. Quaid, "The Assessment of Corporate Criminal Liability on the Basis of Corporate Identity: An Analysis," *McGill Law Journal* 43, no. 1 (1998): 67–114.

22. Larry May, *The Morality of Groups: Collective Responsibility, Group-Based Harm, and Corporate Rights* (Notre Dame: University of Notre Dame Press, 1987), 69.

23. Annette C. Baier, *The Commons of the Mind* (Chicago: Open Court, 1997), 21–40.

can have a rational point of view, can be committed to achieving overall rational unity, and can be susceptible to rational modes of influence, then we should treat them like agency-regarding persons—that is, they are capable of acting like rational agents and treating other persons as rational agents. According to Carol Rovane, it would be hypocritical for individuals who think these are the elements of their own identity as persons not to treat groups with the same characteristics as persons. For example, walking partners owe the group, not just other individuals in the group, an explanation when personal obligations force them to cancel, since the group ideally would have the same agency-regarding respect for any of its members.[24]

One problem with this group ontology is that it ignores the institutional context of group formation and action. Neighbors disagree, build fences, and break off relations, but this kind of analysis abstracts from the institutional structures of power these neighbors inhabit. In fact, actual neighbors inhabit overlapping structures of power. They are usually neighbors within the same school district and the same police precinct, but they rarely work for the same company and may have different national citizenship. The examples of walking partners or house-painting couples ignore the problems that these institutional realities pose for real neighbors with group intentions and responsibilities. It is only when a toxic dump site or something equally dramatic intrudes that the institution-based power relations among neighbors become visible.

Rovane is correct, I believe, that good neighbor groups can be committed to achieving rational unity and can be susceptible to rational modes of influence. Corporations that have unjustly enriched themselves are also concerned with their rational identity, but they seek something less than "rational unity" (what I will call rational coherence) in a more complex institutional environment. The accusation of complicity presupposes an underlying political identity that is not reducible to the various individuals or groups that make up the corporation, hence the notion of an artificial group person.

In other words, some benefits that corporations as artificial group persons enjoy in capitalist societies with a history of severe violence may be the result of a corporate plan to conceal stolen assets or other ill-gotten gains, no matter what individual members or subgroups may say about their own personal knowledge or intentions. These benefits, in addition to their immediate value, also may enhance a corporation's competitive market position long after they

---

24. Carol Rovane, *The Bounds of Agency: An Essay in Revisionary Metaphysics* (Princeton: Princeton University Press, 1998), 49, 131.

initially were acquired and through no personal, isolated fault of the current owners and employees. This phenomenon of corporate complicity, rather than corporate collaboration, does not involve the kind of intentional action that we associate with immoral individual collaboration. Corporate complicity is precisely the kind of entanglement with severe violence that an artificial group like a corporation with the complex structure I have described above is likely to have because of the partial knowledge and control that each of the corporation's constitutive groups has.

A corporation, then, is a group of groups artificially bound together, capable of incurring specific second-order political responsibilities for benefits whose acceptance may perpetuate this tainted legacy. A corporation's plan to conceal tainted benefits does not have to presuppose the desire for rational unity. In fact, given the complex structure of such corporations, there probably will be serious disagreements among the groups that make up this artificial group person. In order to survive as a corporation with a coherent (not unified) identity, however, there must be some consensus among these groups that the plan was permissible and the benefits are worth retaining. The discovery of tainted benefits can tear the corporation apart, with some groups adamantly opposed to them and others ready to accept them as part of an unchangeable past.

What is to be done about these benefits? Consider the benefit of competitive market advantage. This is something that builds up over time and cannot be disassembled and redistributed any more easily than the transportation and industrial infrastructure of a society can be moved around. Beyond the mechanical problems facing restitution and compensation, it is not likely that corporations that have been complicit can all be put out of business without serious ripple effects that may harm the very persons reparations are supposed to help. One alternative to being held morally and legally responsible for these ill-gotten gains is to take responsibility for them in a democratic sense.

Regardless of their degree of responsibility for causing or facilitating past atrocities, corporations often benefit in ways that carry these benefits forward, for which they ought to take political responsibility. If, for example, they have benefited from the employment of slave labor (as Blackmon describes so well in the case of slavery and forced labor in the United States), then they have at a minimum a present responsibility to participate in the redistribution of those benefits so that they and their descendants (corporate and individual) do not continue to profit from a past injustice that will persist and multiply.[25]

---

25. Ruti Teitel makes a somewhat different argument. She argues that when states have neglected to correct past wrongs, they become implicated in them, and the original wrong becomes an

What we have here is a web that encompasses corporate accomplices, forced and slave laborers, and perpetrators. Like Primo Levi's "gray zone,"[26] corporate complicity defies the urge to either convict or excuse. Because corporations are not full moral persons, it would be wrong to convict them of collaboration, thereby allowing them to shield other wrongdoers. On the other hand, because they are not mere instruments of individual groups or persons, it would be wrong to excuse them from all political responsibility for their acts of complicity.

Institutional political responsibility rests on recognition of the unhappy presence of the past in any democratic transition, new or old, and our inability to disentangle fully the political responsibilities different groups have for moving democracy forward in this context. Taking specific, second-order political responsibility more seriously may eventually encourage complicit corporations to accept backward-looking moral duty and legal liability, but its primary purpose is to meet the forward-looking, shared political responsibilities for the benefits that flow from institutional complicity in severe violence. Ultimately, "the political community as a whole," not just individual corporations, must recognize this responsibility if corporations are to be held accountable. Thomas McCarthy, arguing for reparations for slavery in the United States, has put it very well:

> Thus, the responsibility to rectify the continuing harms of past racial injustice accrues to the political community as a whole, not only because those wrongs were generally state sanctioned and frequently state implemented, but also because present members who share inherited benefits must by the same logic share inherited liabilities. Our national inheritance was in considerable part unjustly acquired at the expense of African-Americans; and, as a result, it is now unfairly distributed in respect to them. The issue here is not whether individual citizens' ancestors owned slaves, or whether they have personally benefited from discrimination against blacks, but that they now share in and benefit from an unjustly acquired and unfairly distributed national inheritance. *This is not a matter of collective guilt but of collective responsibility; and reparation is not a matter of collective punishment but of collective liability.*[27]

"unrepaired state wrong." By not repairing the wrong, the current state lends new legitimacy to it and thereby implicates itself in the original harm. See Teitel, *Transitional Justice* (New York: Oxford University Press, 2000), 142.

26. Primo Levi, *The Drowned and the Saved,* trans. Raymond Rosenthal (New York: Vintage, 1988), 36–46.

27. Thomas A. McCarthy, "Coming to Terms with the Past, Part II: On the Morality and Politics of Reparations for Slavery," *Political Theory* 32, no. 6 (2004): 759–60; see also McCarthy, "Vergan-

11. Slavery and Forced Labor

Unlike the infamous case of I. G. Farben,[28] there is a set of more recently filed cases of corporate complicity with the Nazi Holocaust that illustrates the usefulness of the concept of specific, second-order political responsibility. Several German corporations that continue to benefit from their past relationship with the Third Reich have been subject to lawsuits brought under the traditional tort law concept of liability. Insurance companies, banks, and manufacturers who exploited slave labor have been the primary targets in these suits. Their collaboration not only kept them in business, it also helped to finance the Nazi war effort and extermination plan. Litigation against these corporations has fallen into three categories. Some plaintiffs have sought recovery of lost property or insurance policies that were never paid off. Other plaintiffs and their heirs have sought to recover damages and back pay based on the claim that these corporations have unjustly benefited from unpaid labor. Finally, some plaintiffs have argued that corporations that violated international human rights by collaborating in the most abhorrent Nazi practices should have to pay a certain kind of reparation. Manufacturers of the lethal gas used in Nazi death camps, for example, and companies that purchased, melted down, and resold gold taken from concentration camp victims would be liable for damages in this third category.

One of the most important cases in this last category was the 1999 class action suit *Burger-Fischer v. Degussa AG* brought in U.S. district court. The Degussa Corporation smelted gold looted from Nazi death camp victims and manufactured Zyklon-B cyanide used in gas chambers. In 1998, the corporation offered to make humanitarian payments to its former slave laborers. This gesture was rebuffed as inadequate, and the class action suit was filed in U.S. district court on the grounds that Degussa's conduct had violated international treaties, fundamental human rights laws, and customary international law.[29]

Before this suit was dismissed as a nonjusticiable political question, the German government in fall 1998 had approached Stuart E. Eizenstat, then U.S. deputy

---

genheitsbewältigung in the USA: On the Politics of the Memory of Slavery," *Political Theory* 30, no. 5 (2002): 623–48.

28. I. G. Farben, the large German chemical company, collaborated closely with Nazi officials in planning the invasions of Czechoslovakia and Poland. It made use of slave labor in manufacturing, including the production of the pesticide used in the gas chambers. Joseph Borkin, *The Crime and Punishment of I. G. Farben* (New York: Free Press, 1978), 148–54. More generally, see Frank M. Buscher, *The U.S. War Crimes Trial Program in Germany, 1946–1955* (New York: Greenwood, 1989).

29. *Burger-Fischer v. Degussa AG*, 65 F. Supp. 2d 248 (D.N.J. 1999). See Derek Brown, "Litigating the Holocaust: A Consistent Theory in Tort for the Private Enforcement of Human Rights Violations," *Pepperdine Law Review* 27, no. 3 (2000): 553–90.

secretary of the treasury, to help them resolve similar class action suits pending in the United States against Degussa and other German companies. After several years of discussions with representatives of other interested governments as well as representatives of the victims and the companies, the German parliament created a foundation, "Remembrance, Responsibility and the Future." The German government and the German corporations equally endowed the foundation, with formal support from the United States. The agreement does not extinguish the claims made by U.S. citizens against German corporations, but rather states that the U.S. government will provide a statement to courts hearing such suits that it is in the "foreign policy interests" of the United States and "legal peace" generally that these cases be dismissed and the plaintiffs seek a remedy through the foundation.[30]

Consequently, almost all the pending tort suits were dismissed on December 5, 2000, on motions by the plaintiffs. Now that the corporations believe that their future legal liability is negligible, they are willing to accept the foundation's settlement terms.[31] Despite the small individual payments and the self-serving behavior of the corporations involved in the settlement,[32] this process neither dissolves corporate wrongdoers in bankruptcy nor merely imposes a fine that allows them to pay off their debt once and for all. It is a process (in its earliest stages) that forces them to acknowledge the benefits that they have continued to enjoy, and to share them with those whose suffering made the benefits possible. In the words of the deciding judge:

> In formulating the framework for the Foundation "Remembrance, Responsibility and the Future," the participants have provided a mechanism for payments to hundreds of thousands of slave and forced laborers, following the initiative of German companies to establish a foundation, which has since been joined by thousands of other German companies. But within

30. *Agreement Between the Government of the United States of America and the Government of the Federal Republic of Germany Concerning the Foundation "Remembrance, Responsibility, and the Future,"* Berlin, Germany, July 17, 2000, http://germany.usembassy.gov/germany/img/assets/8497/agreement.pdf. See also http://www.stiftung-evz.de/eng/. It is important to distinguish between reparations for slavery and forced labor on the one hand and restitution for confiscated property on the other. There has been much less consensus about the latter than the former. For example, see Dan Bilefsky, "Hurdles in Eastern Europe Thwart Restitution Claims: Reluctance to Act on Holocaust Seizures," *New York Times,* August 2, 2009.

31. Roger Cohen, "Last Chapter: Berlin to Pay Slave Workers Held by Nazis," *New York Times,* May 31, 2001.

32. See "Poles Start Receiving Payments for Slave Labor Under Nazis," *New York Times,* June 29, 2001.

the Foundation itself is a "Remembrance and Future Fund" charged with the permanent task "to foster projects that serve the purposes of better understanding among peoples, the interests of survivors of the National Socialist regime, youth, exchange, social justice, remembrance of the threat posed by totalitarian systems and despotism, and international cooperation in humanitarian endeavors." It is this commitment that grounds our confidence in Kierkegaard's words, that "life must be lived forwards."[33]

Group political responsibility for reparations cannot be apportioned without some understanding of the past, but unlike moral and legal responsibility, its special task is not to lose sight of how reparations can move the democratic transition forward.

Degussa and the Remembrance, Responsibility and the Future foundation created to handle cases like this underline the importance of treating corporations as artificial groups. When corporations are complicit in genocide by employing slave laborers, they must be required to explain their acts and address those persons who continue to be harmed in the aftermath of those acts. This certainly could become a charade in which executives hide behind a corporate shield, but it need not. International political cooperation at this level, similar to the cooperation that has brought the International Criminal Court into being, may be able to curb corporate power and include corporations in the process of reformulating the distribution of power and wealth on an appropriate footing with other interested parties.[34]

One alternative is for corporations to investigate themselves and, unlike U.S. Steel in the Cottenham case, make amends. In January 2005 JPMorgan Chase announced that on the basis of research commissioned from the History Associates research company, the bank was publicly apologizing "to the American

33. Opinion of U.S. district court judge William G. Bassler, *In re Nazi Era Cases Against German Defendants Litigation,* 198 F.R.D. 448 (D.N.J. 2000).

34. In contrast to French, Jeffrey Nesteruk and David T. Risser have argued for a limited holistic view of the corporation, where corporations are complexly organized and have moral obligations to serve interests other than those of their stockholders: "According to the restricted personhood conception, a corporation is a moral agent responsible for its actions, and is not merely the property of its shareholders. Thus, corporate decision makers should recognize that their firms are responsible to a broader constituency than shareholders alone; a constituency including employees, customers, local communities, and the public at large. This recognition reinforces social expectations which encourage corporate decision makers to act more as public trustees, and not merely as agents for the shareholders, in the performance of their corporate roles." Nesteruk and Risser, "Conceptions of the Corporation and Ethical Decision Making in Business," *Business and Professional Ethics Journal* 12, no. 1 (1993): 87. While I agree with their criticism of French, I am concerned with the political responsibility of corporations, not their status as ethical agents or trustees.

public, and particularly to African-Americans" for the role that two of its prede-cessor banks, subsequently acquired by JPMorgan Chase in 2004, had played in the history of slavery.[35] Citizens Bank and Canal Bank had provided credit to plantation owners in Louisiana, accepting as partial collateral 13,000 individuals held in slavery. Between 1831 and 1865 the two banks took possession of approxi-mately 1,250 of these individuals when the plantation owners defaulted. Insisting that "JPMorgan Chase is a very different company than the Citizens and Canal Banks of the 1800s," the bank reviewed its affirmative action policies and estab-lished a new five-million-dollar educational scholarship fund for students living in Louisiana.[36] Compared to U.S. Steel, JPMorgan Chase was both more forth-coming and more generous. But there is an important sense in which the bank's actions in 2005 have not led to political dialogue. The apology is no longer visible on the company Web site, possibly in response to shareholder criticisms in 2007—what goes up on the Web can just as quickly come down, with little trace remaining.[37]

If the German experience is to serve as a model for taking political responsi-bility for the legacy of benefits of severe violence, what more should corporations that unjustly enriched themselves from slavery in the United States do? One thing would be to open their books wider so that all the benefits that have accrued to them can be publicly known.[38]

Just as insurance companies that benefited from the Holocaust have begun to take responsibility for what they have done, some U.S. insurance companies such as Aetna have begun to accept responsibility for this part of the legacy of slavery. For example, railroads that employed slave labor would also be appro-priate targets for this kind of full disclosure. Legal research in the United States

35. David Weidner, "JPMorgan Apologizes Over Slavery," MarketWatch, *Wall Street Journal* Digital Network, January 21, 2005, http://www.marketwatch.com/News/Story/Story.aspx?guid =%7 BEB212AD8%2D4E10%2D4146%2D81CB%2DFE6022404198%7D&siteid=google&dist=google.

36. Jesyca Westbrook, "JP Morgan Chase Creates 'Smart Start Louisiana,'" BlackCollege View .com, February 14, 2005, http://media.www.blackcollegeview.com/media/storage/paper928/news /2005/02/14/BusinessTechnology/Jp.Morgan.Chase.Creates.smart.Start.Louisiana-2472822.shtml.

37. "JPMorgan Chase Slavery Apology to Be Challenged at Company's Annual Meeting," National Legal and Policy Center press release, May 14, 2007, http://www.prnewswire.com/news-releases/jpmorgan-chase-slavery-apology-to-be-challenged-at-companys-annual-meeting-nlpc-shareholder-proposal-says-bank-opens-itself-to-slave-reparations-liability-58124352.html. Not long thereafter, the U.S. House of Representatives issued its own apology for slavery and "Jim Crow" segre-gation. See Darryl Fears, "House Issues an Apology for Slavery," *Washington Post*, July 30, 2008.

38. One important part of the U.S. acceptance of the German foundation was the creation of the Presidential Advisory Commission on Holocaust Assets in the United States. Its extensive report, *Plunder and Restitution: Findings and Recommendations of the Presidential Advisory Com-mission on Holocaust Assets in the United States,* published in December 2000, gave survivors and other interested parties more confidence that the record of collaboration and profiteering from the Holocaust was becoming available. See http://www.pcha.gov/.

in support of legislation and lawsuits seeking reparations for slavery is already uncovering a web of corporate complicity that unites the North and South.[39] The threat of liability suits and bad publicity may prompt more corporations, universities, and governments to create foundations that will serve as a public forum to discuss how best to remember the suffering of slavery and redirect the benefits that have flowed from it. Beyond this, membership in the chartering body for such a foundation would force the corporation to respond to public arguments regarding its past actions and intentions. Engaged in public debate in this way, complicit corporations have the opportunity to demonstrate to other political persons their capacity to respond to political arguments and demands.[40]

To repeat, corporations are institutions that have a specific second-order political responsibility to participate in the design of fair procedures for organizing the benefits that continue to accrue from past undemocratic practices and thereby obstruct democratic transitions at home and abroad. This is an obligation to take appropriate political responsibility for a legacy of tainted benefits by participating, for example, in the creation of a special charter or treaty. When corporate institutions such as universities fail to meet this political responsibility, several things can happen. They can obstruct the democratic process by ignoring their own influence, thereby diminishing the voices of others. They can leave the tainted benefits they enjoy in place, thereby preserving the unjust accumulation of wealth and power that has occurred gradually over time. More subtly, they can fail to notice the ways in which this inequality of accumulated wealth and power communicates a negative political message to those who are not part of the privileged institutional structure.

This is what Thomas Pogge calls an "implicit social attitude" of "official disrespect": "Such wrongs do not merely deprive their victims of the objects of their

---

39. It should come as no surprise that slavery was as much a part of the economy of the so-called free Northern states as it was the Southern economy in the United States before the Civil War. That Northern textile manufacturers, for example, generally were uncritical of Southern slavery was no accident. This part of the legacy of slavery has yet to be written. Many press reports have been issued regarding research in this area by lawyers such as Deadria Farmer-Paellmann and Charles J. Ogletree. On July 24, 2000, Brent Staples published "How Slavery Fueled Business in the North," a *New York Times* editorial summarizing this neglected aspect of the political economy of slavery. According to Staples, in the early 1800s New York City had more slaves than any other U.S. city except Charleston, South Carolina. See also "Symposium: The Jurisprudence of Slavery Reparations," *Boston University Law Review* 84 (April 2004): 1135–1466.

40. To assist this process of democratic transition, economic historians should address the question of who has enjoyed the legacy of benefits from slavery, much as they have done in investigating the efficiency of the plantation system and the health of slaves. See, for example, Robert William Fogel and Stanley L. Engerman, *Time on the Cross: The Economics of American Negro Slavery* (Boston: Little, Brown, 1974).

rights but attack those very rights themselves; they do not merely subvert what is right, but the very idea of right and justice."[41] Pogge stresses the attitudes conveyed through official tolerance of overt violence carried out by death squads and militias, but other forms of official disrespect embodied in unjust accumulation and inequality can be equally demoralizing. For example, when a university decides not to remove or otherwise disassociate itself from the names, pictures, and busts of slave owners on its public buildings, this attitude conveys a message to some members of the political society that the harm done to them does not outweigh the good that these slave owners and their descendants have purportedly done for the institution. In contrast, by distancing itself from these figures, the institution conveys a very different political attitude about the relative importance of these harms and benefits. The University of North Carolina, Chapel Hill, has provided information on its official Web site on "Slavery and the Making of the University."[42] Brown University in Providence, Rhode Island, has made a substantial effort to acknowledge and take responsibility for its own complicity in the local slave trade, through various local programs and through endowment programs for students in the Providence public schools.[43]

There are other ways that corporate institutions and their members can contribute to development as democratic political education, sometimes in the most unlikely places. In poor countries such as Mali where extractive industries notoriously have done well at the expense of the majority poor population, new institutional responsibilities have been identified to improve democracy.[44] For example, under the heading of corporate social responsibility, mining companies have begun to seek public-sector partners and confer with community organizations, human rights organizations, and other stakeholders before beginning their work. By anticipating and reducing untoward social as well as environmental impacts, these corporate institutions are able to reduce some of the harmful political, social, and economic consequences of mining. If mining companies can do this, certainly universities can. Instead of contributing to the movement of educated workers from poor countries to the countries where they do their

41. Thomas Pogge, *World Poverty and Human Rights* (Cambridge, Mass.: Polity, 2002), 59.

42. "Slavery and the Making of the University," Manuscripts Department, University of North Carolina, Chapel Hill, University Library, Chapel Hill, N.C., http://www.lib.unc.edu/mss/exhibits/slavery/index.html.

43. University Steering Committee on Slavery and Justice, Brown University, Providence, R.I., http://brown.edu/Research/Slavery_Justice/.

44. Eyolf Jul-Larsen and others, *Socio-economic Effects of Gold Mining in Mali: A Study of the Sadiola and Morila Mining Operations* (Bergen, Norway: Chr. Michelsen Institute, 2006), http://www.cmi.no/publications/file/2340-socio-economic-effects-of-gold-mining-in-mali.pdf. I am indebted to Felipe Tejeda for useful discussion on this topic.

graduate and professional research, universities can design programs that (1) ensure that students return to their native countries to complete their degrees after an enriching experience at a better-endowed institution abroad, and (2) provide opportunities for future research and scholarly collaboration with faculty at the better-endowed institution.

Should institutions, especially transnational corporations that have this capacity, be entrusted with the authority we otherwise entrust to the state? Onora O'Neill argues that within limits and in certain circumstances, transnational corporations should have this authority.[45] Where states are too weak or too corrupt to carry out certain functions, whether it is in health and education or in communications and transportation, transnational corporations may be our best bet. This is not just a matter of privatization or outsourcing public services with blind faith in the efficiency of the market. Depending on what exactly the goal is, transnational corporations (like international nongovernmental organizations) may have the capability to carry out this responsibility. In the case of graduate and professional education, research universities may be able to manage the freedom to travel of students from poor developing countries more effectively and wisely than a state agency that is less familiar with the problems of "brain drain" from poorer countries. They would not be exclusively responsible for this function. Rather, they would have to work with other institutions, and their faculty and students participating in the exchange programs and other international research projects would share this political responsibility as well.

45. Onora O'Neill, "Global Justice: Whose Obligations?" in *The Ethics of Assistance: Morality and the Distant Needy,* ed. Deen K. Chatterjee (New York: Cambridge University Press, 2004), 242–59.

PART 2

Recognizing Complicity

4 BEYOND SYMPATHY

Theories of citizenship and responsibility like those discussed in the previous two chapters can help us identify the possible scope of our shared political responsibilities as everyday bystanders to global problems such as famine, civil war, and genocide, but they do not go far enough. There is a gap between theoretical justifications of these political responsibilities and our abilities and efforts to recognize them as *our* responsibilities. After a brief overview of this motivational problem, I discuss three ways in which everyday bystanders may come to recognize their political responsibilities as the beneficiaries of severe violence.

12. Motivation

Hugh LaFollette and Larry May, following the eighteenth-century philosopher David Hume, have argued that bystanders have a shared moral responsibility to help chronically malnourished children, regardless of whether they are responsible for their suffering. Their argument is built on an individual natural sentiment of sympathy for suffering children, which they extend in the following way: if you have sympathy for one child who is suffering because she is denied basic educational opportunities, they argue, then you should feel an analogous sympathetic responsibility to contribute to educational institutions that offer the best strategy for educating as many needy children as possible without making undue sacrifices of your own.[1]

1. Hugh LaFollette and Larry May, "Suffer the Little Children," in *World Hunger and Morality*, ed. William Aiken and Hugh LaFollette, 2nd ed. (Upper Saddle River, N.J.: Prentice Hall, 1996). On

Onora O'Neill believes arguments by analogy such as this are not enough. As complicated as causal arguments about responsibility for suffering may be, they can and should be made only where injustices such as violence, coercion, and deception have occurred. She offers this description of one such complicated hypothetical case of responsibility:

> For example, a system of food aid and imports agreed upon by the government of a Third World country and certain developed states or international agencies may give the elite of that Third World country access to subsidized grain. If that grain is then used to control the urban population and also produces destitution among peasants (who used to grow food for that urban population), then those who are newly destitute probably have not been offered any opening or possibility of refusing their new and worsened conditions of life. If a policy is imposed, those affected cannot have been given a chance to refuse it: had the chance been there, they would either have assented (and so the policy would not have been imposed) or refused (and so proceeding with the policy would have been evidently coercive), or they would have been able to renegotiate the terms of trade.[2]

According to O'Neill, a cultivated Humean sympathy like the one LaFollette and May describe is not enough to motivate shared and institutional responsibilities to the chronic problems of adults who have been harmed in these ways. Two more rational duties exist: a strong duty (what Kant called a "perfect duty") not to condone, participate in, or otherwise support an unjust offer or policy, complemented by the additional responsibility (what he called an "imperfect duty") of beneficence. This responsibility of beneficence is not merely the option to give charity, O'Neill stresses, though it is also not a matter of legal obligation. Like "perfect duties" of justice, it rests on a well-reasoned respect for individual autonomy and an analysis of the institutional causes of suffering.[3]

Hume's original conception of sympathy, see Philip Mercer, *Sympathy and Ethics: A Study of the Relationship Between Sympathy and Morality with Special Reference to Hume's Treatise* (Oxford: Clarendon, 1972).

2. Onora O'Neill, "Ending World Hunger," in *Matters of Life and Death*, ed. Tom Regan, 3rd ed. (New York: McGraw-Hill, 1993), 264.

3. "Clearly the vulnerable position of those who lack the very means of life, and their severely curtailed possibilities for autonomous action, offer many different ways in which it might be possible for others to act beneficently. Where the means of life are meager, almost any material or organizational advance may help extend possibilities for autonomy. Individual or institutional action that

If we ground responsibility in antecedent causes, I prefer O'Neill's analysis of the suffering of those she aptly describes as "impoverished providers." She calls this a "practical approach" to responsibilities because it does not rest on speculative metaphysical assumptions about individual identity. It is grounded in the practical assumptions that we make when we act in the world. When we join and support institutions we also assume certain things about the types of persons who will be affected by our actions. If they are customers, we assume that they will respond to advertising in certain ways. Our actions are different if they are students, patients, or immigrants. In her words, "We lead our lives with little concentration on the metaphysics of the person. Yet it is quite clear that we view many others as agents and as subjects of experience. Although we do not always articulate or establish the assumption that others are agents or subjects of experience, these assumptions are embedded in our action."[4] According to O'Neill, this practical approach should guide any analysis of responsibilities to impoverished providers, whether they are distant strangers, unfamiliar neighbors, or future generations.

Thomas Pogge also prefers antecedent causal responsibility over sympathy, charity, and beneficence. He rejects the presumption that poor nations today are primarily responsible for their own problems, and its correlate that citizens in rich countries are usually innocent bystanders to global poverty. On the contrary, he argues that the rich often are deeply implicated in global poverty through their participation in and the benefits they derive from harmful global economic institutions and practices. The more the rich participate in and benefit from the current global economy, the more they perpetuate and aggravate global economic poverty and inequality.[5] According to Pogge, any denial of this responsibility is a matter of cognitive incompetence or self-deception. In terms of

---

aims to advance economic or social development can proceed on many routes. The provision of clean water, of improved agricultural techniques, of better grain storage systems, or of adequate means of local transport may all help transform material prospects. . . . While the central core of such development projects will be requirements of justice, their full development will also demand concern to treat others as ends in themselves, by paying attention to their needs and desires." O'Neill, "Ending World Hunger," 269.

4. Onora O'Neill, "Distant Strangers and Future Generations," in *Self and Future Generations: An Intercultural Conversation,* ed. Tae-Chang Kim and Ross Harrison (Cambridge, UK: White Horse, 1999), 65.

5. See, for example, Thomas Pogge, *World Poverty and Human Rights* (Malden, Mass.: Polity, 2002). Consistent with this emphasis on institutionally mediated causal responsibility, Pogge also has written that "with a better understanding of the role global institutional factors play in the persistence of severe poverty, many would take this problem much more seriously." Pogge, "'Assisting' the Global Poor," in *The Ethics of Assistance: Morality and the Distant Needy,* ed. Deen K. Chatterjee (New York: Cambridge University Press, 2004), 280.

motivation, knowledge of the causal roles played by the international trading and borrowing privileges accorded by rich countries to poor, often authoritarian regimes should be enough to make anyone who is not chronically self-deceived take global political responsibilities more seriously. Knowledge should be sufficient for virtue.

Regardless of whether one prefers a Humean or Kantian explanation for the sentiments of justice and beneficence, and whether one takes a practical or more metaphysical approach to the justification of responsibilities, LaFollette and May are correct that one purpose of all these philosophical theories is to motivate those who do have responsibilities for suffering and violence to recognize these responsibilities and begin to act on them. As yet, this has not happened. More needs to be said about the obstacles to recognition, especially for beneficiaries, and the motivation to overcome them. I will consider three ways to prompt everyday bystanders into thinking more self-critically about their shared and institutional political responsibilities. There may be many others, but these seem to me to be the most pervasive and potentially effective in the current context.

The first are simulations designed to reach a relatively wide audience. They often begin with an image of a helpless individual victim and then walk the viewer or reader, step-by-step, through the process of rescue. They put a human face on otherwise abstract facts and statistics,[6] and conclude with clear instructions for alleviating suffering. One such image is that of six-year-old Mark Kwadwo, a Ghanaian child who was sold into forced labor by his family. Two days after his story ran in the *New York Times* and was posted on the *Times* Web site as part of a virtual tour of child labor in Ghana, the "Letters" section included several presumably representative reactions by readers. According to one reader, "It is especially wrenching to read of the desperate comments that Mark and the other boys whispered to the reporter, probably the only sympathetic adult they have ever encountered." Another wrote, "I surprised myself by falling into tears after finishing your article. For me, the most profound moment was reading that Kofi Quarshie, 10, believes that his parents sold him because they didn't like him." Both readers, moved by sympathy, pleaded for "a little bit of guidance toward action."[7]

---

6. On the relative ineffectiveness of statistical information to elicit sympathetic reactions, see Paul Slovic, "'If I look at the mass I will never act': Psychic Numbing and Genocide," *Judgment and Decision Making* 2, no. 2 (2007): 79–95.

7. Sharon LaFraniere, "Africa's World of Forced Labor in a 6-Year-Old's Eyes," *New York Times,* October 29, 2006; and "Letters," *New York Times,* October 31, 2006.

Simulations can have a similar effect even on seasoned observers of scenes such as these. It is not just the human face, but the simulated journey it leads us on. Concluding a brief tour of one refugee camp in Sudan, Jeffrey Gettleman of the *New York Times* wrote:

> The saddest sight I see is a young woman sitting by herself with her baby. She has not built her shelter yet. She has a few things—a battered plastic jerry can, a charred pot blacker than charcoal, a small supply of dried okra and a mat. In my mind, I picture all of it bundled up and lashed down on top of a truck, along with 200 other bundles just like it.
>
> Her husband has been killed, I am told, and she has come with the others, packed in like corn. She is not talking to anyone. And I have nothing to say, either, no questions to ask. I write nothing down. Everything is so heartbreakingly obvious that it hurts just to look.[8]

Simulations of scenes such as this attempt to give sympathetic audiences a way of seeing that is more than merely heartbreaking. They draw the viewer in, often through video game or Web formats (discussed in more detail below), and then provide advice for political activism or crisis management. While the most common medium for this is the Internet, print media have begun to catch up.[9]

Simulations—whether in print or electronic form—are built around a sympathetic image that leads us into a vicarious relationship with the victims. The danger with simulations is that they may be too game-like and thereby trivialize the victims' experience. The second way of prompting everyday bystanders to recognize their responsibilities for severe violence is through more static representations such as photographs, paintings, and sculptures of suffering individuals and displaced persons. They also attempt to evoke sympathy, although they require more interpretation; it is not just a matter of navigating a Web site and following instructions. Unlike simulations, representations of severe violence seem caught on the horns of a different dilemma: they must either emphasize the

8. Jeffrey Gettleman, "Touring a Camp's Circles of Loss," *New York Times,* November 5, 2006.
9. The close-up photo of a young child's face adorning the cover of *Not on Our Watch: The Mission to End Genocide in Darfur and Beyond,* written by actor Don Cheadle and former Clinton administration staffer John Prendergast, has this kind of emotional effect. It is followed by a clearly formatted account of the Darfur genocide, various groups that have been involved in lobbying for humanitarian intervention, and tips for new activists. Cheadle and Prendergast, *Not on Our Watch: The Mission to End Genocide in Darfur and Beyond* (New York: Hyperion Books, 2007). Prendergast is also the cofounder of the humanitarian aid organization the Enough Project, http://www.enoughproject.org/.

scale of severe violence and risk making its victims anonymous and therefore less sympathetic, or focus on the plight of particular individuals and risk obscuring the magnitude of the problem.

Third, there are dramatic reenactments in which the narrative line and voices are more complex. Like artful representations, if they are to motivate bystanders, reenactments require more careful interpretation than do simulations. Done and interpreted well, I argue, some reenactments can evoke empathy, not just sympathy. That is, reenactments can help bystanders see, feel, and understand severe violence from a perspective alongside "impoverished providers" without becoming either self-absorbed with their own moral status or oblivious to the differences that remain between themselves as bystanders and those who suffer most from severe violence.

There is nothing essentially more effective about any one of these three methods of political education. Even mass media simulations can evoke a greater self-critical awareness of complicity and spark political dialogue. They certainly have the potential to quickly reach a much larger audience of everyday bystanders. On the other hand, some reenactments can be so didactic that they fail to reach their selected audience. In other cases, such as the reenactment of the Abu Ghraib tortures in photographs and film, they provide a stage for self-conviction and pleas for mercy. I will refer to some flawed examples of each of these three methods, but only to shed more light on the compelling cases. In the end what is needed is a range of critical simulations, representations, and reenactments required to reach everyday bystanders blinded by a culture of simulation (see chapter 7). For the moment, I want to explain the differences between simulation, representation, and reenactment.[10]

13. Simulation

Consider the virtual refugee camp sponsored by Médecins Sans Frontières (MSF). It is a series of images from a tour of a refugee camp in which "you" are asked questions like "Where will I live?" "Where will I find water?" and "Where will I find food?"[11] Then you are faced with wide-eyed and hungry children who look

10. For an introduction to performance art that stresses its relationship to social change, see Richard Schechner, *Performance Theory* (New York: Routledge, 1988); and Victor Turner, *The Anthropology of Performance* (New York: PAJ, 1986).

11. Médecins Sans Frontières/Doctors Without Borders, *A Refugee Camp in the Heart of the City*, http://www.refugeecamp.org/home/. For a more interesting and less melodramatic photographic and comic art narrative about the generally laudable work of MSF in Afghanistan, see Emmanuel Guibert, Didier Lefèvre, and Frédéric Lemercier, *The Photographer*, trans. Alexis Siegel (New York: First Second, 2006).

puzzled and sad. After the tour you can "learn more about food aid," including how to get it and how much to get. The needs for nutritional balance can be quantified. Shipments can be estimated. Arrangements can be made. You are cautioned not to forget the refugees: "Above all listen to their opinions and allow them to describe their needs."

Something very important happens on this virtual tour. The simulation begins by addressing us as potential refugees ("Where will I live?" "What if I get sick?"). We are encouraged to identify with parents desperate to find food for their hungry children. But as we search for information, we discover that this is not about us, but about "them." We gradually become the representatives of agencies responsible for medicine, food, and clean water. We are there to help the refugees. We have identified and sympathized, and now we are asked to step back and help fix the problem.

A more interactive video game that also simulates life in a refugee camp is *Darfur Is Dying*, produced by mtvU, MTV's college network as part of a contest to design the best humanitarian video game. Like the MSF virtual tour, the game attempts to lead the player toward greater activism and engagement, in this case with regard to the genocide in Darfur.[12] The first move is to choose a victim's persona, after which you must try to outrun the Janjaweed (armed gunmen). If "you" are a young girl, then you are quickly caught and probably raped. If you want, you can try again, only to be caught and raped again. When you do resign yourself to life in the refugee camp, it proves to be not much better. Then, after glimpsing the fear and frustration that defines life in Darfur, the player can watch an interview with a Darfurian who breaks down in tears. Finally, if you are finished impersonating the virtual characters in the game, you can take real action by sending a message to the president or your congressional representative. There are instructions for starting a divestment campaign on your own college campus or submitting a new game of your own to MTV.

Darfur Is Dying has received considerable publicity, but as a video game it is not technically sophisticated. It is not so much a game as it is a virtual experience

---

12. "In partnership with the Reebok Human Rights Foundation and the International Crisis Group mtvU launched the Darfur Digital Activist Context, an unprecedented competition bringing together student technology and activism to help stop the genocide in Darfur. . . . *Darfur is Dying* is a narrative-based simulation where the user, from the perspective of a displaced Darfurian, negotiates forces that threaten the survival of his or her refugee camp. It offers a faint glimpse of what it is like for the more than 2.5 million who have been internally displaced by the crisis in Sudan." See http://www.darfurisdying.com/aboutgame.html. See also "Come Clean 4 Congo," a video contest cosponsored by YouTube and the Enough Project, http://www.youtube.com/enoughproject/.

of genocide. No matter which character you choose, you always end up suffering ignominiously. Consequently, *Darfur Is Dying* is not likely to persuade those who do not already feel an obligation to "take action"; in fact, it is just as likely to offend by trivializing what suffering victims are facing in Sudan and nearby refugee camps.

One can imagine a more sophisticated and interactive simulation, something like the popular video games *SimCity* and *SimLife,* which can have a more profound effect because the players' choices do make a difference. Whereas *Darfur Is Dying* exhorts visitors to the site to write letters and support divestment campaigns—things that displaced persons in refugee camps cannot do—a hypothetical *SimDevelopment* video game could place you in a situation in which you have choices appropriate to particular roles in the development process. *SimDevelopment* could convince everyday bystanders that should they decide to donate money, MSF managers and doctors would use their contributions wisely. Political education in this case, as with the MSF site described above, is education for managing the problems of refugees. This is what is called a "serious game." Local governments in North America have created them both to educate citizens about the challenges and choices that city managers must face and to collect information from citizens on pressing public issues.[13] The United Nations World Food Programme has a serious game as well, *Food Force,* which combines the interactive elements of a fast-moving video game with the types of content found on sites such as the MSF refugee camp virtual tour.[14]

Food Force begins with an aerial reconnaissance mission over a drought-stricken territory that is also troubled by civil war. The player receives a score indicating how well the mission has been accomplished, and then moves on to plan the food supply, airlift it in, and eventually construct a self-sufficient village that will not require humanitarian assistance. For each mission, the player receives a score based on how many photographs are taken, how many bags of food are dropped, and finally how well-balanced and self-sufficient the new village is. Little dexterity is required, although there is a timer to heighten the feeling that the refugees' needs are critical. After each mission, the player receives a brief evaluation and usually is invited to try again. At the end of the last mission, the player can submit the total score and compare it to the best scores on record.

13. For example, the city of Guelph, Ontario, uses a serious game, *GuelphQuest Online,* for this purpose. See http://guelph.ca/living.cfm?subCatId=1615&smocid=2193.

14. *Food Force,* United Nations World Food Programme, http://www.food-force.com/. I am indebted to Seth Morton for very helpful discussion on the subject of serious games and for bringing to my attention several of the examples in this section.

While the movements of the figures in the game are not especially lifelike, the stakes are high and the final mission resembles a hypothetical *SimVillage* game in which the player gets a fairly accurate idea of just how difficult it is to establish a self-sustaining rural economy, even with relatively generous provisioning. By creating a new narrative for this troubled region, the player learns not just who to ask for help but also how to reflect critically on what is being done.

It remains an open question, however, whether this serious gamer understands some of the other obstacles beyond the logistics facing humanitarian intervention, especially problems such as how to mediate among conflicting factions on the ground in the refugee village itself. It is also not clear whether the player becomes simply more motivated to play serious games, but does not become more motivated to examine how what he or she is already doing contributes to the need for humanitarian intervention in the first place.[15]

14. Representation

Representation can be used as a generic term for all three of the forms of political education I am describing in this chapter. I want to use it more narrowly, however, to refer to a range of artful representations that are neither simulations nor reenactments.

Let me begin with a famous example from nineteenth-century British romantic landscape painting by J. M. W. Turner descriptively titled *Slavers Throwing Overboard the Dead and Dying—Typho[o]n Coming On [The Slave Ship]*. The narrative context of this 1840 painting is crucial for understanding its emotional impact. Because slavers would have been denied insurance payments for slaves lost to illness, they often threw their sick captives overboard. They could then fabricate a story of escape or rebellion that would allow them to collect on their losses. "Hope, Hope, fanacious, Hope!" Turner wrote of this scene, "Where is thy market now?" John Ruskin, equally outraged by this cash nexus, interpreted *The Slave Ship* in an essay in his 1846 collection *Modern Painters*: "Purple and blue, the lurid shadows of the hollow breakers are cast upon the mist of night,

---

15. Yet another species of these serious simulations is the "advergame" that purports to teach a valuable lesson at the same time that it gently plugs a product. *Planet Green Game,* put on the Web by Starbucks Coffee Company and Global Green USA in 2007, is a good example. Each player tries to accumulate points by making environmentally sound decisions for the small community of Evergreen. Like other serious games, this one provides instructions for how to "take action" based on what the player has learned, and references to Starbucks are tucked discretely inside a pull-down menu. See http://www.planetgreengame.com/.

which gathers cold and low, advancing like the shadow of death upon the guilty ship as it labours amidst the lightning of the sea, its thin masts written upon the sky in lines of blood, girded with condemnation in that fearful hue which signs the sky with horror, and mixes its flaming flood with the sunlight, and, cast far along the desolate heave of the sepulchral waves, incarnadines the multitudinous sea."[16]

Ruskin focused not on the small bodies of the drowning slaves but on the slave ship itself. The ship is a vehicle for his interpretation of Turner's use of color, and it is through these colors, Ruskin argued, that our emotions are represented and heightened. We do not feel sympathy or sadness for the drowning slaves, but a rush of violent emotion as the guilty ship is consumed by an ocean of flames, attacked by carnivorous sea creatures, and buried in a sea of flesh. If we are witnesses to this scene, Ruskin seems to be saying, we do not remain bystanders. Nature expresses our emotional outrage and condemns the slave ship.

Compare the painting by Turner with a later series of photographs collected in the 1941 volume *Let Us Now Praise Famous Men,* by James Agee and Walker Evans, which catalogued the poverty and illiteracy of white tenant farm families in Alabama during the Great Depression and the New Deal period in the United States.[17] Evans's untitled, black-and-white pictures of these families stand in sharp contrast to Turner's minute silhouettes of slaves being thrown overboard to their death. Evans's figures are unflinchingly captured in pitiful surroundings, their blank stares and motionless, emaciated bodies testifying to the hopelessness of their lives. It is no wonder that some commentators have criticized these photographs as intrusive and condescending. As if to forestall such criticism, the authors begin with two quotations, one from Shakespeare's *King Lear* and the other from *The Communist Manifesto* by Marx and Engels. One line from *Lear* stands out above the rest: "Expose thyself to feel what wretches feel." This is more than an admonition; it captures Agee's desire to feel empathy for the poor and his imperfect recognition that he cannot fully feel what these wretches feel. Then, after quoting the final lines of *The Communist Manifesto,* Agee and Evans write in a footnote: "These words are quoted here to mislead those who will be misled by them." That is, Agee and Evans say that they are not fighting

16. John Ruskin, *Modern Painters,* vol. 2 (1846), reprinted in *Selections from the Writings of John Ruskin* (n.p.: Obscure Press, 2007), 157.

17. James Agee and Walker Evans, *Let Us Now Praise Famous Men* (1941; repr., Boston: Houghton Mifflin, 1969). The indentured servitude documented by Agee and Evans did not rise to the level of slavery in the United States and therefore is not exactly a representation of severe violence in the sense I am using this term.

for a cause. They caution the presumptuous reader that "neither these words nor the authors are the property of any political party, faith, or faction."[18] Don't criticize us for not organizing a social movement or joining a political party to change these woeful conditions; this, they seem to be saying, would only make things worse.

Sadly, Evans's cold images and Agee's opaque, sometimes self-absorbed interpretations cannot help us "feel what these wretches feel" any more than Agee did: "It seems to me curious, not to say obscene and thoroughly terrifying, that it could occur to an association of human beings drawn together through need and chance and for profit into a company, an organ of journalism, to pry intimately into the lives of an undefended and appallingly damaged group of human beings, an ignorant and helpless rural family, for the purpose of parading the nakedness, disadvantage and humiliation of these lives before another group of human beings."[19] Rather than take responsibility for the voyeuristic way in which they used their subjects, Agee unloads on his readers. His "self-disgust," he tells us, is not with his own ignorance or failure to make good arguments; it is "in my inability," he says, "to state it even so far as I see it, and in my inability to blow out the brains with it of you who take what it is talking of lightly, or not seriously enough."[20]

Both Ruskin and Agee struggled to interpret two different but related representations of violence (slavery and indentured servitude). Ruskin hoped to bring home the emotional and rational elements of Turner's representation of the slave trade. Agee attempts to remind us of our own humanitarian responsibilities for the inhuman conditions that Evans framed in black and white, but he does not shy away from pointing out the flaws in the poor white tenant farmers he has gotten to know. Neither Ruskin nor Agee, I would argue, has succeeded. Ruskin convicted the slave ship with the same passion that Agee would like to "blow out the brains" of his readers. Ruskin ignored those whom I have called everyday bystanders; Agee condemns them along with himself, as if this would somehow right the wrong.

When Agee comes across a black couple walking alone and tries to approach them, presumably for an interview, he realizes for an instant just how little he feels what they feel. He tells us that he apologized for frightening them, but they do not respond. Then he writes:

18. Ibid., xix.
19. Ibid., 7.
20. Ibid., 307.

They just kept looking at me. There was no more for them to say than for me. The least I could have done was to throw myself flat on my face and embrace and kiss their feet. That impulse took hold of me so powerfully, from my whole body, not by thought, that I caught myself from doing it exactly and as scarcely as you snatch yourself from jumping from a sheer height: here, with the realization that it would have frightened them still worse (to say nothing of me) and would have been still less explicable; so that I stood and looked into their eyes and loved them, and wished to God I was dead.[21]

If Evans's photographs represent a failure to sympathetically project himself into the world of his subjects, this testimony by Agee indicates a failure to empathetically discuss his responsibilities as a citizen and a writer for the poverty he hopes to represent to a wider public.

Robert Coles tells us that *Let Us Now Praise Famous Men* was a "talisman" for white civil rights workers in the American South after it was reissued in 1960.[22] It gave them strength to know that others like Agee and Evans had gone before them. Further, he continues, it was passages like this one that impressed 1960s African American civil rights leaders in the South. Agee's confession was not one that southern blacks ever had heard from southern whites.[23] While it may be true that Agee's tormented prose struck a responsive chord in Coles and his generation, many of whom risked their lives and did express great empathy for the poor blacks and whites they had gone south to help, it is no less true that Agee's attempt to interpret the cold, uncharitable images in *Famous Men* today more than ever seems, to use Sontag's words, "impertinent—if not inappropriate."

Coles provides more detailed but no less ambivalent commentary on the work of Agee and Evans in *Doing Documentary Work*. He criticizes Agee for his "bile, his seemingly hopeless inconsistencies, his self-accusations, his search for targets at which to aim his bitter, tart asides." But then just as quickly Coles argues that "we know in our heart of hearts (as Agee knew) that we ourselves won't be where we now are (as volunteers, as members of Vista or the Peace Corps) for the rest of our lives; far from it."[24] My take is very different. Agee's remark reminds us why it is important to sustain democratic acquaintances and make them part of our everyday lives, as Addams did at Hull-House;

21. Ibid., 42.

22. Ross Spears and Jude Cassidy, eds., *Agee: His Life Remembered,* with a narrative by Robert Coles (New York: Holt, Rinehart and Winston, 1985), 97.

23. Ibid., 99–100.

24. Robert Coles, *Doing Documentary Work* (New York: Oxford University Press, 1997), 55. A recent attempt to capture the lives of the poor that has some of the same weaknesses of *Famous Men* and some interesting racial differences is William T. Vollmann's *Poor People* (New York: Ecco, 2007).

Fig. 1   A malnourished, dehydrated woman waits her turn in the hospital in Gourma-Rharous, Mali, 1985. Photo by Sebastião Salgado.

otherwise, occasional acts of partial sympathy will breed irrational guilt and prostrated "self-disgust."

Now consider a very different representation of severe violence, with different strengths and limitations. On his Kodak-sponsored *Migrations: Humanity in Transition* Web site (2000), the Portuguese photographer (and former World Bank economist) Sebastião Salgado is quoted as saying "I want to show the immigrants' dignity, to show their courage and entrepreneurial spirit and to demonstrate how they enrich us all with their individual differences."[25] Salgado's pictures are riveting, whether he is showing a sea of humanity on the move or small children gathered around a slow-burning, toxic charcoal fire. There is indeed a quiet dignity in their suffering. But it is not as clear that our sympathy for them depends on an understanding of their "individual differences." Despite the unflinching criticism of exploitation and alienation in Salgado's photographs, there is something missing in the portraits of these impoverished workers and their children.

This is even more evident in an earlier project of his (designed to raise money for Médecins Sans Frontièères) that includes this photograph of a woman in the hospital of Gourma-Rharous, Mali, in 1985.

25. Sebastião Salgado, "Migrations: Humanity in Transition," *Photo District News*/Kodak "Legends" site featuring Salgado "Migrations" project, http://www.pdngallery.com/legends/legends10/.

In Malian culture, to cover one's head with one's hands is an act of desperation and near surrender. Yet Salgado has found a way to avoid this conventional interpretation. There is no doubt that she is in pain and in need of comforting. The tilt of her head and the shape of her mouth suggest a perplexity without anger or resentment, despite the suffering she is enduring. Her hands and the cloth together form an arch over her body, not just a cradle or sling for her head. There is strength in the way the veins of her hands and wrist parallel the lines in the cloth she has used to shelter herself. Because of this self-supporting human structure, we are able to show more sympathy for her than we can for the emaciated children and cadaverous adults in the other photographs by Salgado in this same collection. They seem to be all but dead; she still seems to be with us.

The effect of Salgado's photographs on us as bystanders is an overwhelming sense of sadness, but in this particular case we do not want to turn away. We are not speechless. We want to put our feelings for her into words. Political education in this case is an education in more lasting sympathy, but it is still not clear who benefits most from this act of sympathy. She remains isolated and anonymous, her story disconnected from the stories of other victims of famine, and we are left dangerously close to contemplating our own capacity for sympathy and, once more following Sontag, imagining our own innocence.

15. Reenactment

Ubu and the Truth Commission by William Kentridge and Jane Taylor is a 1997 multimedia play done in collaboration with the Handspring Puppet Company.[26] I want to focus on one set of figures, the puppets in *Ubu,* because of what they tell us about empathy for those who suffered most under South African apartheid. I will compare this work to several other photographs by Salgado in order

26. Handspring Puppet Company, http://www.handspringpuppet.co.za/. A revealing contrast to the multimedia *Ubu* is a recent all-star benefit concert "Requiem for Darfur." In the words of one reviewer, "Verdi's great work, presented not just as a prayer for the dead but as a call to compassion and purpose, came through affectingly. The apocalyptic Dies Irae ('The day of wrath, that day will dissolve the world in ashes') is always chilling. But it is hard to describe the effect of hearing this ferocious music while seeing a photograph by Ron Haviv projected on the wall behind the performers: it showed a painting by a Sudanese boy (now a refugee in Chad) of his home village burning, with bodies on the ground and attacking militia on horses." Anthony Tommasini, "Making Music for Those Without a Voice," *New York Times,* January 24, 2007. As moving as this adaptation of the now-familiar *Requiem* is, it is not empathy we feel but sorrow for the innocent victims and outrage toward their oppressors.

Fig. 2   A witness puppet testifies in *Ubu and the Truth Commission:* "Someone came and told me, they are burning your son." Jane Taylor, William Kentridge, and the Handspring Puppet Company. Photo by Ruphin Coudyzer.

to sharpen the difference between representations and reenactments of severe violence.

Just as it is all too easy to misconstrue extreme hunger and life-threatening disease when one has not experienced them firsthand,[27] it is all too common for those who sympathize with the poor to imagine that they are poor because they have no work (or choose not to work). In fact, it is often the poorly paid, unrelenting work—the manual labor from morning until night—that wears the poor down and pays them so little that they cannot afford the food in the market. Here is one such figure who was the victim of apartheid violence portrayed in *Ubu and the Truth Commission.*

27. For a clinical description of various forms of dying, see Sherwin B. Nuland, *How We Die: Reflections on Life's Final Chapter* (New York: Vintage Books, 1993).

Fig. 3   Looking down on the mine workers in the Sierra Pelada gold mine, Brazil, 1986.
Photo by Sebastião Salgado.

One can see in the dark eyes of this woman and the turned-down corners of
her mouth a level of comprehension. This is not a blank stare; she almost dares
us to justify the loss and suffering she has endured. She is not covered, emaciated,
and anonymous as is the woman in the Salgado photograph. Even if we do not
know her name, she speaks for herself.

Compare this puppet's expression with two other Salgado pictures of mine
workers in the Sierra Pelada gold mine in Brazil in 1986. These photographs are
of interest because there are elements of both simulation and reenactment in
them. On the one hand, not only are the mine workers anonymous, but they
are simulating a conveyor belt. In the first photograph we see the sacks of earth
moving en masse up the side of the mine. The figures carrying them on their
backs at once resemble World War I infantry troops climbing out of a massive
trench and slaves weighed down by the sacks of earth that await them every
waking hour of every day.

In the second mine workers photograph we see the machinery underneath
the weighed-down backs of these faceless laborers: the driving legs, interlocked
and straining under this load, with little footing underneath.

Unlike the simulations of refugee camps that are designed to evoke a matter-
of-fact, problem-solving attitude, this human conveyor belt is a kind of cyborg

Fig. 4   A close-up of the legs of the mine workers in the Sierra Pelada gold mine, Brazil, 1986. Photo by Sebastião Salgado.

in reverse: The mine is a machine made out of human parts. We do not see the world from the perspective of the miners, but we have a better idea of what it looks like from the panoptical point of view of the owner. Our anger outweighs our sympathy, and in this sense the photograph resembles Turner's slave ship painting.

Now return to *Ubu* and compare these Salgado representations of dehumanized suffering to a scene in which two puppeteers silently manipulate a hand-and-rod puppet, creating the illusion that they are watching intently as the puppet acts under his own power. They are bystanders whose connections to this impoverished-street-vendor-cum-housekeeper are unspoken yet fully understood by the audience. Intermittently, Kentridge's redrawings of the puppet's meager possessions are projected onto a rear screen, moving by themselves from place to place to underscore the illusion that the puppeteers have no connection to the action.

In this multilayered scene, the trader puppet also works for Ubu and his wife, who appropriate the physical objects on the table as if he was serving them dinner. Ma and Pa Ubu are played by live actors in the role of former "mixed-race" functionaries in the South African apartheid regime. They do not yet know whether they will be called to testify before the Truth and Reconciliation Commission (TRC), and so they quarrel as they plot their escape, oblivious to the figures

Fig. 5   A trader puppet in *Ubu and the Truth Commission* silently setting up the goods of his street-side store in the middle of Ma and Pa Ubu's dinner table. Jane Taylor, William Kentridge, and the Handspring Puppet Company. Photo by Ruphin Coudyzer.

(represented by puppets) whose lives they depend on. The deeply lined faces of the mute puppets tell another story. Even though his body is consumed by the details of his daily labor, the worker's intent expression remains distinctively his own. The puppeteers are the epitome of unreflective everyday bystanders. They work alongside the trader puppet, earning their living by holding him in his place, yet never seeing him eye to eye.

In this reenactment of events surrounding and informing the TRC's proceedings, the puppets convey the purposelessness of their suffering and servitude. Their sobriety contrasts with the manic, carnivalesque antics of the Ubus, who fear they will be called before the TRC for complicity, and the faces of the puppeteers, who know they will not be. But their heads are not bowed. We are not just invited to see, feel, and understand the world from the point of view of these puppets; rather than sympathetically prescribe a remedy for their condition, we are challenged to understand our complicity in their suffering through both their actions and the silent movements of their handlers and the objects projected behind them.

Admittedly, it is possible to interpret simulations and representations of suffering so that bystanders have a more acute understanding of the scale and depth of severe violence, and also so that we are more aware of the limits of simulations and representations. Beyond this, however, we also need interpreters and narrators of reenactments of severe violence who can forge bonds of acquaintance between everyday bystanders and others whose suffering they gradually may be able to recognize as part of their own lives. One place this can happen is in undergraduate education, and those of us who have taken on teaching as a vocation have a responsibility to blend these idioms together in what Michael Oakeshott calls a conversation—that is, in the distinctive way in which human beings become acquainted with one another.[28]

In a university in which there are opportunities to teach and learn from students and colleagues from regions of the world where severe violence is part of everyday experience, we can become more acquainted with our own contributions to and benefits from this violence. We can begin to recognize our own shared political responsibilities without becoming distracted by questions of guilt-ridden doubt or overwhelming feelings of sympathy. But becoming acquainted takes time and careful effort.

It also requires imagination. To help everyday bystanders see themselves within a new framework of responsibility and citizenship, critical reenactments and their interpretations by citizen-teachers must be conveyed in a poetic voice. The hunger and pain of impoverished providers do not have to remain ineffable, but it takes a powerful poetic imagination to express them persuasively. I discuss this at length in §23. Rather than try to define what counts as poetry—since I believe that we often do not realize how common poetry is in our ordinary spoken language and popular music—let me offer an example of one artist who uses it to stimulate our imagination in this way.

Alfredo Jaar is a performance artist born in Chile who has conducted several long-term projects, including community-based projects in South Africa and Rwanda. He calls them public interventions, and his personal Web site retells these stories in a poetic voice. The Web site opens with eight lines from a poem by William Carlos Williams that expresses the need to use poetry as a medium for political education:

> It is difficult
> to get the news from poems
> yet men die miserably every day

28. Michael Oakeshott, "Education: The Engagement and Its Frustration," in *The Voice of Liberal Learning,* ed. Timothy Fuller (New Haven: Yale University Press, 1989), 54–55.

for lack
of what is found there.[29]

Once the Web site visitor clicks the poem's final word, which is presented in red type (all others are in white), the text is then replaced by Jaar's prone silhouette, outlined in white chalk as if he were the victim of a crime. The silhouetted form slowly awakens, looks up to a star-filled sky dominated by Earth, dives upward, flies through space, and disappears into the African continent.

The next screen contains a passage from a poem by the twentieth-century Romanian writer E. M. Cioran, "Degradation Through Work," which includes the following: "I am simultaneously happy and unhappy, exalted and depressed, overcome by both pleasure and despair in the most contradictory harmonies."[30] These lines capture Jaar's ambivalence toward our everyday routines: they can exhaust and deaden us at the same time that we can take pride and comfort in our most modest accomplishments. But Jaar is not ready to stop there; he realizes that Cioran himself was a contradictory figure and that his poetic insight must be held up to a critical light.

Cioran's early attraction to authoritarianism gave way to an existential alienation very unlike Jaar's commitment to collaborative work with poor communities. When we click on Cioran's words, one small box at a time, they are replaced by one of three large group photographs of young workers and children (the site cycles through the three photos, presenting a different one to the viewer on subsequent visits). Some of the figures are soiled and tired, possibly even degraded by work, but not defeated; others are beaming and seem to be imagining another world; and still others are embracing casually in the aftermath of severe violence. Jaar does not dismiss Cioran but uses his ambivalence as a lens through which to see beyond the rhythms of everyday work and visualize that "thronged and common road" Jane Addams imagined. Whether in the form of a Web site like Jaar's, installation art, or political theater, the visual poetry of a critical reenactment sometimes can help us imagine new forms of democratic acquaintanceship.

---

29. Alfredo Jaar, http://www.alfredojaar.net/. The quotation is from William Carlos Williams, "Asphodel, That Greeny Flower," in *Journey to Love* (New York: Random House, 1955), 41.

30. E. M. Cioran's "Degradation Through Work," written in 1934, may also be found in his *On the Heights of Despair,* trans. Ilinca Zarifopol-Johnson (Chicago: University of Chicago Press, 1992), 104–5.

5 BYSTANDER ALLEGORIES

In this chapter I focus on the allegories of bystander responsibility that have dominated rich-nation public discourse on severe violence. These allegories have been the underlying uncritical codes of the simulations and representations of responsibility that were discussed in the previous chapter, and they inform the undemocratic culture of simulation to be discussed in chapter 7.

Allegory, from the Greek meaning "other" (*allos*) and "to speak in public" (*agoreuein*), is typically a narrative rich in detail and designed to prompt public imagination. Allegories of responsibility help us talk with one another in a public forum about types of individual and collective responsibility. While some may prefer to describe the texts that I call allegories as myths, I believe that they have in fact prompted public imagination and dialogue, and so can be loosely described as allegories.[1]

Allegories occur most commonly in literature, the paradigmatic cases being Plato's allegory of the cave in *The Republic,* Dante Alighieri's *The Divine Comedy,* and George Orwell's *Animal Farm.* But allegories can also occur in film (e.g., Fritz Lang's *Metropolis*) or painting (Jan Vermeer's *The Art of Painting*). The greater the metaphorical detail and the more coherent the narrative, the more generative power the allegory has. Between the shadows on the wall in Plato's cave and the sun outside, there are numerous sources of light and dark. These

---

1. Although I rely heavily on literature, poetry, and film throughout this book, the following arguments about the limitations of contemporary allegories of responsibility in development theory are not attempts at postmodern deconstruction in the fashion, for example, of Jacques Derrida or Paul de Man. See Paul de Man, *Allegories of Reading: Figural Language in Rousseau, Nietzsche, Rilke, and Proust,* new ed. (New Haven: Yale University Press, 1982). For a postmodernist reading of U.S. Cold War political discourse as allegory, see Frederick M. Dolan, *Allegories of America* (Ithaca: Cornell University Press, 1994).

connected details enable the reader to make creative comparisons between life in the cave and the experiences of students in classrooms, prisoners in jail, voters in polling stations, or audiences in theaters.[2] The allegories of responsibility considered in this chapter help us interpret some of the connections between acts of severe violence and the many agents responsible for them, without being constrained by a single metaphor.

Peter Singer's famous allegory of the drowning child places high utilitarian demands on individuals to aid and rescue those in need,[3] although Singer has argued recently that these demands are not as unrealistically high as some of his critics have contended.[4] At the opposite pole are Bernard Williams's stories built around the value of individual life projects. In this chapter I begin with two variations on Singer's allegory. The first is a morally naive (and economically sophisticated) exhortation by Jeffrey Sachs to respond to the preventable deaths of millions of children as we would to a disease afflicting our own child. The second is a more nuanced, consequentialist allegory suggested by Amartya Sen about a mother who must make a decision about food for her own child when other children are starving. In contrast to Singer, Sachs, and Sen, Williams's stories presuppose controversial ideas about institutional as well as individual responsibilities. While I disagree with Williams's conclusions, his elaboration of the stories of bystander responsibility in place of cryptic allegories is more appropriate for the culture of reenactment that I describe in chapter 8.

16. Allegories of Rescue

"If it is in our power to prevent something bad from happening," Peter Singer argued in 1972 in the case of famine, "without thereby sacrificing anything of comparable moral importance, we ought, morally, to do it."[5] Singer has qualified this principle on the margins over the years, but he has more or less resolutely

---

2. Plato's allegory has inspired many literary and artistic works, including William Kentridge's 2005 installation *Black Box/Chambre Noire* at the Deutsche Guggenheim museum in Berlin. Another is the novel by José Saramago, *The Cave,* trans. Margaret Jull Costa (New York: Harcourt, 2002).

3. Peter Singer, "Famine, Affluence, and Morality," *Philosophy and Public Affairs* 1, no. 1 (1972): 229–43. But see Liam B. Murphy, *Moral Demands in Nonideal Theory* (New York: Oxford University Press, 2000), for a discussion of collective responsibilities for beneficent action when we cannot count on others to do their part.

4. Peter Singer, *The Life You Can Save: Acting Now to End World Poverty* (New York: Random House, 2009).

5. Singer, "Famine, Affluence, and Morality," 231.

stuck to the main idea. To defend this principle, not just illustrate its force, Singer describes a situation in which he is walking past a shallow pond in which a child is drowning. He argues that the cost of muddying his clothes is certainly more than offset by rescuing the drowning child. Extending this principle to distant strangers, complicating the situation by adding other passive bystanders, and worrying about one's effectiveness as a rescuer—none of these circumstances changes the moral principle. Numbers, Singer steadfastly asserts, make all the difference in the world.

The primary objection to Singer's utilitarian theory of humanitarian sacrifice, and what lies behind Williams's argument, is the belief that from the point of view of moral persons, the lives and interests of some other people are and should be more important than the lives and interests of other people. We would not want to live in a world in which parents, for example, did not feel a stronger moral obligation to their own children than to others. Jeffrey Sachs responds to this objection by saying that even if we allow for this kind of "agent-centered prerogative,"[6] there is still plenty of room for improving our moral response to the harsh suffering of others, especially innocent children. Too many people are dying and living miserable lives because, through no fault of their own, they cannot meet their most basic needs. There is nothing mysterious about this problem, he argues, and there are no magic bullets that will fix it. The necessary healthcare, education, sanitation, food, and water can be "costed out," and the amount of money rich nations would have to invest to get the poor out of their traps, according to Sachs, will not significantly lower the rich nations' standard of living. We can afford it.[7]

Sachs seems baffled and at times morally outraged that his fellow citizens, especially those in power, do not get the message. In his campaign to raise support and funding for his "millennium village" strategy to meet the United Nations' Millennium Development Goals, he has relied on a version of Singer's drowning child allegory. In a lecture to the Washington, D.C., Center for Global Development (streamed on their Web site), Sachs presented a slide showing children

6. The concept of an agent-centered prerogative is found in the writings of Samuel Scheffler. Both Scheffler's view and parallel arguments leading to limitations of the Singer principle, such as Liam Murphy's argument from fairness and Jean Hampton's egoistic argument, are reviewed by Richard J. Arneson, "Moral Limits on the Demands of Beneficence," in *The Ethics of Assistance: Morality and the Distant Needy,* ed. Deen K. Chatterjee (New York: Cambridge University Press, 2004), 33–58.

7. Jeffrey D. Sachs, *The End of Poverty: Economic Possibilities for Our Time* (New York: Penguin, 2005), 288–328. See also Pedro Sanchez and others, "The African Millennium Villages," *PNAS* 104, no. 43 (2007): 16775–80; and Edward R. Carr, "Millennium Village Project and African Development: Problems and Potentials," *Progress in Development Studies* 8, no. 4 (2008): 333–44.

who were afflicted with a complex of preventable diseases and dying in a sub-Saharan African hospital:

> This was a visit to Zomba Central Hospital in January. You are seeing children lined up like sardines in a coma dying of malaria. This is not a normal picture. This is not a normal circumstance in the world. This is a tragedy and utterly controllable and we have done very little up until now to control it. There is no excuse for this but there is also no possibility of economic development unless we can address these basic challenges of disease and hunger. One child after another in a coma. Probably most of them dead the day after our visit. Hundreds of children crowded into this ward. Hungry, parasitized not just by malaria but soil helmens, by schisto, by onchocerciasis, by a host of controllable diseases that we have not seen fit to lift a finger to control. . . . Now the fact of the matter is that millions of people are dying right now because they are too impoverished to stay alive. They are not getting enough food. They are not getting safe drinking water. They are not getting access to basic health services. They are not getting access to a bed net to protect them from malaria or a $1.00 dose of artemisinin and combination therapy to cure them of malaria when it hits.[8]

When Sachs is among like-minded development professionals, as he was in this setting, he lets his guard down and allows his metaphors to go too far (e.g., "sardines in a coma," "lift a finger"). He believes that it is just inhuman (as well as contrary to our strategic political interests) not to make the modest contributions it would take to remedy extreme poverty. Here is the allegory:

> Now my proposition, which is very unpopular in this city, is that this actually involves some upfront investments to solve. If we actually took the lives of these children at a tiny fraction of the seriousness that we took the lives of our children, and I believe we should, not only for the human dimension of it, not only because we promised, but because as the Major General recently told me from the European Command. He cannot begin to do his job helping to provide security vis-à-vis Africa with a hungry

8. Jeffrey Sachs, "The Millennium Village Project: A New Approach to Ending Poverty" (transcript prepared from audio recording), presented at the Center for Global Development, Washington, D.C., March 14, 2006.

continent. Because the generals are completely on to this case though our political leaders are not.[9]

All it would take, Sachs opines, is a "tiny fraction of the seriousness" that we have for our own children. We would not let our own children suffer and starve like this. If this argument doesn't move you, he notes, then at the very least you ought to realize that a hungry Africa poses a security threat to richer countries. But the real point for him is that these images of children dying from preventable diseases and preventable starvation have an irresistible motivational force, if you just let yourself look at them the way you would look at your own children. You don't need a complex moral theory, just the courage to look the facts in the face: "We are leaving people to die by the millions and that is literally what we have been doing. And I am seeing them dying, many more than I want to see, and I expected to see in my life. Children dying before my eyes and I recommend that you go see it too so you could see what we could be doing."[10]

He confesses that he never thought of development this way when he was prescribing free markets and trade liberalization for Poland twenty years ago. He now realizes that in many of the regions of sub-Saharan Africa, there just are not enough natural resources and no means on hand for these people to replenish or supplement them by themselves. If we don't believe it, we should go see for ourselves. Sachs has seen dying children. If you see them too, you

9. See the "Partnership to Cut Hunger and Poverty in Africa" statement by Julie Howard, delivered to the United Nations Economic and Social Council Special Event on Food Crisis in Africa, New York, October 27, 2005, http://www.un.org/docs/ecosoc/meetings/2005/docs/Howard%20Speech-%20Food%20Crises-%2027%20October%202005.pdf: "In private discussions I find our partner members in the U.S. and in Africa increasingly worried about the priority accorded to the Millennium Village concept and the absence of high-level discussion about the relative merits of this model against the historical program experiences of many United Nations development agencies and other agencies. The Villages have raised the media profile of African development in a very important way. But U.S. and African public and private sector experts worry that the simple message that infusions of resources targeted locally will solve development problems glosses over some very hard lessons learned with integrated rural development and similar approaches over the past 30+ years. Giving away free seeds, fertilizer, healthcare and education at the village level provides dramatic results in the short term but quickly proves unsustainable without the larger set of public investments and without consideration about how to engage the private sector. How will services be paid for and who will provide them in the future? In Zambia, Malawi, Mozambique and else-where, prolonged distribution of free agricultural inputs and services has significantly damaged the incentive for private sector providers to enter the market. There are concerns, too, that the approach takes badly needed attention away from the big-ticket, less glamorous items for which public investment is desperately needed—infrastructure, institution building, improving gover-nance, capacity building. Mr. President, we regard these as important questions and hope that they might merit further discussion at the highest levels."

10. Sachs, "Millennium Village Project."

will come to the same conclusions he has. But since most people won't go themselves, Sachs is bringing the starving children to them.

What would we have to do to get serious, one village at a time? Unlike Singer, who suggests something like an across-the-board sacrifice above a certain annual individual or family income, Sachs prefers a sharply progressive taxation scheme. The issue is not whether the rich countries can afford to give more foreign aid, but whether we as individual citizens in rich countries have the political will and the economic science to do it right, one village at a time.

It is the last part of Sachs's plan that has raised the most questions among those sympathetic to his appeal. Even if we see what he sees and feel what he feels, there are problems with a "millennium village" strategy to meet the Millennium Development Goals. Each village will indeed do better if it is the beneficiary of large infusions of foreign aid. The question is for how long? Will the villagers be able to keep it up once the aid stops? Sachs insists that these are not give-aways or paradoxical aid packages that undermine local capacity building or the creation of legitimate institutions. They are "clinical" cures that will lift villages out of the poverty trap, one by one, so that then they can sustain themselves under their own power. To accomplish this, Sachs acknowledges, villagers must participate in the planning and they must also invest some of their own capital in the development project, whether it is a new school or just a new truck for the village. They will be investment partners and they will acquire new governance skills in addition to needed new resources.

Sachs's critics are not convinced. Villages may escape the poverty traps they are in now (low rates of savings, high birth rates, and the inability to reach the minimal thresholds needed for transportation infrastructure), but what will keep them from slipping back once foreign aid is directed away from them and toward other needy villages, even with the new skills and commitments they have acquired as millennium villages? Who will provide the credit, the birth control, and the road repair once the aid runs out?

Sustainable development will require finding ways for villages to enter the regional or global economy so that they can begin to generate a surplus themselves that will pay for schools, healthcare, road repair, and other basic needs on an ongoing basis. This may mean switching over from subsistence farming (e.g., sorghum and millet) to cash crops that can generate foreign exchange. It may mean exporting some of their own human capital to foreign countries so that they can receive remittances from their most promising young people working abroad. Some villages may want to embark on this path even though it will involve difficult choices and sometimes will be culturally and politically wrenching.[11]

11. Ibid.

Persuading these villagers to believe that they can preserve their freedom and the integrity of their village life and have sustainable development at the same time may be misleading, and ultimately it may make it even more difficult for them to escape their current poverty traps.

These hard choices, Sachs believes, can be made when we face the suffering and starving children at Zomba Central Hospital. Does the sight of dying children like our own somehow make these choices more possible? As sincere as Sachs is about having villagers take responsibility for how development aid is used village by village, his allegory of responsibility focuses our attention on the individual responsibilities of parent donors for their own starving children. This kind of paternalism is understandable when one thinks of those who are in need as helpless "sardines in a coma." It is misplaced in this context, however, and because it reinforces Singer's one-time emergency allegory of child rescue, it may even work against Sachs's own humanitarian goals.

At a theoretical level, what Singer and Sachs have in common is that they rush too quickly to what they think are irresistible moral intuitions. In Singer's case it is that the urgent need to be rescued is just that—it overrides other needs that are not comparable, and does not lose its urgency because it occurs far away. The moral intuition is one of equality, what Richard W. Miller calls a right to equal concern. The allegory of the drowning child dramatizes this overriding need for equal concern but in the process avoids hard questions about institutional entanglement. Perhaps, as Miller has argued, there are less urgent but more obligatory responsibilities that less distant fellow citizens have for one another because of the coercive legal structures they share. And these responsibilities may rest on a right to equal respect, not the concern that is more appropriate for family and friends. These are open questions. They depend on how much less the urgent needs of distant strangers depend on similar global structures than the urgent needs of fellow citizens depend on shared national structures of power. They also depend on what benchmark of equality is most appropriate. Equal concern and equal respect, as Miller notes, are not identical and should not be combined into one single right. But these questions do not arise for Singer; in his view, there is no time to spare for these institutional issues.[12]

Sachs's impulsiveness is even more apparent. His intuitions are not especially egalitarian. He portrays unnecessary suffering as a tragedy, not a drowning accident, and his intuitive response is a blend of paternalism and market faith. The

---

12. Richard W. Miller, "Moral Closeness and World Community," in Chatterjee, *Ethics of Assistance*, 101–22.

metaphors of "traps" and "ladders" dominate Sachs's argument in the sense that he believes that once we pull these childlike villagers out of the traps they are in (once the children come out of their comas), whether because of mistakes they have made or because of opportunistic behavior by others (including their own fellow citizens and leaders), and once we give them one foot up on the ladder of development, then other incentives and forms of assistance will do the rest. To let them languish in these traps is inhuman; after all, we would not treat a trapped animal this way. To leave them grasping for the rungs of a ladder that is out of reach is equally inhumane. There is no clear moral intuition here similar to Singer's concern for the accidental victim. In Sachs's allegory we are simultaneously parents, hunters, and climbers who should take pity on helpless victims. For both Singer and Sachs, however, the intuition that the needy actually will have to make hard choices from the very start about their own development path is overshadowed by their urgent and tragic present circumstances.

Amartya Sen is well aware of these hard choices and realizes that the poor must be able to participate in them if their suffering is to be mitigated in a sustainable way. But he does not liken development to a one-time emergency rescue mission, a clinical intervention, or even more long-term parental oversight. "Development as freedom," he argues, should cultivate the capability to choose among alternative paths of human functioning above a basic level of survival.[13] When confronted with the question of who is responsible for making this happen, however, Sen also falls back on a parent-child allegory, albeit one that does not have the problems of Singer's and Sachs's allegories.

Sen's theory of capabilities is a theory of individual substantive (not just formal) freedom, and he says that this kind of freedom is a prerequisite for responsible human agency. That means that the freedom to live a healthy life, for example, must include adequate access to food, medical care, and a clean environment. Individuals who are substantively free will be able to make responsible choices—that is, sound judgments about their own well-being. Further, individuals who are substantively free can be and ought to be held responsible for their choices. It is this second sense, of being responsible *for* one's choices (as opposed to being capable of making responsible choices to do certain things), that is critical to his account of development as freedom.

Sen argues that individuals are not to be held responsible for impersonally maximizing their own utility. That kind of consequentialism does not capture

---

13. In *Development as Freedom* (New York: 1999), 54–55, Sen offers a parable that also stresses the importance of agency and choice: a woman, Annapurna, must choose between three job applicants, all of whom have an urgent need for employment but for different reasons.

how people actually make moral decisions, and so we shouldn't try to force them to choose this way. Instead, they can and ought to view the world from their position as "situated consequentialists," for whom a picture of a good state of affairs *simultaneously* includes rights, duties, and conceptions of the person.[14] Such situated individuals are responsible for respecting human rights, honoring moral duties, and furthering human well-being:

> The demand of situated evaluation requires that a person not ignore the particular position from which she is making the choice. Consider, for example, the parent of a child for whom she is choosing a particular baby food. The requirement of situated evaluation does not, in any way, vindicate smugness about one's contingent level of ignorance, and does not deny the need for the person to find out, if reasonably possible, more about what others know or see (e.g., that the baby food with which the parent is familiar might have been shown to be harmful). Nor does it deny the relevance of broader sympathies (for example, a parent may well ask whether it is right that her child should have the benefit of some baby food to which other children do not have access). What is denied is the possibility of ignoring the person's own responsibilities in her particular situation, in this case that of being a parent of this child.[15]

Parents can be held responsible for negligence when they fail to know and act on knowledge they reasonably ought to have. That is what it means to be a responsible parent in a particular situation. This responsibility, Sen asserts, does not preclude a parent questioning the rightness of the social distribution of baby food, even if that might mean less food for her own baby. The individual responsibility for one's own baby's well-being should not "deny the relevance" of having sympathy for the well-being of babies in general who have less food than one's own. Depending, presumably, on the urgent needs of other less well-fed babies, a moral duty to aid others could override a parent's responsibility to feed her own baby the most nutritious food. This would not be negligence, and using the simile of development as freedom, the same reasoning ought to apply to the shared responsibilities of peoples across national boundaries.[16]

14. Amartya Sen, "Symposium on Amartya Sen's Philosophy: 4 Reply," *Economics and Philosophy* 17, no. 1 (2001): 60–61.

15. Amartya Sen, "Consequential Evaluation and Practical Reason," *Journal of Philosophy* 97, no. 9 (2000): 484.

16. See, for example, T. M. Scanlon, "Symposium on Amartya Sen's Philosophy: 3 Sen and Consequentialism," *Economics and Philosophy* 17, no. 1 (2001): 39–50.

If we are concerned with the question of responsibility for harm done to the children of others and not just the responsibility of the parent to provide for his or her own child, then Sen's account of responsibility (and negligence) is not enough. He tells us we should not neglect our own children, and we can do this without losing sympathy for those who may suffer because they have less than our own children. What about those children and their families who cannot afford the available baby food for more complex reasons, regardless of whether we purchase a lot of baby food for our own children? To call this a "passive" or "negative" responsibility seems to miss the point. As consumers and citizens we participate in political and economic institutions that make this situation the one that we and the parents of poor children actually face together. There seems to be a much more complex relationship between the effective demand of the poor for food for their children, the nutrition and health of poor children, and their substantive freedom in general than simply how strong our sympathies toward them may be in comparison to our felt responsibility to feed our own children.

This individualism in Sen's account of responsibility is surprising given that he is well aware of the fact that substantive human freedom, including the freedom of poor children, depends in large part on social arrangements that individuals separately have little control over.[17] Gender relations within the family and the political organization of women, for example, may affect the actual health of babies just as much (if not more) than the affordability of baby food for poor families.[18] In the same article in which he describes the individual responsibilities of the situated consequentialist, Sen writes:

> The need to examine the relative importance of different consequences (including well-beings, freedoms, rights, and so on) that may compete with each other in evaluative assessment does arise in many different contexts. We live in an interdependent world in which the realization of our respective freedoms interconnects in a variety of ways, and we cannot treat them each as an isolated island. The discipline of consequential evaluation forces us to take responsibility for our choices, since our actions influence other people's freedoms and lives as well as our own. The reach of our responsibility includes asking certain questions, such as

17. Sen, *Development as Freedom*, 288.
18. For a description of the gap between rising income and continued child malnutrition, see James Tefft and others, "Linkages Between Child Nutrition and Agricultural Growth in Mali: A Summary of Preliminary Findings," *Policy Synthesis* 64 (April 2003), http://www.aec.msu.edu/agecon/fs2/polsyn/number64.pdf.

those concerning the relative importance of different rights or freedoms the realization of which may impinge on each other.[19]

What is noteworthy about this analysis of our "interdependent world" is that "our responsibility," as Sen calls it, is not equally interdependent. When it comes to social responsibility, Sen warns us that "any affirmation of social responsibility that *replaces* individual responsibility cannot but be, to varying extents, counterproductive. There is no substitute for individual responsibility."[20]

This seems like an odd formulation for someone who has written so eloquently on public action and the need for it to provide communication, health, education, and transportation infrastructures to avoid famine and hunger. Aren't these social responsibilities? And when professionals organize to form groups such as Physicians for Social Responsibility, are they counterproductively substituting social responsibility for individual responsibility? Wouldn't it be more accurate to say that they are acting more responsibly by recognizing the need for collective action and shared social responsibility? Just as some actions lead to a complex pattern of effects, so too do some actions stem from a complex web of causes and antecedent conditions that cannot be reduced to the sum of individual responsibilities.

A people can incur legitimate social responsibilities for the capability deprivation of others, regardless of individual moral duties. This is what development is very often about. That is, reconstructive and conciliatory development, not merely humanitarian aid, is needed to remedy the severe violence that has been generated in complex patterns over time and that continue into the present. Part of the individual *and* social responsibilities of democratic citizens in this context is to make educated choices about the constitution of power and the patterns of violence that development simultaneously creates. To see more clearly how these patterns shape political responsibilities, I turn to Bernard Williams's account of responsibility.

17. Individual Integrity

Williams does not deny that there are "remote" causes and effects surrounding our actions, and that we may well be responsible for them in some sense. From a moral point of view, however, he does not think they are significant.[21] The

---

19. Sen, "Consequential Evaluation," 500.
20. Sen, *Development as Freedom,* 283.
21. Bernard Williams, "A Critique of Utilitarianism," in *Utilitarianism: For and Against,* ed. J. J. C. Smart and Bernard Williams (New York: Cambridge University Press, 1973), 94.

significant issue for him is the way in which consequentialist reason focuses exclusively on "states of affairs" at the expense of understanding the moral importance of individual commitments, projects, and integrity for assigning responsibility for actions leading to these states of affairs. Even though Williams warns us that we should not be held prisoner by a simplistic model of human agency,[22] he still believes that we should focus our attention on non-problematic, more proximate causes and effects—that is, those cases where doing or not doing something clearly results in certain consequences. I hope to show how Williams's own examples rely on understated and unstated assumptions about a more complex and interdependent world than he recognized.

Specifically, Williams argues, it is the attribution of responsibility for not doing something ("negative responsibility") that reveals the most troubling limitations of consequentialism. Consequentialism, along with its utilitarian varieties, depreciates the importance of individual feelings, convictions, projects, and life commitments. It encourages a kind of moral alienation by severing the relationship between a disembodied, rationalist conception of happiness and the emotionally rich projects organized according to the deeper commitments that make a happy life. In effect, it alienates agents from their moral feelings and their actions. Further, consequentialism pretends to be impartial by treating negative and positive responsibility equally, regardless of who the agent happens to be (i.e., it is agent-neutral), but in practice it is guilty of "discounting one's reactions, impulses, and deeply held projects in the face of the pattern of utilities, not merely adding them in."[23]

Williams made this non-consequentialist argument against negative responsibility in 1973, but it has remained influential in ethics primarily because of the two examples he introduced: George, a chemist opposed to doing research on chemical and biological warfare, and Jim, a botanist who accidentally stumbles on a grim village scene while doing fieldwork in South America, have become fixtures in undergraduate ethics courses and in the literature of applied ethics. Philosophers and practitioners have used these examples to dramatize the limitations of utilitarian cost-benefit analysis and to sharpen the sympathies of professionals for their clients and patients.

Williams is well aware that he has begged some important questions in these two cases. He acknowledges that not all possible choices are available to these

22. "We deceive ourselves if we suppose that public practices of ascribing responsibility can be derived from an antecedent notion of moral responsibility, or that the idea of the voluntary is uniquely important to responsibility." Bernard Williams, *Shame and Necessity* (Berkeley and Los Angeles: University of California Press, 1993), 67.

23. Williams, "Critique of Utilitarianism," 118.

fictional actors, and the question as to how they got themselves into these situations in the first place is not on the table. He tells us that we are not allowed to rewrite the scripts, just to write the next scene. Writing the next scene, however, requires that we fill in some of the unstated portions or gaps in the existing scripts.

Let me begin with George, described as a somewhat-frail, unemployed chemist who has depended on his wife to support a family that is clearly showing the strains of this arrangement. George is offered the opportunity to do research on chemical and biological warfare (CBW) but is opposed to it in principle. He ponders the possibility that he could take the job and drag his feet, thereby keeping a more zealous advocate of CBW from doing harm in that position. George's wife, whose views we are told need not concern us in any detail, is indifferent with regard to CBW research.

There are actually two ways in which negative responsibility arises in this case. One is how responsible would George be if he didn't take the job and a more zealous new employee caused more harm than George would have caused in that position. Because the harm done by George's likely replacement is harm done in the future and "elsewhere," Williams thinks that it is not as weighty as immediate harm to real persons. This allows us to conclude that George's commitment not to support CBW clearly outweighs whatever differential impact his replacement might have. This judgment, according to Williams—not any utilitarian calculation about the happiness of all concerned (George, his replacement, his wife and children, and the beneficiaries and victims of CBW)—is what ought to determine George's responsibility.

The unstated part of this script is the project and the commitment of George's likely zealous replacement. This individual deserves the same respect as a person that Williams wants us to give to George. But all we know is that he is zealous about CBW. We don't know why and we don't know anything about the context in which CBW research is being conducted. Before we can decide whether George ought to be negatively responsible for the possible future harm done by his zealous replacement, we have to know more about this person's projects and commitments. Before we can judge whether George's commitment to his life project would make him responsible for his replacement's actualized commitment to his counterproject, or whether George is just stepping out of the way, we have to know more about this counterproject.

This is not just a request for more information about remote future consequences, which Williams rules out of order; it is information that we need about the present hypothetical context if we are to judge whether George's commitment not to do CBW research ought to be honored, even if it allows his replacement to pursue an alternative project (conceivably the proliferation of CBW). If CBW is inherently unethical because of the danger it poses to combatants and noncombatants alike, that would answer the question. If, on the other hand, CBW is the only effective tool for combating a naturally occurring deadly micro- scopic organism, the answer might be otherwise. Then we might say that by declining the job George is unwittingly facilitating the work of a kindred spirit. He is negatively responsible for the moral benefits of CBW. Williams, arguably, assumes that CBW is inherently unethical and thereby dismisses the project of George's replacement as purely immoral zeal.

But this is not the only question of negative responsibility George faces, and probably not the one that concerns Williams most. The more immediate issue for George is how responsible in a negative sense would he be for the further suffering of his family in the event that he refused to take the CBW job but did not find a comparably paying job. Is George responsible for their suffering by turning down the only job he can get at this time, even though the causes of their suffering would be overdetermined by, among other things, the existing tension between him and his wife because of his unemployment and her demanding job, the job market for chemists in general, and his frail bodily constitution?

Here the missing part of the script is not the relationship between George's pacifist commitments and the counterprojects of others. It is not a matter of whether George should be held responsible for someone else's projects, even if his own is only making it more possible for that person to carry out his or her work. The issue is not what bearing George's project has on the well-formed projects of others. Rather, the issue is how his joint project with other family members—making a life together—is to progress. Further, this joint project depends on a more complex institutional context, not just how George, his wife, and their children feel about their future together. Whether they have a future together at all will depend on forces beyond their control, including the labor market for chemists, the public and neighborhood support networks for families, and possibly even the geopolitical system that has fostered CBW. To know how negatively responsible, if at all, George is for exacerbating problems at home, one must locate his project within this context. There is no counterproject to juxtapose against George's pacifism, but only a complicated web of social rela- tions that gives his project its interpersonal meaning for him and others. When Williams dismisses George's wife's views with a casual remark that she does not think there is anything "particularly wrong with research into CBW," he excludes a relevant part of the story: not what George does to his wife, but what they do together based on reasons they share.[24]

That is the case of George, and it is clear why Williams seems less interested in it than his other case, Jim and the Indians, in which Jim the botanist accidentally comes on a village in which soldiers are interrogating villagers they suspect of antigovernment protests. In Jim's case there is a counterproject, that of the government captain Pedro, which is what is missing in the case of George. The question now, argues Williams, is unavoidable: what is the relationship between Jim's project as an innocent botanist and Pedro's project of suppressing protests by villagers against the government. There are immediate consequences to real people if Jim does not "help" Pedro by executing one of the random villagers being held hostage so that the other nineteen will be allowed to live. In this case, Williams admits that his own analysis of the situation could result in the same judgment that utilitarianism countenances: Jim should compromise his integrity to save the nineteen Indians. But, Williams stresses, what we learn from an analysis of the competing projects and commitments is that the very idea of negative responsibility, as utilitarians have used it, is deeply flawed.

When we ask how Jim's project is related to Pedro's, one thing Williams answers is that Jim is only an instrument that Pedro uses to carry out his project of counterinsurgency. On this interpretation Jim doesn't really kill a single villager, but rather he does something (shoot the gun) so that Pedro can have the villager killed and strike fear into the hearts of the remaining nineteen. Williams also suggests that we ask what effect Pedro's counterinsurgency project has on Jim and presumably his academic project. The answer is that it alienates Jim from his moral feelings and his own actions. This is what it means for Jim to become an instrument in Pedro's project. Utilitarianism accepts this instrumentalization when it traces responsibility either positively from Pedro's orders through Jim's firing of the gun to one dead Indian or negatively from Pedro's orders through Jim's refusal to shoot to Pedro's execution of all twenty Indians. In either case, Williams says, Jim "is the agent of the satisfaction system who happens to be at a particular point at a particular time: in Jim's case, our man in South America."[25]

In the case of Jim and the Indians there is little uncertainty about the counterproject, and Williams has little doubt that Jim's integrity will suffer if he becomes

---

24. See Christine M. Korsgaard, "The Reasons We Can Share: An Attack on the Distinction Between Agent-Relative and Agent-Neutral Values," in *Creating the Kingdom of Ends* (New York: Cambridge University Press, 1996), 275. This is an example of the emphasis on shared reasons and social relations that feminist ethics of care have stressed.

25. Williams, "Critique of Utilitarianism," 115.

implicated in the killing. Should he accept this suffering for the sake of the lives of nineteen others? Williams implies that he probably should, but we should know what we are asking Jim to do, and we should not talk about his negative responsibility for the death of those nineteen if he is unable to make this sacrifice. Either way he is not morally responsible because it is Pedro's project, not Jim's, that is controlling what Jim does.

Williams's critique of negative responsibility is strictly speaking not an anti-consequentialist argument. Williams calls it non-consequentialism, but in fact it is quite consistent with the kind of situated consequentialism that Sen advocates. And as in Sen's consequentialism, Williams permits his moral actor to recognize the larger distributive problems while also honoring other non-consequentialist values—in these cases a duty to uphold one's own integrity, not (as Sen's example highlighted) a special duty to one's own child. What are missing in Williams's two cases are precisely the interpersonal projects and social networks that we fleshed out for the case of George. They also are at work in the case of Jim, but are overshadowed by the duel between Jim and Pedro. In the background of that clash between projects are similar institutionalized patterns of power and violence to those that structured the case of George, as well as similar questions about shared reasons and shared responsibilities.

Botanists who take the risks that Jim does are not romantics on a quest for the meaning of "being." Yet we know very little about Jim's real project. Does he work for a large pharmaceutical company doing research on genetically modified organisms? Does he work for a petrochemical company assessing the environmental damage of its oil-drilling projects? In what sense, then, is he an "honored guest," as Pedro says? Is this phrase to be taken as an ironic comment on Jim's complicity with the government in relocating villagers? Or is Jim an environmentalist who is doing research to support the protests of villagers against government and corporate policies? Answers to these questions are relevant to Williams's argument. They are not just requests for information about possible future consequences; they are questions about the context of development, the social meaning of research technology, and the structures of power and the patterns of violence personified by Pedro and Jim. This is why we would want to know what the Indians think in this case. If they recognize Jim as someone working in solidarity with their cause, they might say one thing to him. If they perceive him as an "honored guest" of the government they might say another. The moral world, as Christine Korsgaard has correctly noted, includes Jim, Pedro, and the Indians.[26] It

26. Korsgaard, "Reasons We Can Share," 296.

includes the institutional actors as well—the government and Jim's sponsors. Whatever Jim does, it will be as a result of reasons he shares with some of these others as well as the reasons of others that he rejects.

It is not surprising that in 1973 Williams made explicit the CBW research project George resisted. Protests against the Vietnam War were reaching their zenith, and resistance to U.S. forces and the Saigon government continued to grow. In this context, controversies over the use of Agent Orange and other forms of chemical and biological warfare were being seized on by organizations such as Vietnam Veterans Against the War and other protest groups. Williams's audience could immediately identify with George and the moral dilemma he faced.

Not so with Jim, even though his situation is more dramatically alluring. The case of Jim and the Indians vaguely recalls a colonial past, not a divisive wartime present. Were Jim to appear today, questions about ecotourism, environmental ethics, counterinsurgency, and globalization would have to be confronted. Is Jim studying genetic pollution from Bt crops? Is he studying the effects of genetically modified organisms on monarch butterflies? Botany today is no more innocent than CBW research was in 1973. Jim's case may be better, as Williams says, for discussing the shortcomings of the utilitarian conception of negative responsibility. But this is in part because, unlike the case of George, its complex political structure is obscured by a decontextualized conflict between government forces and villagers to whom Jim has no real connection. Williams claims we do not have to know how George or Jim got to their respective points in their lives in order for his argument against negative responsibility to hold. On the contrary, "CBW" does tell us something about George's situation in 1973. The narrative in Jim and the Indians is less revealing, and so the conflict between Jim's project and Pedro's project appears to be clearer. In fact, this is an illusion. Read in today's context, botany is very much a part of the history of development and technology. Today Jim is hardly an accidental honored guest. He and the institutions that sponsor his research are part of this history.

In this chapter I offer two short stories that illustrate the complexity of bystander political responsibility at the individual and institutional level. Unlike the bystander allegories of Singer, Sachs, and Sen, they locate individual responsibility within an explicit institutional context. Unlike the stories that Williams tells to debunk "negative responsibility" for severe violence, these stories illustrate how bystanders from both rich and poor nations are sometimes politically responsible for severe violence through the benefits, large and small, that they may enjoy.

18. Jim in the Grand Marché

Imagine Jim thirty years later. He received tenure, and he no longer did field-work. His research career had just crested, and he decided to get back to undergraduate teaching. He wanted to introduce his students to the world, just as he was introduced to it as a young botanist. But he recalled his earlier encounter with Pedro and the Indians, and decided that he'd take his students to a safer place.

Jim led the first-ever study abroad program to a very poor country in West Africa. The title of his program was Ethics and Development in West Africa. He had ten undergraduate students from several universities in the United States, none of whom had ever been to a country like this before. The program lasted two months, and most of the time the students studied ethical problems that arise in agriculture, education, and visual culture. Among the sites they visited were an agricultural research station fifty kilometers outside the capital city where scientists are experimenting with new strains of drought-resistant sorghum, a community school that emphasizes instruction in native languages, and an artists' collective that provides apprenticeship programs for unemployed youth while trying to market contemporary textile art and consumer goods that are based on traditional patterns and use traditional techniques and materials.

The program was based in the capital city during the rainy season, and students lived in a conference center located in a quiet neighborhood twenty minutes from the city center and its bustling market, the grand marché. After the first week, during which Jim was very careful not to let the students (eight women and two men) wander off on their own to explore the city, he agreed to take six of them shopping in the market. They would also have to change money, and he was told there was one ATM in the city that accepted Visa debit cards.

After hailing two cabs and negotiating the fare for the group of seven, they set off across the bridge that separated their neighborhood from the city center. Traffic moved at its customarily unpredictable pace, scattering pedestrians one minute, stalling for no apparent reason in a roundabout the next. The closer they got to the grand marché, the slower the trucks and cars moved and the more daring the motorbikes became. The drive itself was a lesson in the ethics of development, and Jim tried to point this out as they approached their destination. It was clear that the capital city was strained well beyond capacity. Its infrastructure was not equipped to handle the large number of residents who had migrated from the countryside over the last twenty years. Small children rushed the taxis at every chance, trying to sell telephone calling cards and mangoes. Adults watched from the curb, where they were selling large, multicolored plastic tubs used for washing, cooking, and eating; similarly multicolored teapots used for boiling water or for toileting; walls of fabric; and assorted small household items. Small children who were not selling were either sleeping on the side of the road or leading disabled, older adults through the traffic as they begged for money. It was noontime in the middle of the week. Except for Jim and his students, there were no tourists to be seen. Jim knew, however, that many of the people in the street were immigrants from other West African countries who had fled the civil wars there. As inhospitable and impoverished as this capital city was, its political climate was relatively stable for the moment.

Jim's taxi drivers did not know exactly where the ATM machine was, but they did know the grand marché. So, without much local currency and slightly nauseous from the exhaust fumes, Jim and his charges disembarked, ready to browse and anxious to find the machine that would take their Visa cards. They got lucky, and after only fifteen minutes in the hot, muggy, muddy streets lined by open sewers on either side, an elderly tailor pointed to a large, stone-faced building across the street from his makeshift stall on the edge of the market. The ATM was obviously working since there was a line of four African women in colorful, well-ironed dresses standing outside the small booth that housed it. Jim and his students crossed the busy street, and one by one they withdrew the daily maximum: two hundred U.S. dollars' worth of local currency. Their good fortune did not go unnoticed.

As they crossed back to the grand marché they were met by Moussa and Fakara, two tall African men in their mid-twenties who spoke enough English to offer their services as guides through the market. Jim was immediately skeptical, but he knew from experience how easy it was to get lost in the market. He tried to negotiate a price in advance for the services of these two freelancers, but there was some confusion and the students were clearly very anxious to get out of the traffic and begin shopping. Before he knew it, they were shopping.

After two hours wandering through the grand marché, the students were weighed down with overpriced jewelry, small wood carvings, and other nonessentials. They were also very tired and hungry. Moussa and Fakara offered to take them to a small restaurant that served Western food. After a half-hour trek into one of the neighborhoods bordering the grand marché, they ended up in a small cul-de-sac with no restaurant in sight. Residents on the street looked with amusement at this group of soggy white foreigners, hugging their backpacks to their chests, hanging on to their new purchases, hoping to find a piece of dry ground to sit on, and somewhat unhappy. When Jim asked Moussa and Fakara what they planned to do now, the two guides shrugged and said the restaurant must have closed. They wanted their fee, they said, because they had to return home. They said the fee was twenty dollars per person for the two-hour tour, or one hundred forty dollars.

Jim was stunned. He thought they had said forty dollars total for the tour. His students were on a shoestring budget, as was he. He had no idea where they were at this point, and he was worried about both the health and the physical safety of his students. He feared that if he refused to pay the fee, then at best Moussa and Fakara would not help them find their way to a street where they could get taxis back across the river; he didn't want to think about the worst they might do. It was mid-afternoon, and the call for prayer could be heard in the distance over a loudspeaker. The street was suddenly becoming more crowded, and everyone seemed to be walking in the same direction, probably toward the mosque.

Jim did not want to ask the students to pay such a high price, but he wasn't sure how Moussa and Fakara would respond to any effort to bargain hard at this point. They were visibly impatient. He could start asking for directions from the local residents, but it was prayer time now, and even before that he had sensed that they were not especially interested in his troupe; this was not the grand marché, and they had very little to sell to the students. Or he could try to convince the students that they should think of their predicament as an activity just like the ones they would have at the agricultural research station, the community school, and the artists' collective. In that case, it was well worth what Moussa and Fakara were charging. As relatively wealthy foreigners they could afford this special, if unplanned, immersion experience.

Now consider this story from Sen's perspective. Jim clearly had several individual responsibilities that he failed to meet. He should have planned the trip to the grand marché more carefully and prepared the students for young men like Moussa and Fakara. If he was going to hire the two men, he should have negotiated more carefully.

His social responsibilities were more complex. From the perspective of a situated consequentialist, one might argue he had a responsibility to consider the value of the high-priced tour for his students and its value for the two guides. Given their relative positions, was he responsible for paying one hundred forty dollars for a walking tour of the grand marché? Or was the responsible thing to do to confront the guides and demonstrate to them and the students that regardless of who is involved, everyone has a right to be treated fairly? One might argue that despite the sour taste left in the mouths of Jim and his students if they paid the full price, the net gain for the students would still be very high and the net gain for the guides probably higher than what they would have received otherwise. Looking at the rights, duties, and overall well-being of all the parties "simultaneously," on balance the responsible thing to do would have been to pay the one hundred forty dollars. Even without a meal at the end, the enlightening visit to the grand marché and the valuable lesson learned from the transaction (always negotiate the price in advance) outweighed the bad feelings of being taken advantage of.

What would Williams say about Jim in the grand marché? How does this encounter with development differ from the collision between Jim and Pedro that Williams pictured in 1973? To answer these speculative questions, it is safest to begin with what Williams might say that a utilitarian like the ones he had imagined would say. Williams's utilitarian foe could describe what happened this way: Moussa and Fakara intentionally led Jim and his students into a dangerous neighborhood and tacitly threatened Jim. If Jim did not extract twenty dollars from each student, Moussa and Fakara would abandon them, and he in effect would have put the students in danger. Jim would have spared the students the exorbitant price, but he would be negatively responsible for whatever new harms came their way.

Williams, presumably, would reject an interpretation of the story based on the concept of negative responsibility. He could argue that Moussa and Fakara were pressuring Jim to give up his own project as a teacher and become a mere instrument in their hustle. Jim would not be responsible for the danger they would be in if he decided not to capitulate to Moussa and Fakara. He certainly would have regretted it if anything untoward had happened, as he already regretted his failure to negotiate a clear price at the beginning of the tour. But regret is not the same as moral responsibility.

There are two problems with this hypothetical Williams interpretation. First, Jim had an ongoing set of responsibilities to his students. He was not operating on his own, as seemed to be the case when he encountered Pedro decades ago. But, in fact, he was not alone in the earlier case either. He was sponsored, employed, or funded by an institution that would hold him responsible, and which itself could well be held responsible for what he did. In the grand marché case, Jim's university, not just Jim, would be held responsible if something unfortunate happened as a result of this immersion experience. Jim's project was not his alone.

Second, Jim once again was in a situation in which there were already expectations, suspicions, and even obligations in play. In a poor country in which tourism is not established and in which study abroad students are a novelty, the expectations of the various parties are likely to be very different from one another. In the hypothetical Williams interpretation, it appears that Jim was naive and disorganized, and Moussa and Fakara were the ones exercising power and threatening violence, albeit indirectly. But from the perspective of Moussa and Fakara, the structures of power might look very different. Jim and his students had access to the ATM machine, they had foreign passports, and they had connections. Once Moussa and Fakara realized that they were not going to receive a high price for their services (roughly equal to the average annual income of one adult in their country), their first reaction might be to flee. They did not want to be accused of mistreating, threatening, or endangering this group of foreigners who might be well-connected.

In this alternative reading, Jim had a responsibility to situate the grand marché in a more revealing historical context for his students. The grand marché, no less than the overcrowded streets through which he and his students traveled on their way there, had a history. Who buys and sells in these stalls? How does information travel within this system? How much does it cost to rent space? Where does the merchandise come from? Where do the proceeds from sales go? Who are the freelance guides like Moussa and Fakara? How did they end up in this situation? Why aren't they in college or regularly employed? The violence that Jim and his students felt threatened by was very different from the violence that Moussa and Fakara experienced every day as they looked for customers in the grand marché. Similarly, the power that Jim and his students had to withdraw cash from the ATM and purchase goods cheaply was not the same as the power that Moussa and Fakara had by virtue of their local knowledge of the unmarked alleyways and streets.

Development as democratic political education will not eradicate these conflicts and differences. But it can make them more visible, and it can focus attention on their sources and open up a discussion of their possible resolution. Complicity may seem too strong a word for the shared responsibilities that teachers like Jim and their institutional partners (corporations and universities) have for this situation—that is, only if we think of responsibility in either a moralistic or a legalistic way. Complicity is the occasion for democratic engagement and self-critical reflection. As a reminder of our participation in the generation of structures of power and the enjoyment of their benefits, whether they are large dams irrigating transgenic crops, foreign-owned textile plants manufacturing clothing made with this cotton, or sprawling, ramshackle markets where clothing and other synthetic products are sold, the term "complicity" is all too appropriate.[1] The grand marché is a tourist attraction for a few, a source of livelihood for many, a home for the homeless, and a symptom of the violence that a transforming political economy brings with it for others. The exchange between Jim, Moussa, and Fakara, no less than the earlier exchange between Jim and Pedro, is embedded in this larger world. As a citizen-teacher, it was Jim's political responsibility to introduce his students to this complex power structure of institutions that they themselves benefited from and now had a hand in making.

19. Ousmane at the Crossroads

Jim and his students survived the grand marché, and for the students the study abroad program proceeded without any further major mishaps. All the students

---

1. See William G. Moseley and Leslie C. Gray, eds., *Hanging by a Thread: Cotton, Globalization, and Poverty in Africa* (Athens: Ohio University Press, 2008).

were sick at least once during the program. They gradually became more comfortable in smaller neighborhood markets, and they avoided the grand marché. Transportation by taxis and small vans proved to be necessary, but was unreliable at best. Sometimes bargaining over a fare proved just as frustrating, if not as frightening, as the encounter with Moussa and Fakara.

In order to provide backup transportation and emergency service, Jim purchased a used car that he drove behind the taxis and vans they rented on their occasional excursions in the capital city. He initially allowed one or two students to ride with him but quickly learned that this was not a good idea. If one white expatriate driver attracted the attention of the police, three of them in the car together were sure to result in their being stopped. In fact, the taxis and vans turned out to be a backup for Jim, rather than the other way around. Here's why.

Jim bought the car from a mid-career official at the U.S. embassy ending his tour of duty. The car had borne diplomatic license plates and still had not cleared customs when Jim took possession of it. Getting the customs duties fully paid proved to be an expensive mystery, and it took time as well as a few small bribes. This meant that while he waited for the car to be processed, Jim had only a temporary registration and no license plates, not even a piece of paper in the rear window. One result of this was that Jim regularly would be whistled over by police officers directing traffic at major intersections in the capital city. If he was with the rest of the program in their taxis or van, the taxi driver or van driver would negotiate a very small bribe and they would be on their way. When Jim ventured out on his own, however, he was much less able to resolve the problem either as quickly or as cheaply. This was an annoyance and often an inconvenience; in one case it turned out to be more than that.

It was early Saturday morning one month before the end of the study abroad program, and Jim was driving back from the ATM, where he had withdrawn a large amount of money in the local currency for the program's final activities. One of the four police officers at a familiar busy intersection whistled him over. There were several cars and vans already parked along the side of the road, waiting to negotiate with the police. Two drivers were standing outside their vehicles, engaged in heated arguments with the police. A few others seemed to be taking it in stride, and one was actually walking back toward his car with his arm draped over a police officer's shoulder.

Jim was in a hurry and in no mood for this petty extortion, locally referred to as "tea money." He knew exactly what was going to happen, and it did. The police officer who whistled him over approached from behind on the passenger side. Jim reached over and cranked the window down. The officer asked for the registration and Jim's driver's permit. Jim handed him the three-month-old wad of paper, twice renewed, that served as his temporary registration, and also his bent-up AAA International Driver's Permit. The police officer looked them over, checked the registration number against the stickers on the right-hand side of the windshield, and then said somberly that while the papers were in order Jim did not have a license plate, which would cost the equivalent of twenty dollars. Jim said, as he had said for three months, that the license plate could not be issued until the permanent registration arrived, which had still not happened. Further, the temporary registration was properly renewed and so he didn't have to pay anything. The officer then turned and started walking back toward the corner with Jim's temporary registration and driver's permit in hand.

Jim popped out of the car and quickly caught up with the police officer. He insisted that the officer return his papers now. The officer just ignored him and indicated to one of his fellow officers when they reached the corner that Jim's car had no plates. They both agreed he owed twenty dollars. After what felt like five minutes of silence to Jim, he pulled out the equivalent of two dollars from his wallet and gave it to the officer, who reluctantly took the money and gave him back his documents. Jim hurriedly walked back to his car from the corner, and as he approached it, a woman who was cooking millet cakes on the side of the road over a small charcoal grill laughed and pointed down at Jim's flat right rear tire.

Jim looked into the crowd along the roadside to see which of the young men there would fix it for him. Two young men approached separately. One had a broad smile but did not offer to help. The other looked more tired and did offer to help. Jim opened the trunk, and the second man, Ousmane, quickly jacked up the car, removed the flat, and put on the spare. He told Jim to wait five minutes and he would get the flat fixed at a little shop around the corner. Given the frequency with which Jim's tires went flat, Jim thought that this was the best thing to do, even though he was in a hurry and still in a lousy mood because of the tea money.

As Jim waited by the open trunk of the car for Ousmane, the other man cautioned Jim that he should not pay more than one or two dollars for the work and the repaired tire. Jim thought that was about right and thanked him. A few more minutes went by and Jim happened to look at the front seat of his car. The window was still open on the passenger side and his backpack was gone. Jim became frantic. He rushed around the car exhorting the crowd to help him find the thief. They looked on incredulously, not able to understand him very well. He raced to the corner. Ousmane still had not returned. He found the police officer who had extorted the small bribe and demanded his help at the same time that he accused him of being in league with the thief. The policeman indicated that Jim should report the theft to the officer in charge of the four-person crew, who was standing in the middle of the intersection directing a sea of vans, motorcycles, and taxis. It was mayhem, yet Jim managed to wade out into the middle of the crossroads. After a near-tearful retelling of the events, including a detailed description of the contents of the backpack (passport, computer, several thousand dollars in cash and traveler's checks, airline tickets for all his students), Jim demanded that all four officers at the scene begin a sweep of the neighborhood. The crew chief told Jim to "keep his cool" and report the incident at the local police station about two kilometers away.

At this point Jim was beginning to feel faint. It was very hot. The exhaust fumes were intense, and Jim was soaked through with nervous perspiration on top of his normal daily layer of sweat. Suddenly Ousmane turned up in the middle of the intersection, proudly presenting the repaired flat tire but puzzled by Jim's appearance. Jim tried to explain to the crew chief that Ousmane was the Good Samaritan, not the thief, and at this point Ousmane put things together himself. He helped Jim get safely through the traffic back over to his car, put the repaired tire in the trunk, and offered to conduct a one-man search throughout the neighborhood. Before Jim could dissuade him, Ousmane was off, racing around the corner with his own small backpack flapping over one shoulder.

Jim sat mournfully in his car inventorying everything that had been stolen, wondering what he should do next. Probably, he thought, he had to get a police report if he was going to recover anything under his own home owner's insurance policy or from the university. This hardly consoled him since his own papers and e-mail correspondence, not just documents and materials for the study abroad program, were on the computer, and his small backup memory stick was also in the stolen backpack. Ousmane returned after a half hour. He was drenched in sweat but had nothing else to show for his efforts. Jim asked him if he knew where the police station was, and Ousmane offered to go there with Jim. They set off, driving back through the intersection past the police officer who had pulled Jim over in the first place, who glanced in their direction.

After repeating his story and describing the contents of the missing backpack to two different clerks who each recorded the information in longhand in large notebooks, Jim and Ousmane were told to wait with about twenty-five others in a large room with long, backless wooden benches. An hour later, they were called into a small office where a plainclothes police officer asked Jim to repeat his story a third time. The officer then turned to Ousmane and asked him for some identification. Ousmane produced his own driver's license and another identification card that Jim did not recognize. After a cursory glance, the officer locked both documents in a small safe. Ousmane was visibly upset and asked for them back. The officer told him he would get them back shortly.

In the ensuing conversation about the identity of the other person who had approached Jim at the corner, the one Jim and Ousmane both said could have been the thief, Ousmane volunteered to search for this alleged perpetrator himself. Since the police didn't seem anxious to do anything, Jim was delighted to accept Ousmane's help. As they left the station, the investigating officer told Ousmane that if he did find the culprit, he should call the station house immediately. Ousmane seemed to be cheered by this, as if he had just been deputized, and for the moment he seemed less depressed about having lost his papers. Jim and Ousmane exchanged cell phone numbers and parted ways.

The next morning Ousmane called Jim. He said he had found the real thief. While combing the grand marché, where he thought he could trace Jim's stolen computer, Ousmane said he encountered another man who had been there at the crossroads when the backpack was stolen. At this very moment, Ousmane said breathlessly over the phone, the man was standing next to two brand new motorcycles. Ousmane said that he knew this man, and that the only way he could afford two new motorcycles was if he had purchased them with stolen money.

Jim told Ousmane to remain calm and not give the man any reason to flee. In the meantime he would contact the police station and try to get someone to come with him to the grand marché. Miraculously, that is how it worked out, and three officers took the suspect (and his motorcycles) into custody that afternoon. Jim and Ousmane were asked to wait until a hearing could be arranged later that evening, after the police had searched the suspect's apartment for other stolen property. Jim was asked to pay the investigating officer twenty dollars to cover the cost of the search, which he did. Through all this, Ousmane's spirits rose steadily. At several points he asked to have his identification cards back, only to be told that he would receive them in due time. Jim urged him to be patient because it was only a matter of time now before they would have the whole thing settled.

The apartment search turned up nothing suspicious, let alone any of Jim's property. The suspect called his employer who came to the station with the bills of sale for the two new motorcycles, and the suspect was released late that same night. Jim and Ousmane were told that the investigation would continue. Ousmane once again asked for his driver's license and identification card back. He said he was a chauffeur and could not possibly get a job without them. He was told to wait.

By the middle of the next day, Jim thought he had devised a plan for replacing his stolen documents and students' tickets; getting reimbursed for the stolen property, cash, and traveler's checks; and also procuring a replacement computer from his university almost immediately. It would be an inconvenience, he told his students, but there was a lesson to be learned: pay attention to details and don't let petty official corruption distract you. The police are poorly paid, he told his students, and this is how they supplement their salaries. In effect, bribes like these are small transportation and safety taxes levied on expatriates. Further, if he had locked his car before he chased after the police officer who took his temporary registration and license, the theft probably would not have occurred.

While Jim was looking on the brighter side, Ousmane's troubles had just begun. His wife and two-year-old child depended on him for their income, and his occasional chauffeuring jobs just barely put food on the table. He had not worked for several weeks when he was standing at the corner where Jim's tire went flat, waiting in hope of something coming his way by chance. The opportunity to help a distraught expatriate, he thought, might lead to something. Even a small tip for fixing a flat tire would be better than nothing. It turned out to be much worse than nothing.

The investigation did continue. Jim was called back to the police station and asked if Ousmane had contacted him. Jim said that in fact Ousmane contacted him regularly, asking him to tell the police that he had nothing to do with the incident and that they should return Ousmane's papers. As Ousmane became more insistent, at one point bringing his wife and daughter to Jim's home to show him how the family was suffering because of all this, Jim began to fear that he would do something violent. When he told this to the investigating officer, there was no discernible reaction as far as Jim could tell. At the end of the interview, Jim asked what they planned to do. He was told the investigation would continue.

Jim didn't hear from Ousmane for two weeks. Then the police called and asked Jim to come in for another hearing. This time it was Ousmane who was being charged. While the police had found no stolen property in his home, as far as they could tell, they still believed that his behavior had been designed to throw them off the trail of the real perpetrator, with whom Ousmane had been working since the beginning. Ousmane would be held as an accomplice to the crime pending further investigation.

When Jim inquired at the police station right before the departure of his students, he was told the investigation was continuing. He had no way of contacting Ousmane's wife, and neither she nor Ousmane ever contacted Jim again. He was much more careful about locking his car doors during the remainder of the study abroad program, and after he got his permanent registration and license plate the police never once stopped him for tea money. He liked to tell his students that he had learned his lesson. Of course, he felt bad that Ousmane's wife and child were having a harder time of it, but he told himself that a lot of people in the capital city were struggling as well, and he just didn't know what to think about Ousmane's role in the whole affair. Maybe the police were right and the investigation ought to continue. If Ousmane was part of an organized group of thieves who preyed on expatriates, then he should be taken off the street. The last thing this poor country needed, Jim wrote in his final report, was to scare away well-run study abroad programs that brought hard foreign currency into the country. Jim got all his property replaced as well as the lost money when he returned home.

From a classical utilitarian perspective one might argue that in "Ousmane at the Crossroads" Jim is better off having learned his lesson, recovered most of his property, and completed the study abroad program, and while Ousmane and his family may be worse off, the net effect on everyone may be positive. As a situated consequentialist one might argue that Jim did the right thing. He was aware of the costs to Ousmane and his family, and he was also aware of the relative inconvenience to his students because of the theft. He tried to balance helping Ousmane with leading his program responsibly. When it was no longer clear what role Ousmane had played in the incident, his responsibilities to his students dominated his decision. Finally, even from a hypothetical Williams perspective, Jim did the right thing: he did not use Ousmane as an instrument but tried to respect the integrity of his life projects as much as he could (i.e., raising a family and finding work as a chauffeur); Jim also supported Ousmane until the presumption that he was innocent was called into question by Ousmane's own aggressive behavior.

This is how it might look from Jim's perspective. His individual responsibility to himself and to his students eventually outweighed his responsibility (and gratitude) to Ousmane, but not without a full awareness of the consequences of this individual responsibility for Ousmane. Jim is not negatively responsible for what the police did to Ousmane, nor is he passively responsible for the fate of Ousmane's family.

What about other shared responsibilities, in particular the responsibilities that Jim incurred by virtue of his participation in the study abroad program? What decisions has Jim's university made that one might argue raise the question of individual and institutional political responsibility in this case? One such decision involves transportation. The decision to use inexpensive vans, taxis, and one private car to transport students during the study abroad program was an institutional decision, not just an individual decision made by Jim alone. The program could have rented one larger, more expensive van for all program activities and provided Jim with a chauffeured car with license plates. Instead, they chose to keep costs down. Jim accepted this approach, even though it included special inconveniences for him.

How does this decision, only one of many we might examine, look to Ousmane? On the one hand, one might argue, Ousmane's meager and occasional income depends on drivers like Jim having trouble at the crossroads. He was there that Saturday waiting to be asked for help by a stranger. On the other hand, for the many drivers like Ousmane who are out of work, it would be much better if programs such as this employed licensed chauffeurs and registered vehicles. Then Ousmane would have a better chance for regular employment. An institutional decision to save money was also an institutional decision not to contribute to the development of the rental transportation system in this country. Jim was only half right about the benefits of his well-run study abroad program to the host country as a whole. Yet the students in the program never discussed this question. Any responsibility on their part for the transportation system seems far-fetched to them at best, yet they benefited by the decision to hold transportation costs down. But to Ousmane's family and to Ousmane himself, watching from his detention cell and wondering when he will be able to work again, it is hardly far-fetched.

The other question that Ousmane might be asking is who is the real Good Samaritan, who is the accomplice, and who is the perpetrator in this case? How, Ousmane wonders, did an act of benevolence on his part lead to him being accused of wrongdoing? Should he have remained simply a bystander, not offering to help Jim? Wouldn't he be better off now? Should he have avoided Jim after the incident, rather than coming to his house with his wife and child demanding help? Gradually he realizes that he didn't have much of a choice, especially once he lost his license and identification papers. He needed Jim just as much as Jim needed him.

The concept of need is very important if we are to understand the role of everyday bystanders in this situation.[2] Ousmane was not a bystander by chance. He was at the crossroads waiting for a problem that he could help solve. His

---

2. Garrett Thomson provides a clear statement of the meaning of "fundamental needs" in his article by that name in *The Philosophy of Need*, ed. Soran Reader (New York: Cambridge University Press, 2005), 175–86.

livelihood depended on it. He needed work. He was an everyday bystander in the sense that every day he waited for work in this way. It was a form of day labor without a crew chief. If Ousmane weren't available, standing by as it were, Jim would have to develop another way of handling emergencies. But since day laborers are paid so little, it made little economic sense for Jim to do otherwise. He could always count on someone like Ousmane to fix his flat. In other words, Ousmane's role as bystander was much more integral to this situation than the conception of the innocent accidental bystander might lead us to believe. That does not make Ousmane a victim of Jim's self-centered and myopic concern with his students at the expense of Ousmane and his family. But it does mean that Jim and Ousmane were in it together in a way that Jim failed to realize, and in a way that goes beyond Jim's relationship to Moussa and Fakara.

The importance of needs also points to the larger institutional significance of these stories about individuals. Jim and Ousmane, for example, did not need each other out of sympathy or kindness, but because of the material and psychological needs that are fostered within the institutions they inhabit. While needs have a certain objectivity and priority over wants, they also are discursively negotiated ways of coming to terms with social scarcity and conflict. Ousmane didn't personally need Jim any more than Jim needed Ousmane in particular. What they needed were ways of addressing their pressing economic concerns without neglecting their obligations to their family and students, respectively. They learned these forms of address the way we learn how to speak any language fluently: through meaningful engagement with others with the same needs. This was not Jim's first time at the crossroads, and it certainly was not Ousmane's either. They recognized each other almost immediately through their interdependent needs.

Second, Jim and Ousmane are themselves metonymic symbols of institutions. "Jim" is a symbol of universities offering students an enriched study abroad experience while struggling to find healthy linkage agreements with universities in the host countries. "Ousmane" represents the manual labor force, struggling to make a subsistence living in the overpopulated capital city of a resource-poor country. Sometimes the two meet on the street. Often, they encounter each other in the hallways, classrooms, and vehicles that just barely keep this linkage agreement going. "Jim's" students find their host institution under-equipped and poorly maintained. "Ousmane" and his fellow workers find their guests unrealistic and often unable to manage the most elementary task (e.g., fixing a flat), but for the moment these are the only guests they have.

If we are to work out the full consequences of this encounter, we must consider the political responsibilities of institutions like Jim's university and not only the petty corruption that seems to have triggered these unhappy events. One place to begin is by educating the students, who have unwittingly benefited from the existing linkage agreement and the fragile web of connections that reaches all the way down to our everyday bystanders, Jim and Ousmane. These stories of bystander responsibility—"Jim in the Grande Marché" and "Ousmane at the Crossroads"—are replayed daily. The challenge for a democratic political education is to reenact them in a more complete institutional context rather than simulate them as the travails of individuals.

PART 3

Making Acquaintances

While simulations and games such as *Food Force* and *Darfur Is Dying* are not inherently depoliticizing, within the context of a wider culture of simulation that privileges expert knowledge, these well-meaning technologies play into the hands of narrow allegories of rescue. Who better than Sachs's development professional to tell us how much food is needed, how many schools ought to be built, or where the next dam ought to go? Prometheus redivi.

The Promethean myth is usually analyzed in relationship to the question of the neutrality of technical and scientific knowledge. In this chapter I examine several interpretations of the Aeschylean version of the myth in *Prometheus Bound* in relationship to the question of responsibility. These reenactments, unburdened by allegories of rescue, introduce a more democratic orientation toward technology and development than currently exists in our culture of simulation.

20. Technology

Simulations are, first of all, technologies with all the complexity and ambiguity that concept carries with it. Darin Barney calls attention to the puzzling nature of the modern concept of technology: One root, *techne,* refers to the artificial creation of things that do not already exist in nature. The other half, *logos,* refers, among other things, to the activity of discovering and gathering up what already exists in nature and is true.[1] The conjunction of these two activities

---

1. Darin Barney, *Prometheus Wired: The Hope for Democracy in the Age of Network Technology* (Chicago: University of Chicago Press, 2001), 27–28.

takes what exists in nature and modifies it so that it is neither all natural nor entirely artificial. Modern technology poses a problem right from the beginning: how can these two seemingly opposed activities of creating and discovering be brought into balance?

This is an especially difficult question for simulation technologies. For example, do simulation technologies that allow urban planners to anticipate and solve social problems create a world in which problems in the built environment are the most visible at the expense of other social problems, or do they simply enable the planners to see architectural problems more clearly? How does one learn to cope with and navigate within this space? Risk and cost-benefit analyses of particular simulation technologies only scratch the surface. One must still have a means of weighing competing risks, costs, and benefits against one another, especially when the costs and benefits refer to very different conceptions of how we view ourselves and our communities.[2] The problem of evaluation, however, goes deeper than this. In Sherry Turkle's words, "We make our technologies, our objects, but then the objects of our lives shape us in turn. Our new objects have scintillating, pulsating surfaces; they invite playful exploration; they are dynamic, seductive, and elusive. They encourage us to move away from reductive analysis as a model of understanding. It is not clear what we are becoming when we look upon them—or that we yet know how to see through them."[3] How do modern biotechnologies and information technologies affect politics, and specifically political responsibility? Have state policies and social movements been shaped in the image of these "seductive" cyborgs and other less human, "pulsating" simulations, or can we "see through" these proliferating technologies and act responsibly?

Cyborgs that simulate the human organism have evolved beyond prosthetics and implants to the point where organic and inorganic materials now are blended all the way down to the molecular level. According to Rodney Brooks of the MIT Computer Science and Artificial Intelligence Laboratory, "We are on a path to changing our genome in profound ways."[4] We are, in other words, changing how we think of what it means to be a human being. A new dualism, consisting of our genetic code on one side and our contingent bodies on the other, has

2. Gordon Graham, *The Internet: A Philosophical Inquiry* (New York: Routledge, 1999), 48–56.

3. Sherry Turkle, "Seeing Through Computers: Education in a Culture of Simulation," *American Prospect* 8, no. 31 (1997): 82.

4. Rodney A. Brooks, *Flesh and Machines: How Robots Will Change Us* (New York: Pantheon, 2002), 236.

replaced the older, Cartesian mind-body distinction and represents a serious rival to contemporary monistic metaphysics.[5]

Instead of asking how well computers can simulate real persons or how well GMOs can simulate organic species, I wish to ask, following Turkle, what kind of citizen we become when we see the world of power and violence through simulations that explain, predict, and justify our political actions. Simulating the growth of an individual shrub under certain natural and artificial conditions seems innocuous. The implications of simulations are more visible when we consider them writ large; for example, simulating climate change under certain levels of air pollution or the effects of a new dam on the ecology of a river valley are simulations that concern me. I would argue that these simulations are just as important for political responsibility as the simulations that we use to train policy makers to handle decisions about the acceptable level of collateral damage in counterinsurgency and counterterrorism warfare. The answer I will offer is that simulations, whether they are used to test agricultural biotechnology or justify the implantation of nanotechnology, may adversely affect our capacity to recognize ourselves as responsible everyday bystanders. Simulations are not necessarily antidemocratic or depoliticizing, but reliance on them to make sense of power and violence has the effect, I will argue, of unduly distancing citizens from politics and obscuring their complicity as everyday bystanders.

We think of flight simulators, for example, as cockpits in which pilots can train to handle actual flight conditions without the risk of crashing. Video games now are used to train sharpshooters in the same risk-free way. A simulation is a method of creating a set of habitual, optimal responses to a range of probable future events without risk of actual damage. Ideally, a simulation differs from the real event only in terms of the risks involved. According to Jean Baudrillard, however, simulations are more than training vehicles. The codes and programs that run the simulation "vehicle" become internalized, multiply, and eventually stabilize the social system. The result is a society of simulations. This not fully deterministic process is reflected in the built environment as well as the behavioral codes that individuals have internalized: "The two towers of the W.T.C. are the visible sign of the closure of the system in a vertigo of duplication, while the other skyscrapers are each of them the original moment of a system constantly transcending itself in a perpetual crisis and self-challenge."[6] There is no original

5. N. Katherine Hayles, "The Condition of Virtuality," in *The Digital Dialectic: New Essays on New Media,* ed. Peter Lunenfeld (Cambridge, Mass.: MIT Press, 1999), 73.

6. Jean Baudrillard, *Simulations,* trans. Paul Foss, Paul Patton, and Philip Beitchman (New York: Semiotext[e], 1983), 136–37.

tower and its duplicate; no difference between the real thing and the copy. Both are "originals" running the same program and vying for pride of place in a dizzying process that miraculously achieves homeostasis. This image of the World Trade Center now is all too revealing of the flaw in Baudrillard's argument. Simulations are not self-contained semiotic jousts that end in a standoff. They exist in an actual world, sustained by scarce resources and vulnerable to external demands and challenges.

In less monumental language, Turkle has argued that simulations are indeed more than risk-reducing flight simulators. They are pervasive in our culture and they govern how we do business.[7] The stakes involved in using them are much higher than simply flunking out of flight school. Simulations create political dispositions and reinforce controversial political assumptions. For example, simulated neighborhood places such as virtual cafes and chat rooms, not unlike simulated towns such as those in *SimCity* video games, are two steps removed from actual political life.[8] If the modern shopping mall is a simulation of the traditional town square, then the virtual café is a more high-tech simulation of the shopping mall. Just as the shopping mall drains the town square of some of its democratic political content (e.g., the loosely structured and unpredictable conversations that occur in some town or neighborhood public squares), virtual public space exacerbates this process of urban development by burying controversial political assumptions about the role of expert planners, and the relationship between popular protests and city services, under the rules of the simulation game.[9]

These are two simulations of a democratic politics that suppress or obscure the grittier, violent disagreements that democracies must regularly face. As Turkle suggests, seeing local democratic politics through the lens of a simulation game can be harmful politically in at least two respects. First, players come to believe that political decisions are best made by technical experts, in this case city planners, not by democratic citizens. More worrisome, the assumptions of the game (e.g., raising taxes leads to riots) become assumptions players gradually

7. Beginning with a supply chain management game developed at MIT in the 1960s, the "beer game" (now available on the Web at http://beergame.mit.edu/guide.htm), simulation games have evolved and spread exponentially as teaching tools. See, for example, Joakim Eriksson, Niclas Finne, and Sverker Janson, "Evolution of a Supply Chain Management Game for the Trading Agent Competition," *AI Communications* 19, no. 1 (2006): 1–12.

8. Sherry Turkle, "Virtuality and Its Discontents: Searching for Community in Cyberspace," *American Prospect* 7, no. 24 (1996): 50–57.

9. On the political significance of the modern shopping mall, see my *Intimacy and Spectacle: Liberal Theory as Political Education* (Ithaca: Cornell University Press, 1994), 224–31.

accept in actual democratic politics even when there are good reasons to question the legitimacy of these assumptions outside the simulation game. Not unlike *SimCity* and its offspring (including the genetic engineering game *SimLife*)[10] are the more serious and sophisticated simulations that policy makers themselves use to determine combat strategies in war and budget strategies in bureaucratic politics. While some simulators are used to train fighter pilots and other combat soldiers, more complex strategic simulations are used to determine the advisability of larger troop movements. The same kind of formal modeling is used to determine strategies for combating infectious diseases, developmental disabilities, the dilapidation of urban housing stock, and economic downturns. Prior to Hurricane Katrina on the U.S. Gulf Coast, the Federal Emergency Management Agency ran a simulation, "Hurricane Pam," to prepare the residents of New Orleans and other population centers for such an event.[11]

According to Turkle, a culture of simulation does not merely desensitize youth or make them trigger-happy. In this culture, citizen-players internalize and rationalize the antidemocratic assumptions of the politics game as expert policy making and uncritically accept the Promethean myth that technology is a god-challenging, democratizing weapon. Tolerance for an acceptable level of collateral damage, no less than AIDS, diarrhea, and famine, becomes part of the cost of doing business in an imperfect world. Gradually, the actual effects of these forms of violence become less tangible and responsibilities for them seem to be detached from actual persons, except the most blatantly guilty. Culpable individuals who seem overly enamored of Promethean fire can be said to have struck a Faustian bargain—that is, the thrill of doing "big science" leads them astray.[12] While perhaps true for a few scientists, this is not an adequate explanation for the pervasiveness of this culture, nor does it suggest a remedy on the political level, where responsibilities are much more differentiated and cannot always be reduced to intentional, voluntary actions. "We deceive ourselves," Bernard Williams claims, "if we suppose that public practices of ascribing responsibility can be derived from an antecedent notion of moral responsibility, or that the idea of the voluntary is

10. See Ken Karakotios and Michael Bremmer, *SimLife: The Official Strategy Guide* (Roseville, Calif.: Prima, 2003).

11. See the FEMA news release dated July 23, 2004, "Hurricane Pam Exercise Concludes," http://www.fema.gov/news/newsrelease.fema?id=13051. I am indebted to Eric Gorham for bringing this to my attention.

12. Freeman Dyson accused J. Robert Oppenheimer of succumbing to a Faustian bargain in his role as leader of the Manhattan Project. See the film by John Else, *The Day After Trinity: J. Robert Oppenheimer and the Atomic Bomb* (1981). See also Graham, *The Internet*, 39–61.

uniquely important to responsibility."[13] In this sense, the Greeks did have something to teach us about responsibility, despite their obvious cultural prejudices and democratic shortcomings. Our search for a deeper grounding of responsibility in a true moral ontology of the self has blinded us to the fact that "the responsibilities we have to recognise extend in many ways beyond our normal purposes and what we intentionally do."[14]

21. *Prometheus* Reenacted

A good place to begin the search for an alternative to simulation technology is with attempts to reinterpret the founding myth of the culture of simulation, Aeschylus's version of the Prometheus story. *Prometheus Bound* represents the struggle of Athenian democracy against authoritarian rule. Aeschylus had fought in the Athenian war against the Persians and personally witnessed the overthrow of tyranny in Athens and the establishment of democracy there in the fifth century B.C.E. He appropriated the myth of Prometheus, the popular hero who saved the human race from extinction, with Athens's collective struggle in mind. As Aeschylus tells it, Zeus becomes increasingly annoyed with Prometheus; not only has he gone against Zeus's wishes by rescuing human beings, but he also will not divulge information about Zeus's own future demise. There are two important themes in this ancient tragedy that highlight the importance of democratic political education: suffering and hubris.

Prometheus's suffering, like the suffering of human beings, is a necessary precondition for the invention and deployment of new technologies. Without it, there would be no development of language, science, and everyday technologies, all symbolized in the play by fire. According to George Thomson, "If Prometheus has to suffer, it is because man himself has suffered in the course of his advancement. Without suffering he would have lacked the stimulus to invention."[15] The implication is that a democratic political education that prepares the demos to overthrow a tyrant's rule, yet not falter themselves, is an exacting process. The creation of new dispositions is not simply a matter of acquiring new reflexive responses through conditioning. It requires something more

---

13. Bernard Williams, *Shame and Necessity* (Berkeley and Los Angeles: University of California Press, 1993), 67.

14. Ibid., 74.

15. George Thomson, *Aeschylus and Athens: A Study in the Social Origins of Drama* (1940; repr., New York: Haskell House, 1967), 327.

psychologically difficult: a conscious suffering that will motivate the demos to overcome long odds.

Second, not only did Prometheus endow human beings with a blind hopefulness that could sustain them during difficult times, but some of that blindness rubbed off on him. He hoped to use his own knowledge to establish a political regime more sympathetic to "the many," but his pride made it impossible for him to seek a political compromise with Zeus. The closing dialogue between Prometheus and Zeus's messenger Hephaestus, who seems to be pleading with Prometheus to seek out some common ground, suggests that Prometheus, the erstwhile benefactor of the human race, has lost sight of his primary goal: it is more important that he refuse to make any concessions to Zeus, even a formal apology, than advance the cause of democracy.

Despite this hubris, Aeschylus closes his play on a relatively optimistic note:

> Such is the storm Zeus gathers against me,
> Ever nearer approaching with terrible tread.
> O majestical Mother, O heavenly Sky,
> In whose region revolveth the Light of the world,
> Thou seest the wrongs that I suffer![16]

The same optimism can be seen in high-tech, self-styled Prometheuses today such as Ray Kurzweil, an inventor, corporate executive, and philanthropist who has used information and biotechnology to merge the human species with technology in order to overcome seemingly natural barriers. With his help, more of those who have lost their sight can learn to play musical instruments. Those with life-threatening degenerative diseases can be restored to a fully functioning role in society. Even those who are healthy but apparently lack artistic talents can be taught to paint and write poetry with the right technological assistance. Suffering can not only be alleviated, it can be outwitted. We do not have to make do with our natural limitations if we are willing to explore the world through a new set of scientific magnifying lenses.[17]

Now, compare Kurzweil with Mary Shelley's Dr. Frankenstein, whose character is thoroughly corrupted and who fails to meet his responsibilities, both private and public. First, Shelley suggests that Frankenstein has a parental obligation to his cyborg "monster." He gave birth to it in a figurative sense and consequently

16. Aeschylus, *Prometheus Bound,* trans. George Thomson (New York: Dover, 1995), 47.
17. Kurzweil Technologies Inc., "A Brief Career Summary of Ray Kurzweil," http://www .kurzweiltech.com/aboutray.html.

ought to nurture it and prepare it for life in the world. Even with natural off-spring, the responsibilities of parents are limited. They do not last beyond the minority years usually, and even then parental responsibilities will vary with social circumstances, as will the consequences of failing to meet those responsibilities. Perhaps the larger question here is what constitutes neglect. Parental responsibilities that protect children against abuse are relatively clear compared to what constitutes neglect. Is neglect just a milder form of abuse, or is it more like criminally negligent behavior in laws governing behavior toward other adults who have no special relationship to one another? If Dr. Frankenstein failed to meet his parental responsibility, it was not because of abuse; if it was because of neglect, then the neglect might be a form of negligence, but not necessarily.

This brings us to the second form of responsibility: contractual responsibility. Was there any agreement, promise, or tacit contract between Dr. Frankenstein and the monster that could have remedied the relationship but was broken? The monster clearly believes Dr. Frankenstein's promise to create a mate for the monster was binding. Dr. Frankenstein thinks that the new couple might create future generations of monsters that would threaten human survival, but the monster is not persuaded that such a fear constitutes grounds for this kind of dereliction of contractual duty. The monster's case is not entirely clear; a contract to produce a truly dangerous organism, no matter what the intentions of the party to whom it is to be entrusted, could certainly be ruled unenforceable.

This leaves the last type of responsibility, authorial responsibility. The author of something genuinely new, whether it is a technology or a text, has some responsibility for its impact and reception. A dangerous technology ought to be labeled and restricted, and the inventor has some responsibility to provide the information needed to make the appropriate regulatory decisions even if others have the final say. Similarly, the author of a scandalous or disturbing text has some responsibility not to deceive readers into thinking it is something it is not. Once again, this is a shared responsibility, and the consequences of defaulting on it will vary considerably. If parental responsibility raises questions about the meaning of neglect and contractual responsibility raises questions about enforceability, then authorial responsibility raises questions about liability. How liable should an author be for expressing ideas, either in print or in some other medium? Is the author of a published and freely available chemical formula as liable as the manufacturer of the chemical when it proves to be toxic and readily available? If authors wish to have intellectual property rights that will protect their ownership of ideas, formulas, signs, and symbols, must they also accept liability for harm that comes from the dissemination of this property, even if the author did not intend the harm but could have reasonably foreseen it?

Perhaps what determines which of these three forms of responsibility makes the most sense is a prior assumption about what kind of entity the monster is: a dependent child, a functioning adult, or a piece of property. This may account for the open-endedness of the text and the indeterminacy of Shelley's view of responsibility. One attempt to resolve this indeterminacy by applying it to modern biotechnology is Bernard Rollin's *The Frankenstein Syndrome*.[18] Rollin draws from Shelley's cautionary tale three possible types of objections to genetic engineering of animals. The first, that these artificial animals are unnatural, he dispatches without too much trouble. The second, that these practices are risky and perhaps represent a Faustian bargain, is more inconclusive. The third, which takes us back to the question of responsibility, is that biotechnologies have undervalued the responsibility that we have to what we create. It is not at all clear what these responsibilities are, how they are shared, and what their limits may be. Rollin does not simply dismiss the idea of a new generation of Frankenstein monsters, but he does help us see that this kind of fearfulness is akin to a phobia or syndrome that can be controlled if we take a closer look at what we could possibly mean by unnatural genetically engineered animals and the risks we run in creating them. His analysis is less helpful in thinking through the question of democratic responsibility for mass political violence, however, because like Shelley, his concern is primarily with the individual responsibility of the expert scientist.

To refocus attention on the issue of political responsibility that was paramount in Aeschylus but lost amid concerns for parental and authorial responsibility in Shelley, consider two contemporary critical reenactments of the Prometheus myth: a post-9/11 dance performance done by the Paul Taylor Dance Company (PTDC) titled *Promethean Fire,* and Tony Harrison's 1998 film *Prometheus*. PTDC's *Promethean Fire* underscores the importance of limiting technological aspirations in order to build a ground-level political solidarity, while Harrison's *Prometheus* calls attention to the dangers of such political solidarity when it is driven too far by technophilia.[19]

18. Bernard E. Rollin, *The Frankenstein Syndrome: Ethical and Social Issues in the Genetic Engineering of Animals* (New York: Cambridge University Press, 1995).

19. Tony Harrison, "Fire and Poetry," introduction to the screenplay for his film/poetry *Prometheus* (London: Faber and Faber, 1998), xx–xxi: "The flames that created reverie create nightmares. The flames that once created man's capacity for dreaming are now fueled by tragedies, and

In June 2002 the Paul Taylor Dance Company performed *Promethean Fire,* its response to the 9/11 attacks.[20] According to *New York Times* dance critic Anna Kisselgoff, the program notes contained a quote from Shakespeare's *Othello*: "fire that can thy light relume." The dancers are introduced as vertical structures, but "whatever vertical forms existed in the imagination as humans, skyscrapers and girders, all suddenly begin to collapse." Despair and then hope are illuminated by a bright red light. After pairing up in rage, "the dancers cartwheel and swivel on one knee, transforming a jubilant diagonal of five couples into the final pyramid-like grouping. A structure rebuilt."[21] What is striking about the visual images of this collapse and reconstruction in dance is the contrast between the verticality of the opening scenes, the energetic dyadic bonding after the collapse, and the reconstruction that emphasizes a broader foundation and more complex latticework of arms and legs. In one early frame the dancers seem to blossom from the center, sprawling outward to each side and gazing vaguely away from the audience. There is very little dramatic tension in this image, although the figures seem held together in a fanlike pose. Later, in a more tightly strung formation, they are linked together, arms crisscrossing and eyes front and center. There is confidence in their full faces, but not hubris in this act of solidarity. They are looking out at "the Light of the world."

The danger here is that these final images are premature. It is still not clear how much solidarity there is in the wake of the events of September 11, 2001. There has been bickering, corruption, and more serious divisions on the ground. Lights have flickered on and off as 9/11 has been used demagogically to justify the war against Iraq. It is this kind of inconclusive and ambiguous situation that the English poet and playwright Tony Harrison strives to capture from an earlier, pre-9/11 time through the images of a world-traveling Prometheus, a giant statue forged from the bodies of British miners (dead at the hands of Thatcherite policies) that visits environmentally ravaged middle Europe; and

---

the expression we seek from their contemplation has to imagine those worst things in the dancing fires that cast our shadows into the next millennium. And if I say that the fire offered by the Prometheus of Aeschylus had not yet acquired the accretions of our bestial and barbaric human history, I would have to add that I think that Aeschylus gazed into what, for him in the 5th century B.C., was an equivalent historical destruction, the eradication of an entire civilization in the razing of the city of Troy. . . . The gift of fire was already ambiguous to Aeschylus."

20. *Promethean Fire,* Paul Taylor Dance Company, available as a PBS performance on YouTube: part 1, http://www.youtube.com/watch?v=-6xLydZmOBM; part 2, http://www.youtube.com/watch?v=ChUWgScmb2A.

21. Anna Kisselgoff, "Promethean Light Illuminates Hope," review of *Promethean Fire,* Paul Taylor Dance Company, New York, *New York Times,* June 10, 2002.

Fig. 6   The climactic moment in *Promethean Fire* by the Paul Taylor Dance Company, written and performed in response to the attacks of September 11, 2001. Photograph © 2002 Louis Greenfield.

its alter ego, a chain-smoking, barely surviving British miner who insists on defending the titan and his own free will. As one critic has noted, "To smoke is a sign of working-class identity and even solidarity . . . and the ultimate sign of personal liberty which the old man refuses to yield to his capitalist masters. Yet it is ultimately forced upon him by big business concerns . . . and is of course killing him." Fire built eastern European socialist societies, but by 1989 they had fallen under their own weight. Fire produced industrial England, but the Thatcher policies of the early 1980s had broken the union. The promise of material progress that Prometheus held out, east and west, has been broken, yet his progeny's consuming spirit remains. Why?[22]

Harrison offers neither redemption nor consolation as an answer. The obstacles to a resurgent working-class politics, east or west, are formidable. You can't get very far on the slogan "Smokers of the world unite!"[23] Yet the spirit of the old miner (in the form of a young boy) accompanies Prometheus's statue nonetheless. Their visit to Auschwitz is especially important, for there the

22. Edith Hall, "Tony Harrison's *Prometheus:* A View from the Left," review of *Prometheus,* by Tony Harrison, *Arion,* 3rd ser., 10, no. 1 (2002): 131.

23. Harrison, *Prometheus,* 30.

commemorative candles of the dead shine on Prometheus's golden body. The scene provokes the following comment from Hermes, who has accompanied the statue and the young boy on a tour of Zeus's triumphs over the human race:

> Flames when they are used for light
> most undermine Lord Zeus's might.
> Zeus particularly dislikes
> such stolen fire in little spikes
> like these, fire that renews
> the eagle-ravaged hearts of Jews.
> Why? Why is it fire that they choose?
> These candles that can help them cope
> with history and lack of hope
> are anathema to Führer Zeus
> who hates fire's sacramental use,
> Jews flaunting in Lord Zeus's face
> the fire he'd meant to end their race.
>
> Zeus and his henchmen have a fit
> whenever they see candles lit.
> The only time they don't is when
> they're in the hands of Zeus's men,
> who happily apply their heat
> to the soles of prisoners' feet.
> Every "human rights abuse"
> had its proud origin in Zeus,
> who deemed that Man was only fit
> for dumping dead in a mass pit.[24]

The light of these commemorative candles represents the resistance of human beings to the oppressive use of technology by Zeus and his armies. Not only do they light the way into the future, Harrison suggests, but they can help human beings "cope with history and lack of hope." It is significant that this ray of hope does not shoot out as a powerful beam of light; it emanates gently from several small candles. The message here may be that the responsible thing to do, when faced with the tyrannical violence of Zeus, is not to launch monumental counter-measures but instead try to forge a collective response on the ground.

24. Ibid., 61.

In contrast to the final scene in Aeschylus's *Prometheus Bound,* Hephaestus and Prometheus in Harrison's *Prometheus* engage in a heated democratic dialogue. The outcome is neither compromise nor consensus, but it does indicate a capacity for deliberation and argument in which Aeschylus and certainly Shelley had little faith.[25] What fails to emerge in Harrison's interpretation is a coherent conception of democratic political responsibility and state or corporate accountability. All the actors have been introduced: the union, the Thatcher government, Western capitalism, and Eastern state socialism. But the lines of group responsibility and state and corporate accountability are still to be drawn. Even the Promethean coal miner has become dependent on an individualized conception of responsibility and agency that is taking him to his grave. There is little prospect of reconstruction and development for the human race as it chokes itself to death, one puff at a time.[26]

Perhaps it is time to reconsider the wisdom of the Promethean myth of progress and responsibility, in all of its various forms, as the sole lens through which we understand our political responsibilities for technology. It may be that like other "second creation" myths,[27] its enshrinement of individual responsibility obscures our vision of a more sustainable democratic future. What may be needed, I have been arguing, is a form of critical reenactment that enables bystanders to recognize a broader notion of accountability that applies to the states and corporations whose actions affect populations that have no voice at all in the governance of these bodies.[28] Bernard Williams has argued that Sophocles, through *Ajax, Oedipus Tyrannus,* and *Oedipus at Colonus,* was able to masterfully reenact a set of myths in such a way that his audience could come to terms more effectively with the incomprehensible forces around them. "The interaction of character or individual project with forces, structures, or circumstances that can destroy them," Williams concludes, "can retain its significance without the presence of gods or oracles."[29] The same is true for modern-day

25. Harrison, "Fire and Poetry," xx–xxi.

26. There has been a vigorous debate over whether Marx uncritically advocated a kind of Prometheanism in his own writings and ignored the limits that the natural environment can and should place on development. One example of this criticism is Leszek Kołakowski, *Main Currents of Marxism* (New York: Oxford University Press, 1978), 412–14. For a defense of Marx and Marxism on this subject, see Paul Burkett, *Marx and Nature* (New York: St. Martin's Press, 1999); and John Bellamy Foster, *Marx's Ecology: Materialism and Nature* (New York: Monthly Review Press, 2000).

27. David E. Nye, *America as Second Creation: Technology and the Narratives of New Beginnings* (Cambridge, Mass.: MIT Press, 2003).

28. Robert O. Keohane, "Global Governance and Democratic Accountability," in *Taming Globalization: Frontiers of Governance,* ed. David Held and Mathias Koenig-Archibugi (Oxford: Polity, 2003), 130–59.

29. Williams, *Shame and Necessity,* 165.

interpreters of our persistent Promethean myths about technology. Modern technology is neither an autonomous god nor a tool that human beings use to try to play god themselves; it is part of the complicated set of often violent "forces, structures, and circumstances" that create new political responsibilities.

8 CRITICAL REENACTMENT

At the same time that a culture of simulation has made it more difficult for everyday bystanders to recognize their institutional roles in situations of severe violence, particular kinds of reenactments—in purpose, content, and voice—make it possible for us as everyday bystanders to have a heightened awareness of our complicity in these situations.

Reenactments can help us understand how we contribute to severe violence as the subjects of development (simulators) and its objects (cyborgs). To counter the culture of simulation, these critical reenactments can create public spaces in which democratic discussion and compromise can occur over the uses of simulation technologies and how they have made taking political responsibility for severe violence more difficult. In this chapter I will use several examples of reenactment in order to describe what makes reenactment a potentially critical alternative to simulation.

The reenactment of severe violence typically involves the testimony of victims and the possible therapeutic effects of this kind of witnessing.[1] While most of the reenactments I consider do include victim testimony, the effects I'm concerned with are those on bystanders to these reenactments, whether they occur on the witness stand or in different venues.

22. Purpose

Like simulations, reenactments involve distancing. Spectators and audiences to reenactments, in fact, occupy a position that is at a greater distance from the

1. Nora Strejilevich, "Testimony: Beyond the Language of Truth," *Human Rights Quarterly* 28, no. 3 (2006): 701–13.

action than do participants in simulations. Reenactments are not hands-on activities. Watching a film or drama that reenacts the operations of severe violence is not like going to a hands-on museum or walking through a reproduction of a refugee camp in real life or virtual reality. But what I will call critical reenactments are multidimensional; they enable the spectator to move back and forth between her local point of view and a larger frame of frame of reference so that she is not seduced by the pulsating, powerful images of herself and others.

This notion of a critical reenactment is what Bertolt Brecht had in mind when he extolled the alienation effect in epic theater at the same time that he railed against Aristotelian theater. Good (i.e., "epic") theater, according to Brecht, disrupts the flow of action and does not encourage uncritical identification with a tragic hero. Instead, the audience is forced to confront the complexity of political life: "Suppose a sister is mourning her brother's departure for war; and it is the peasant war: he is a peasant, off to join the peasants. Are we to surrender to her sorrow completely? Or not at all? We must be able to surrender to her sorrow and at the same time not to. Our actual emotion will come from recognizing and feeling the incident's double aspect."[2]

It is passages like this one that reveal the subtlety of Brecht's argument as well as its limitations. He does not deny the humane tendency we have to identify with the sorrowful sister; he also wants us to recognize that there is more to it than that. Personal attachments never line up neatly in parallel with our political obligations. At the same time, as critics have pointed out, Brecht simplifies the spectator's engagement in this drama. Feeling the sorrow of the sister is a form of empathy, which is not the same as sympathetically feeling sorry for her or even vicariously feeling her sorrow. Further, empathy is not an emotion devoid of cognitive content. Like many other emotional responses, this empathic sorrow is "integrated with perception, attention, and cognition, not implacably opposed to any of them."[3] In order to engage in a conversation with her, we must imagine what it is like to see the world as she sees it, feel the love she feels for her brother, and believe what she believes. We must educate our emotions, not merely succumb to an irrational identification with another, fictional or otherwise.

2. Bertolt Brecht, "Conversation About Being Forced into Empathy," in *Brecht on Theatre: The Development of an Aesthetic,* ed. and trans. John Willett (New York: Hill and Wang, 1964), 271.
3. Murray Smith, "The Logic and Legacy of Brechtianism," in *Post-theory: Reconstructing Film Studies,* ed. David Bordwell and Noëël Carroll (Madison: University of Wisconsin Press, 1996), 133. See also Carl Plantinga, "Notes on Spectator Emotion and Ideological Film Criticism," in *Film Theory and Philosophy,* ed. Richard Allen and Murray Smith (New York: Oxford University Press, 2003), 372–93.

This last point bears repeating. It not only underscores the most important limitation of the Brechtian critique of empathy, but it also indicates how political education can occur through critical reenactments. In his analysis of emotional "engagement" with fictional characters, especially in film, Alex Neill argues:

> In responding sympathetically to others, we may respond in ways that we did not know were "in us." But in responding empathetically . . . we may respond in ways that are not in *us* at all: in ways that mirror the feelings and responses of others whose outlooks and experiences may be very different from our own. Hence empathetic engagement with others may play an important part in the education of emotion. If fiction makes available to us possibilities for empathetic as well as sympathetic emotional engagement, then, that will go a long way toward justifying (as well as explaining) the claim that the value of fiction has a good deal to do with its contribution to the education of emotion.[4]

Reenactments are not necessarily critical of the bystander mentality any more than simulations necessarily support it. Through the following examples and counterexamples, I hope to illustrate this difference between the purpose of critical reenactments and the effects of less critical reenactments and the wider culture of simulation.

To begin, compare the following two reenactments in Claude Lanzmann's 1985 film about the Nazi Holocaust *Shoah*. They both evoke sympathy for the character on-screen: in the first instance it is sympathy for the survivor, Simon Srebnik; in the second, it is sympathy for the Polish aristocrat and resistance fighter Jan Karski. There is also an element of empathy in our reactions to both figures. Lanzmann helps us imagine what it must have been like to see what they saw, believe what they believed, and feel what they felt at the time.

In one scene, villagers in the modern day surround Srebnik in front of the church in Chelmno where he and other Jews of the village had been held before being transported to Treblinka. The same villagers who only moments ago were reminiscing with him about his good fortune to survive are now performing a dual reenactment of the Holocaust and the Crucifixion. Late in the scene, the church organist steps in front of the group and responds to Lanzmann's question, why did all this happen to the Jews? The organist says he does not know, but a rabbi once said that it was because the Jews betrayed Christ. That, the organist,

4. Alex Neill, "Empathy and (Film) Fiction," in Bordwell and Carroll, *Post-theory*, 179–80.

Fig. 7   Simon Srebnik in *Shoah* during a brief pause in the interview between film-maker Claude Lanzmann and Catholics in front of the church in Chelmno, Poland, where the Nazis had rounded up Srebnik and other Jews for execution. Still from *Shoah* (1985), directed by Claude Lanzmann.

insists, was the explanation given by a Jewish leader. At this point the crowd becomes more animated and an older woman takes the argument one step further. She asserts that in fact the Jews brought it on themselves and the Holocaust was justified retribution for the crucifixion of Christ. The Jews got what they deserved. From the look on Srebnik's face and the crowd's hostility, it appears that they are ready to give Srebnik up a second time.

As this conversation with Lanzmann becomes more animated, Srebnik becomes more invisible to his former neighbors and yet more dominant in the frame. As the camera slowly closes in on him, we feel drawn into a silent conversation with him. He appears trapped among these bystanders yet still able to speak to us with his eyes: "Can this really be happening again?"

Srebnik's face is the focal point in what Carl Plantinga would call a "scene of empathy."[5] We empathize with the survivor as he stands falsely accused. We know, as he knows, there is little remorse or sense of responsibility in Chelmno. We

5. Carl Plantinga, "The Scene of Empathy and the Human Face," in *Passionate Views: Film, Cognition, and Emotion,* ed. Carl Plantinga and Greg M. Smith (Baltimore: Johns Hopkins University Press, 1999), 239–55.

Fig. 8   A close-up of Simon Srebnik in *Shoah* in front of the church in which he had been held captive as a youth in Chelmno, Poland. Still from *Shoah* (1985), directed by Claude Lanzmann.

sympathize with him; being surrounded by this chorale of accusing voices clearly is painful for him. But we also can empathize. We can imagine what he saw as a child and what he must have believed was true: that the Chelmno church was an accomplice to severe violence, not a sanctuary from it. This is neither an unmediated emotional identification with Srebnik nor a purely cognitive judgment on our part. Plantinga describes scenes like this as a complex process involving "emotional contagion" as well as cognition and belief. Srebnik's face gives the reenactment its center of gravity, but the process works because the other elements fit together. We know his story; we have seen him singing on the river, retracing his steps in the fields where Treblinka once was, and enduring the callous treatment of his former neighbors once again. One could mistake the look on his face at this climactic moment as a blank stare, a sense of shock. More likely, we imagine, he is wondering how it is possible that we are reliving that horror of his youth.

Compare the way this scene evokes a silent conversation to another scene much later in *Shoah* in which Lanzmann interviews Jan Karski, one of the leaders in the Polish underground. The interview begins with Karski confessing that during his long academic career after the war he never once discussed his role in the resistance or the conditions of the Jews in Poland during the war. Suddenly, he breaks down in tears and walks away from the camera, saying he cannot continue. The thought of retelling this chapter in his life seems to be too much for him to bear. Lanzmann gradually brings him back in front of the camera, and Karski methodically retells the story of his journey back into the ghetto with two Jewish leaders as his guides to gain firsthand information that could be used to rally Allied support for the Jews. In this retelling of his odyssey through the ghetto Karski emerges as a courageous figure, but he expresses very little doubt, let alone remorse, for not providing arms to the Jews. He also expresses condescension, perhaps even revulsion, toward their suffering. The ghetto "was not a world," he tells Lanzmann. "There was not humanity." We feel some sympathy for him but not empathy. Given what he knew, not just what he saw, we find it hard to believe what he believed—that is, to believe that all he could do was be an emissary for the Polish Jews to the Allied leaders. Why did he not also argue for greater assistance from the underground itself? And as a historian and witness, how could he have remained silent so long? It was not just a matter of modesty. In effect, his silence enabled him to conceal his own unbecoming attitudes toward those whose suffering he claims to have been moved to relieve.

These two scenes work on our emotions in different ways. As the camera approaches Srebnik's motionless face, we see him trapped in the church by opportunistic accusers, and his eyes seem to be inviting us to help him understand how this could all be happening again. In the latter scene, as the camera tries again to bring us closer to Karski's experience by closing in repeatedly on his tearful and tense narrative after the initial breakdown, we feel pulled toward him, but the world he witnessed is as strange to us as it was to him. Like him, we are left skeptical and speechless. It is not that one reenactment works and the other does not. Rather, it is that they work in different ways. The reenactment in front of the Chelmno cathedral is a critical interpretation of bystander complicity. The reenactment of Karski's visit to the Warsaw Ghetto is a more direct indictment of the Polish resistance, and tangentially (through camera shots of U.S. government buildings and German industrial plants) the Allies who waited too long and the many German corporations that worked with the Nazis and have since flourished in the postwar period. It is about collaboration, not complicity.

One might argue that Karski's reenactment of his clandestine visit to the ghetto is less ambiguous and more devastating than the reenactment in front of the Chelmno cathedral. Karski describes the ghetto in detail and makes it clear that the Allies knew exactly what was happening to the Jews there yet did not come to their aid. In contrast, the look on Srebnik's face is ambiguous. Is he frightened? Is he disappointed? Is he stunned by what he is hearing? Perhaps all three; it is hard to tell. As an indictment, Karski's testimony is more damning. As a reenactment, however, it does not have as much impact on us as bystanders as Srebnik's return to Chelmno. It is precisely the lack of ambiguity, including Karski's unambiguous failure to address the conduct of the resistance toward the Jews in the ghetto, that constitute the limitations of Karski's reenactment of his visit to the ghetto. Lanzmann lets Karski tell his own story; he does not frame it and re-present it in the same way that he does Srebnik's return to Chelmno. All Lanzmann can do is underline the Allied failures through an ironic panoramic shot of the Statue of Liberty and intimate the guilt of German industrial corporations. There is nothing in Karski's monologue that supports the latter accusation.

Now, to sharpen the contrast between these two scenes in *Shoah,* compare the Karski interview with another reenactment of a visit to the ghetto, the 1943 poem by Czesław Miłosz, "A Poor Christian Looks at the Ghetto":

Bees build around red liver,
Ants build around black bone.
It has begun: the tearing, the trampling on silks,
It has begun: the breaking of glass, wood, copper, nickel, silver, foam
Of gypsum, iron sheets, violin strings, trumpets, leaves, balls, crystals.
Poof! Phosphorescent fire from yellow walls
Engulfs animal and human hair.

Bees build around the honeycomb of lungs,
Ants build around white bone.
Torn is paper, rubber, linen, leather, flax,
Fiber, fabrics, cellulose, snakeskin, wire.
The roof and the wall collapse in flame and heat seizes the foundations.
Now there is only the earth, sandy, trodden down,
With one leafless tree.

Slowly, boring a tunnel, a guardian mole makes his way,
With a small red lamp fastened to his forehead.
He touches buried bodies, counts them, pushes on,
He distinguishes human ashes by their luminous vapor,

The ashes of each man by a different part of the spectrum.
Bees build around a red trace.
Ants build around the place left by my body.

I am afraid, so afraid of the guardian mole.
He has swollen eyelids, like a Patriarch
Who has sat much in the light of candles
Reading the great book of the species.

What will I tell him, I, a Jew of the New Testament,
Waiting two thousand years for the second coming of Jesus?
My broken body will deliver me to his sight
And he will count me among the helpers of death:
The uncircumcised.[6]

Miłosz's "poor Christian," like Karski, expresses his horror at the conditions of the ghetto; he too is struck by the absence of humanity. Unlike Karski, however, this visitor is unable to suppress the fear that he will be discovered. The ominous figure of the "guardian mole," moving among the mounds of dead bodies and remains, is collecting evidence, not to indict the perpetrators but to identify the "helpers of death." In this reenactment, it is the bystander, not the collaborator, who is being scrutinized, and there is no unambiguous verdict.[7]

The challenge that technology poses is one of devising critical reenactments that enable citizens to step back from their comfortable roles as bystanders without ushering them into a simulation in which they mistake technocratic control for political responsibility. Lanzmann's techniques are very different in these two scenes. In Chelmno, Lanzmann uses the camera to recreate a scene in which the figures come alive and interact with one another and with the viewer: Srebnik is looking at us. In Warsaw, Karski is looking at the camera.

6. Czesław Miłosz, "A Poor Christian Looks at the Ghetto," in *The Collected Poems, 1931–1987* (New York: Ecco, 1988), 64–65.

7. My reading of this poem is indebted to the essay by Jan Błoński, "The Poor Poles Look at the Ghetto," in *Four Decades of Polish Essays*, ed. Jan Kott (Evanston: Northwestern University Press, 1990): "Miłosz, when asked what or who is represented by this mole, declined to answer. He said that he had written the poem spontaneously, not to promote any particular thesis. If this is so, the poem would be a direct expression of the terror that speaks through images, as is often the case in dreams and also in art. It makes tangible something that is not fully comprehended, something that was and perhaps still is, in other people's as much as in the poet's own psyche, but in an obscure, blurred, muffled shape. When we read such a poem, we understand ourselves better, since that which has been evading us until now is more palpable" (230).

With the former we are able to converse; toward the latter we feel a mixture of pity and disappointment.

The concept of critical cultural reenactment, then, has three features that distinguish it from simulation: purpose, content, and voice. The *purpose* of critical reenactment is to prompt and enable bystanders to resist the culture of simulation and see themselves as active participants within a more inclusive framework of responsibility. The *content* of critical reenactment draws from prior political efforts to control severe violence, such as the Nuremberg Trials and the South African Truth and Reconciliation Commission hearings. The *voice* of critical reenactment is the poetic way in which it interprets these prior efforts so as to draw the bystander into a conversation with the victim. As different features of the same concept of critical reenactment, the three cannot be separated entirely. As I am discussing the purpose of critical reenactment, I cannot avoid anticipating some of the discussion of content and voice in the next two sections of this chapter.

Having said this, the purpose of critical reenactments of political efforts to control severe violence is to capture the political shortcomings of the official trials and hearings they reenact. Critical reenactments neither exonerate nor convict, neither reproach nor forgive. Instead, through their interpretation of official efforts to come to terms with severe violence, these reenactments complicate citizens' understandings of their relationships to severe violence and the state and corporate institutions that dominate the global political landscape. These tribunals and hearings are themselves laden with dramatic form and content.[8] Critical reenactments of them do not distort their original meaning but widen it for a larger audience. They provide a reading of these tribunals and hearings that—to recall Breyten Breytenbach's expression—can indeed spike the self.

Critical reenactments in this threefold sense are not more iterations in a simulation game. Unlike simulations, they question underlying assumptions of official records and canonical texts. They contest simplifying assumptions and let us listen to our own suppressed doubts. At a motivational level, critical reenactments make their audiences uncomfortable with the role of passive spectator by implicating them in the events that are being reenacted. Their purpose, however, is not catharsis or conviction; it is conversation.

8. For example, see Lawrence Douglas's reading of three famous Holocaust trials in *The Memory of Judgment: Making Law and History in the Trials of the Holocaust* (New Haven: Yale University Press, 2001).

Consider the reenactment of a slave auction.[9] This is not an experience that audiences with historical connections to slavery are likely to view with either detachment or casual interest. If done well, it may extend the circle of complicity beyond the corporations and state and local governments that consciously exploited the conditions of ex-slaves as prison laborers well into the twentieth century, to include individuals and groups who have unwittingly benefited from slavery. In contrast, Civil War reenactment exercises in the United States are more like simulations in the sense that they depend on the repression of competing political interests and moral values. Or consider a reenactment of the shopping mall (itself a simulation of the town square) where the shoppers become cannibalistic zombies, as they do in the 1978 film by George A. Romero *Dawn of the Dead,* which parodies the mesmerizing effects this kind of managed space has on human beings. Reenactments such as this are not campground parties; they make us suspicious of our own intentions and our responsibility as beneficiaries of the work of "impoverished providers."

Under the right circumstances, critical reenactments may enable bystanders, witnesses, and even some survivors to come to terms with their political responsibility for severe violence more honestly and constructively than they otherwise would. It is in this sense that reenactments may function as a form of democratic political education capable of enriching the public discourse at a time when it has become impoverished by a culture of simulation. For example, Peter Sellars has directed Sophocles' *Ajax,* Aeschylus's *The Persians,* as well as Euripides' *The Children of Herakles* with precisely this purpose in mind.[10] According to reviewers, Sellars's reenactment *The Children of Herakles* offers the audience a larger vocabulary beyond individual self-interest for understanding how people become refugees, what it does to them, and how they continue to struggle against this fate. He encourages his audience, and the larger body of citizens with whom they can then discuss this work via the Internet, to understand severe violence at a time when the mass media is simultaneously demonizing and glorifying those who use violence as a substitute for democratic discourse.

9. Leef Smith, "Williamsburg Slave Auction Riles Virginia NAACP," *Washington Post,* October 8, 1994.

10. Gideon Lester, "Balm of Ancient Words," *ARTicles* 1, no. 2 (2002), http://www.american-repertorytheater.org/inside/articles/articles-vol-1-i2-balm-ancient-words: "If you remove culture from the diet of your citizens, as has happened in this country, you shouldn't be surprised that you have the most violent society in the history of the world. If you really wanted to do something for national security you would fund the arts. You can have all the armies and tanks in the world and you are not secure. Security is based on communication, on mutual understanding, on the ability to look somebody in the eye, and this is a cultural program, not a military program."

Intentionally chosen in response to the terrorist attacks of September 11, 2001, and the subsequent wars in Afghanistan and Iraq, *The Children of Herakles* questions the boundaries of political responsibility, not just the state of national security. Sellars has performed this play in Italy, Germany, and France as well as in the United States, choosing countries in which political elections and key public debates have centered on the treatment of refugee populations. In Germany, the play began with stories told by actual Kurdish refugees seeking asylum in Germany at a time when more stringent laws were being debated. In France, the story of an Afghan woman had to be piped into the theater because it was too dangerous for her to appear in public. At the American Repertory Theater in Cambridge, Massachusetts, refugee women from Haiti and Sarajevo introduced Sellars's interpretation of Euripides with their own stories. "The issues raised by the play," Sellars argues, "are international. The refugee crisis entirely exceeded borders. It's the painful contradiction of globalization that now only cash can flow internationally—businessmen can go anywhere but everyone else has to stay put. Meanwhile our economy is supported by virtual slave labor all over the world—we have far more slavery than in the time of Abraham Lincoln. And just like the first abolitionists, people are starting to notice that their economic well-being is based on the servitude of others. At what point does that become unacceptable? At what point are we neighbors?"[11]

At the climactic moment in the play, Herakles' mother, Alkmene, confronts her tormentor Eurystheus, who sentenced Herakles to a life of slavery and his children to exile. Eurystheus appears on stage in a modern prisoner's uniform behind a protective glass panel in a scene resembling the hearings of the United Nations international tribunals created to bring contemporary war criminals to justice. He is convicted, and the "president" of Athens is granted immunity. The audience, like the people of Athens, feels their responsibility to judge and live with their judgments. In this sense the play is a reenactment, not a simulation, designed to prompt a broader sense of political responsibility.

Sellars's *The Children of Herakles* can be didactic at times.[12] Despite its rhetorical excesses, however, Sellars has contested the comfortable assumptions that citizens have about their own responsibilities for severe violence against civilian populations and refugees. The history of modern slavery and the exploitation of refugees in the global political economy compose a living record that we cannot safely ignore. The dispositions these practices have bred are deeply embedded

11. Ibid.
12. Don Shewey, "Peter Sellars's CNN Euripides," *Village Voice,* January 23, 2003.

in political identity, and these instances of past severe violence, if not interpreted, will inform the relationships among future generations inside and outside the boundaries of the territory in which they occurred.

Apartheid, genocide, and slavery are clear-cut cases of severe violence, but they are by no means simple; they epitomize the cruelty of incarceration, murder, and forced labor when it is done systematically to inculcate in its victims the belief that they somehow deserved what they got. Technology has played an important role in these methods for turning enormous harm into hideous cruelty. Technological simulations play a similar role in the systematic severe violence we have seen in Afghanistan and Iraq. Instantaneous battlefield simulations available to today's military strategists, economic planners, and social engineers push refugees to the margins. Imagine a new version of *SimCity*—say, *SimDevelopment*—in which acceptable levels of collateral damage are factored in with the same hypothetical exactness as the costs of restoring electricity and providing clean water, food, and medical supplies. *The Children of Herakles,* unlike *SimDevelopment,* puts the audience in the conversation. They are not asked to prioritize these competing costs from on high or to imagine that they are someone else. As cyborgs, they might be able to adapt and flourish, even in this devastated environment. As fellow citizens they question themselves: at whose expense are they benefiting from this violence?[13]

Ideally, reenactment should help everyday bystanders come to terms with their complicity in the severe violence of these high-tech battleground simulations. The contemporary reenactments of the Prometheus myth, like Sellars's reenactment of the related myth of Herakles, may enable us to view the pervasive practice of simulation and its main character, the invulnerable cyborg, more critically as adjuncts to severe violence, not antidotes for it.

23. Content

Some of the classical and classic texts in political theory have been critical reenactments. For example, in the *Apology of Socrates* Plato reenacts the trial of Socrates in democratic Athens in order to ask not just "How would you, the

---

13. In *SimCity 4,* players build their city in three stages or modes. In God Mode, they shape the very earth that their city will stand on, including fault lines and other natural disasters. Then they shift into Mayor Mode, where they build the infrastructure of the city. Once this is done, they enter My Sim Mode, where they populate the city and assess how well citizen needs have been met. In all three modes, however, they are still viewing the world from the point of view of its creator.

reader, have voted?" but also "What can we, fellow citizens, learn about the internal as well as external threats that a democracy faces during times of war?" In *Eichmann in Jerusalem* Hannah Arendt uses the trial of Adolf Eichmann to raise questions about the nature of evil generally but also about the responsibility of other institutions such as the Catholic Church and even some Jewish organizations for the success of evil forces. The cultural content of these reenactments comes from the object of criticism: both Plato and Arendt dramatize these legal proceedings in order to raise larger political questions beyond the guilt or innocence of the accused.

In her interpretation of the 1961 trial of the Nazi bureaucrat Adolf Eichmann in Jerusalem, Arendt reenacts this extraordinary event, especially mindful that she was living at the height of the Cold War—an age that she had described in 1950 in *The Origins of Totalitarianism* as marked by "homelessness on an unprecedented scale, rootlessness to an unprecedented depth."[14] Many hoped the Eichmann kidnapping and televised trial would do what the Nuremberg Trials had failed to do—convict Nazi Germany of genocide against the Jews, not just of a conspiracy to wage aggressive war—and send a message to all totalitarian regimes that severe violence would be punished, whatever it takes. Instead, Arendt complicates the picture, pressing her readers to see themselves alongside Eichmann, not sitting in judgment on him alone. She insists on the inadequacy of a juridical proceeding for coming to terms with severe violence perpetrated by the state. She describes Eichmann's unthinking "banality" as an example of the inability of human beings in general to make moral judgments when they can only think bureaucratically about what they are doing. This does not exonerate Eichmann, Arendt argues, but it does put his behavior in a less demonic light. It makes him more like the rest of us. She then goes on to insist that guilt and innocence are not so clearly distinguished in situations of mass murder, but that we must nonetheless judge those bureaucratic functionaries, even Jewish officials, who share responsibility for the Holocaust.[15]

It is interesting to compare Arendt's theoretical reenactment of the Eichmann trial with another contemporaneous and more cultural reading of the events by Harry Mulisch. In his reporting on the trial in the weekly Dutch magazine *Elseviers Weekblad*, Mulisch did not portray Eichmann as a thoughtless bureaucratic, and he was less concerned with Jewish collaborators than he was with getting the victims' stories out. But the real difference between these two reenactments

14. Hannah Arendt, *The Origins of Totalitarianism* (New York: Harcourt, Brace, 1951), vii.
15. Hannah Arendt, *Eichmann in Jerusalem: A Report on the Banality of Evil*, rev. ed. (New York: Viking, 1965).

is the larger cultural frame of reference that marks Mulisch's published reports, now translated into English as *Criminal Case 40/61, the Trial of Adolf Eichmann: An Eyewitness Account*. For Mulisch this trial breaks the taboo in Israel on recounting the Holocaust. It also has a less obvious meaning, he argues: it illustrates, almost like a travel novel, how the Reich's marching of a people transformed the traditional German concept of cultural movement (or *Wandervögel*). Mulisch's own travels as he composes this narrative—covering Amsterdam, Berlin, Warsaw, Auschwitz, Buenos Aires, and Jerusalem—parallel Eichmann's odyssey while evading capture. The two journeys mirror the Reich's annexations and conquests. Mulisch cites the inexplicable uneasy feeling he has about Nazi "party Philosopher Alfred Rosenberg [who] officially called life a marching column, which is not interested in where it is marching, just that it is doing so."[16] There seems to be something driving German culture that has swept up both Eichmann and Mulisch and taken them along this path.

Perhaps because of his own family's compromised role during the German occupation of the Netherlands, Mulisch is less accusatory and much more self-critical than Arendt.[17] Both commentators object to reducing Eichmann's significance to his legal guilt or innocence, but Mulisch opens up a much wider conversation, one that treats political responsibility in a more cultural way than Arendt does when she reminds us categorically that new regimes do inherit the "sins of their fathers."

Even in nondemocratic societies, there is a degree of shared responsibility for the sins of our fathers. Hannah Arendt writes in another essay, "When Napoleon Bonaparte became the ruler of France, he said: I assume responsibility for everything France has done from the time of Charlemagne to the terror of Robespierre. In other words, he said, all this was done in my name to the extent that I am a member of this nation and the representative of this body politic. In this sense, we are always responsible for the sins of our fathers as we reap the rewards of their merits; but we are of course not guilty of their misdeeds, either morally or legally, nor can we ascribe their deeds to our own merits."[18] Arendt's point here is that new governments do indeed inherit the debts and other responsibilities of their predecessors, and these are collective debts that can be passed along to distant future generations even though they are not individual

16. Harry Mulisch, *Criminal Case 40/61, the Trial of Adolf Eichmann: An Eyewitness Account,* trans. Robert Naborn, foreword by Debóórah Dwork (Philadelphia: University of Pennsylvania Press, 2005), 74.

17. Dwork, foreword to ibid., xiii–xiv.

18. Hannah Arendt, "Collective Responsibility" (1968), reprinted in *Responsibility and Judgment,* ed. Jerome Kohn (New York: Schocken Books, 2003), 150.

moral or legal responsibilities. Are they shared political or moral responsibilities? She finds these kinds of "collective responsibilities" ambiguous because of the classical resonances these terms retain when we try to apply them to contemporary events. I am inclined to say that her critical treatment of institutions like the Catholic Church as well as Jewish organizations in *Eichmann in Jerusalem* and later responses to her critics reflects a moral rather than a political judgment. But, again, it is hard to be sure which language she herself favors.[19]

Mulisch is no more of one mind about complicity or collaboration than Arendt seems to be. In his novel *The Assault,* a story about the Nazi occupation of the Netherlands and the mysterious murder of an infamous collaborator, the main character observes the capriciousness of key events in his life. It is luck, not the irresistible march of events, that seems to explain things.[20] So much is left to chance that settling accounts can seem arbitrary. Yet Mulisch seems to argue in *The Assault* that the urge to identify and punish complicity, not in round numbers but down to the decimal point, is hard to resist. While not as philosophically and historically erudite as Arendt, Mulisch seems to be more attuned to the cultural dimensions of complicity.

We find similar ambiguities in two recent reenactments of the South African Truth and Reconciliation Commission (TRC) and the United Nations International Criminal Tribunal for the former Yugoslavia. In both cases, critical reenactment depends on its attention to culturally specific details, not universal themes or principles.

William Kentridge and Jane Taylor's collaboration *Ubu and the Truth Commission,* which I have already introduced (§15), is particularly instructive as a way of understanding the goals of democratic political education in an age of severe violence.[21] Kentridge is perhaps best known for his animated film studies of the responsibilities of beneficiaries of apartheid, most notably 1996's *History of the Main Complaint.* In that work, the medical examination of the white tycoon Soho Eckstein takes us inside Soho and back through his entanglement in the violence of apartheid. Soho's diagnosis is performed in the protected space of a hospital room, with Soho surrounded by a wall of sympathetic doctors. But in a coma he is haunted by his own complicity with apartheid as he "drives" back in time. J. M. Coetzee describes the action in Soho's dream this way:

19. In addition to "Collective Responsibility," see the other essays in Arendt, *Responsibility and Judgment,* part 1, "Responsibility."

20. Harry Mulisch, *The Assault,* trans. Claire Nicholas White (New York: Pantheon, 1985).

21. Jane Taylor, *Ubu and the Truth Commission* (Cape Town: University of Cape Town Press, 1998).

A third drive sequence begins. Soho passes by a body lying at the roadside. He passes a roadside fight in which two men attack a third, kicking and beating him brutally (the sequence looks forward to the appalling torture sequences in the 1997 theatre production, *Ubu and the Truth Commission,* with their strong debt to cartoon violence). The points of impact on the victim's skull are marked with red crosses. The skull is superimposed over Soho's, his too, in an X-ray, is revealed to be marked. A whole field of crosses appears on the windscreen, and is wiped away. An eye blinks, with the same effect. In the space of the screen, created by Eisensteinian montage, windscreen and eye and monitor become metonymically the same.[22]

It is this internalized violence that torments Soho and then takes center stage in *Ubu and the Truth Commission.* The challenge, Kentridge suggests, is to render the proceedings of the TRC so that this violence is neither obscured and forgotten nor harmlessly preserved in memory.

Recall that in *Ubu and the Truth Commission,* Kentridge's animated drawings are projected on a screen at the back of a stage on which Taylor's actors, puppets, and puppeteers reenact both testimony before the TRC and the accompanying dramas that surround the official hearings. According to Kentridge, there is a great, unavoidable irony in the TRC's efforts to come to terms with severe violence: "As people give more and more evidence of the things they have done they get closer and closer to amnesty and it gets more and more intolerable that these people should be given amnesty."[23] After severe violence, democratic citizens must learn to interpret and live with this irony. The more effective the TRC is in providing a relatively peaceful public forum for the private stories of victims and perpetrators, the more it denies this irony and the more unacceptable it is as a method for resolving the disputes over intentions and responsibilities that it has opened up. *Ubu* is designed to contest the peaceful closure some advocates of the TRC hoped to achieve, but in a way that advances the process of political dialogue.

The casting and imagery in *Ubu* capture this irony without declawing it. As we saw earlier, the movements and expressions of the long-suffering puppets who testify before the TRC and are exploited by the Ubus are much more human than the human figures, Ubu and Ma Ubu themselves, who venomously battle to

22. J. M. Coetzee, "History of the Main Complaint," in *William Kentridge,* ed. Dan Cameron, Carolyn Christov-Bakargiev, and J. M. Coetzee (New York: Phaidon, 1999), 92.

23. William Kentridge, "The Crocodile's Mouth," in *William Kentridge,* ed. Dan Cameron, Carolyn Christov-Bakargiev, and J. M. Coetzee (New York: Phaidon, 1999), 132.

see who will shred the records and who will use them to buy amnesty. Kentridge observes that the success of the reenactment hinges on this juxtaposition:

> But the question of how to do justice to the stories bedevils all of us trying to work on this terrain. With *Ubu and the Truth Commission* the task is to get a balance between the burlesque of Ubu and Ma Ubu and the quietness of the witnesses. When the play is working at its best, Ubu does not hold back. He tries to colonize the stage and be the sole focus of the audience. And then it is the task of the actors and manipulators of the puppets to wrest that attention back. This battle is extremely delicate. If pushed too hard the danger is that the witnesses become strident, pathetic, self-pitying. If they retreat, they are swamped by Ubu. But sometimes, in a good performance and with a willing audience, we make the witnesses' stories clearly heard and throw them into a wider set of questions that Ubu engenders around them.[24]

In the end Pa Ubu sacrifices the three-headed dog puppet that represents the secret police and other "dogs of war" in order to finagle his own amnesty. He and Ma Ubu sail off into a setting sun animated on the back screen—a sun that is also an open eye that may see them for what they are. We cannot be sure. This tentative promise of a future day of reckoning suggests that the TRC is only the beginning of the story, not the final chapter on apartheid. The theater created by the TRC now includes a wider audience engaged in a more self-critical debate about the limits of amnesty and forgiveness.

One lesson of the TRC is that amnesty and forgiveness can lead to greater divisiveness and recrimination as often as they lead to healing and reconciliation. The significance of critical reenactments like *Ubu and the Truth Commission* is that political education must convey a sense of this unavoidable indeterminacy. In Kentridge's own words, "To say that one needs art, or politics, that incorporate ambiguity and contradiction is not to say that one then stops recognizing and condemning things as evil. However, it might stop one being so utterly convinced of the certainty of one's own solutions. There needs to be a strong understanding of fallibility and how the very act of certainty or authoritativeness can bring disasters."[25]

Critical reenactment must be done in local dialects but in such a way that protects the promise of democracy, even if that ideal cannot be fully realized.

24. Ibid., 139.
25. Ibid.

Kentridge reports this response of one audience member after a performance of *Ubu and the Truth Commission:* "A woman came up to us, obviously moved by what she had seen. She said she was from Romania. We expressed surprise that the play had been accessible to her as it was so local in its content. 'That's it,' she said, 'It is so local. So local. This play is about Romania.'"[26] *Ubu* is no more about Romania than *The Children of Herakles* is about September 11, 2001. But just as adaptations of ancient plays can provide an open-textured language for political resistance and a means for affirming democratic principles of justice, culturally specific reenactments of war crimes tribunals and truth commissions can broaden the meaning of complicity and responsibility so that these terms carry across national boundaries.[27] Their audiences do not fall into the trap of acknowledging the suffering of others only to bring attention to their own capacity for sympathy.[28] Rather than act as judges of guilt, innocence, or sincerity, with the aid of reenactments they may become self-critical participants in a culturally specific dialogue over what they are responsible for beyond the reach of legal indictment and outside the realm of moral forgiveness.

The 1997 film *Calling the Ghosts,* premiered on HBO's Cinemax channel, is about the women raped at the Omarska concentration camp in 1992 and their odyssey to The Hague to testify before the International Criminal Tribunal for the former Yugoslavia (ICTY).[29] The film opens with the main figure, Jadranka Cigelj, herself a victim of ethnic cleansing in Bosnia, raising the question of her "moral obligation" to tell her story and testify against those who raped and tortured her. Gradually, this concern with individual moral responsibility shifts to wider questions of shared responsibility with and for other women who have been victims of severe violence. She worries about her own complicity in severe violence: as she interviews other women (to help them come forward and testify at The Hague), they must reenact their stories, first before her and then in front of the tribunal. Eventually, she realizes that many more women have suffered as a result of severe violence, and that she has been oblivious to their suffering for most of her life. She even wonders whether her own suffering has been a punishment for this callous disregard for the suffering of other women. As she witnesses their confessions, she feels the need to confess her own sins of omission.

26. Ibid.

27. Stephen L. Esquith, "Reenacting Mass Violence," *Polity* 35, no. 4 (2003): 513–34.

28. Elizabeth V. Spelman, *Fruits of Sorrow: Framing Our Attention to Suffering* (Boston: Beacon, 1997).

29. *Calling the Ghosts,* directed by Mandy Jacobsen and produced by Bowery Productions in association with Julia Ormond and Indican Productions, Cinemax, 1997. See also Judith Miller, "Taking Two Bosnian Women's Case to the World," *New York Times,* February 23, 1997.

Cigelj's complicity is not resolved in the film, but instead its near universality is raised as a question for the audience to consider and discuss. Cigelj, like director of the film Mandy Jacobson, is not interested in evoking sympathy for herself and the other victims of ethnic cleansing. They both want to disabuse the audience of any preconceived notions that this violence has been the product of deep ethnic hatred. It is a political weapon, they argue, echoing the words of the ICTY. Both women aim to raise the issue of political responsibility, and not merely extend the bounds of moral sympathy.[30]

Calling the Ghosts thus allows us to see the cultural content of reenactment that distinguishes it from simulation. The film operates on three levels. First, it describes the women's efforts to come to terms with their experience at Omarska, initially by telling their own stories but also gradually by helping other survivors come forward. Second, it portrays these women as witnesses *and* solicitors, who provide, by symbolically reenacting the invasive criminal acts they have tried to suppress, evidence for the prosecution. Third, it confronts the uncomfortable fact that even a survivor can be a bystander to other acts of severe violence and genocide. In this way it creates a new ground on which survivors and bystanders can recognize one another.

Cigelj is the main witness,[31] though she gives very little direct testimony in the film. She does not speak into the eye of the camera. We hear her thoughts in voice-overs or read them in subtitles as the camera follows her journey back inside Omarska and then out again. Family members and journalists corroborate her account, speaking directly into the camera, but Cigelj plays an antipodal role. She shifts back and forth, playing the traumatized witness in one scene, sending "wish you were here" postcards from The Hague back to former coworkers in Prijedor, then suddenly appearing to grieve for herself and women in general.[32]

Cigelj tells how her initial hatred and guilt began to subside, but she never sheds it completely. She and the other main figure in *Calling the Ghosts,* Nusreta

30. Mandy Jacobson, personal communication, April 14, 2005.

31. Roy Gutman, *A Witness to Genocide* (New York: Macmillan, 1993), 144.

32. The scenes oscillate between darkly lit, self-absorbed anguish and bright, festive city life. The musical score carries us up and down in this way, from doleful religious hymns recalling the ghosts of the past to upbeat rock music. The same oscillation occurs between the two major images at the beginning of the film. We see, without explanation, an image of what appears to be a burning field (later we are told it is the traditional Serbian Orthodox religious festival of *Ilie*) and then, we see quickly, Cigelj swimming in the sea under a clear blue sky, washing her face with the water, wondering whether "to stay silent or to speak." Next come family photos of a carefree youth and a naive, irresponsible life: "I was just an ordinary woman" who was "just interested in my home." Then, without warning, we see images of the war. On the importance of oscillation, see Daniel R. Schwarz, *Imagining the Holocaust* (New York: St. Martin's Press, 1999), 140.

Sivac, appear with small handheld tape recorders listening tenderly to the stories of other victims. "Without the live witnesses one can only speculate about the crimes," Cigelj says. But this resolution is only temporary. As women tell them their stories, Cigelj reflects critically on this process of testifying and, disturbingly, their own complicity in the crime: "In order to expose the crime you violate the witness. You don't force her, of course, you beg her to speak. But you do make her live through it again."

Cigelj and Sivac have mixed feelings of empathy, revenge, and guilt because they realize that they have been imitating the objectivity of their victimizers. But they also see themselves as members of the Association of Women of Bosnia and Herzegovina. They are struggling to connect their experience at Omarska to a larger pattern of genocide against women. In the key political moment in the film, Cigelj recognizes that not only is she a survivor of genocide and something of a perpetrator herself when she interrogates potential witnesses, she has also been a bystander: "Before when I read in the newspapers that women were suffering somewhere in the world, I took it simply as news and glanced over it. That is the feeling of guilt I carry all the time."

Cigelj pays tribute to women who have been lost to genocide and who have struggled against it. With each still photo of individual women suffering and protesting throughout the world, the dramatic tension between individual suffering and guilt on the one hand and global responsibility on the other builds, until a poetic web of complex responsibility is visible one frame at a time: "The world watches coldly while everything passes through women's bodies. / Destroying a woman is destroying the essence of a nation. / When they were killing and raping older women they were killing and raping living history. / When they were raping younger women, they were destroying future generations."

Calling the Ghosts is an example of how a reenactment of personal experiences through film can preserve their pathos and authenticity at the same time that it connects these fragments and makes them part of a larger political dialogue about the shared responsibilities of survivors and bystanders. It is an attempt to use visual art and poetic language to transfer our empathy for individuals to a feeling of shared responsibility for those who have suffered because so many have stood by without lifting their voices in protest or solidarity.

Jacobson has translated Cigelj's story of personal suffering, guilt, and vindication into a vehicle for political education. The transfer of empathy is not complete, and the transformation from guilt to vengefulness to solidarity is not stable. In Jacobson's hands, however, successful prosecution is not a matter of closure for individual survivors; their testimony does not settle things once and for all, any more than a guilty verdict does. Framed by Jacobson, their testimony is part of a larger group narrative that helps Cigelj, Sivac, and others like them resist isolation and humiliation.[33]

It is useful to compare *Calling the Ghosts* with another critical reenactment of a criminal tribunal, the film *Bamako* by Abderrahmane Sissako (2006).

---

33. In a parallel film project, *Genocide on Trial,* Jacobson and the Internews Network have addressed the issue of responsibility for the 1994 genocide in Rwanda. The overall goal of the project is "to help Rwandans develop a better understanding of, and the ability to participate in, the global justice system responsible for prosecuting the Rwandan genocide." See Mark Frohardt, Africa regional director, speaking at "Justice After Genocide: Rwanda," U.S. Holocaust Memorial Museum, Washington, D.C., January 29, 2002, http://www.ushmm.org/genocide/analysis/details.php?content =2002-01-29. It began with the filming of the International Criminal Tribunal for Rwanda (ICTR) proceedings but then expanded dramatically. This film, *The Arusha Tapes,* has been shown to approximately twenty-five thousand Rwandans in their villages, town halls, and even prisons. A second film in the project—updating citizens on the formal proceedings, reactions to them, and also alternatives like the traditional Gacaca village reconciliation practices—has also been shown throughout the country. At each screening the audience is engaged in an active discussion about the proceedings and issues, and they also receive information about reactions of previous audiences to earlier screenings so that a national conversation has been taking shape since the ICTR was established. See http://www.gppac.net/documents/Media_book_nieuw/p2_11_rwanda.htm. For an assessment of the very mixed results of the local Gacaca process, see Max Rettig, "Gacaca: Truth, Justice, and Reconciliation in Postconflict Rwanda?" *African Studies Review* 51, no. 3 (2008): 25–50. See also Philip Gourevitch, "The Life After: Fifteen Years After the Genocide in Rwanda, the Reconciliation Defies Expectations," *New Yorker,* May 4, 2009, 36–49.

A long-term study of the Gacaca process and its limitations is the documentary film project directed by Anne Aghion, which began in 2002 and culminated in 2009 with *My Neighbor, My Killer* (Gacaca Productions). Aghion has been able to elicit on film a series of conversations and confrontations between perpetrators who have returned to the villages in which they committed genocide, and survivors who still live in these villages. At times these confrontations turn the tables on the documentarian herself. In one conversation, two women survivors who are participating in the Gacaca process are talking directly in front of the camera, but gradually they seem to let us in on another side of the story:

> But why are they asking us?
> They want to know how we feel about their return.
> Who asks us this?
> Can't you see them?
> These whites, they ask if we are happy, if we feel plenitude.
> Why?
> We are alone in our nights.
> We wander in solitude.
> You wander by day and lie awake at night.
> What can we do?
> That is just how it is.
> Yes, we have no other choice.
> Enough. These whites ask strange questions.
> They ask if the killers come to greet me.

For more details, see http://www.anneaghionfilms.com/.

Bamako is an indictment of the policies of structural adjustment that institutions such as the World Bank and the International Monetary Fund forced on poor debtor countries like Mali. Sissako presents a fictional tribunal held in the court-yard of a poor communal dwelling in Bamako, Mali's capital city, to dramatize the plight of the real victims of decisions made in The Hague and in Washington. Instead of military officers, the defendants on trial are international economic institutions and their leaders. The prosecutors review many of the now familiar arguments against repayment of the debts that were destroying the infrastruc-ture and social services in poor developing countries in the 1990s. We see how hard the local women are working, dying fabric, in the same courtyard in which the mock tribunal is being held. The defense attorney is a buffoon, and witnesses for the prosecution, including one who is played by an actual former minister of culture and longtime critic of neoliberal globalization, Aminata Traoré, speak in articulate detail about the impact of debt servicing on the national budgets of debtor nations.

In *Bamako* the battle lines are clearly drawn; there is no gray zone. For example, we do not hear the voices of Malian employees of national and inter-national nongovernmental organizations that benefit from humanitarian aid programs, some of them funded by the same international economic institutions that drain revenues away from these countries for debt servicing. We do not encounter any of the European expatriates in Mali who work as consultants and private contractors on health and education projects. By treating poverty as a war crime and arguing that the World Bank should be sentenced to extended community service, Sissako implies that the World Bank is no different from the militia fighting for a Greater Serbia. This analogy is misleading. While impoverish-ment can be a tool used by war criminals to accomplish their ends, institutional responsibility for extreme poverty, like institutional complicity in certain war crimes, is not always so overt. In some cases—Ma and Pa Ubu, for example—it is a matter of political responsibility, not legal guilt. To get this across, to get beneath the surface in the way that Mulisch, Taylor, Kentridge and Jacobson do (and Arendt and Sissako do not), the artist also must have a good ear for the voice of the everyday bystander.

24. Poetic Voice

Martha Nussbaum has reminded us that in the search for justice, literature (unlike history and social science) allows us to consider "the possible," and literary imagination, unlike most contemporary brands of philosophy, can summon powerful emotions, not just cool reason, in the service of justice. She argues that Whitman's idea of the poet as an "equable man" is a good model for a poet-judge or poet-legislator.[34] When she cites particular inspirational texts, however, she relies on novels, not poetry. What role can poets play in awakening a greater awareness of the bonds of complicity that tie everyday bystanders to severe violence? Can poetry help bystanders forge new bonds of acquaintance among themselves and those who suffer from severe violence?

If poetry is to have these critical and constructive roles, it must do its work alongside scientific investigation and historical understanding. Heightening the bonds of complicity without attaching them to reliable knowledge and sound judgment can undermine what Michael Oakeshott has called the larger democratic "conversation of mankind" and lead to greater violence.[35] The poetic element in critical reenactments must complement, not replace, a sound understanding of the institutional structure of neoliberal globalization and the cultural roots of particular instances of severe violence. Poetry can heighten our feelings of political responsibility, but it must do so in collaboration with these other modes of knowledge.

According to Breyten Breytenbach, the "artist's responsibility" is not to be the erudite moral conscience of society but to resist clichés and lies with concrete precision: "Nowhere are sunsets as pretty as in a language that has had its eyes poked out. The word becomes wall—no longer, as it ought to be, instrument and means of seeing. You have to spike the self incessantly, you have to probe and to prod the numbness, you must pickle the heart, you have to resist, you have to fight the leveling or the buying and the forgetting brought about by commonplaces."[36] This power to use words as counter-weapons does not come easy. Poets, like all artists, work and rework their material, purging it of deadwood and hollow-sounding phrases, stripping it right down to the bare bone. Only then can it "spike the self" and "pickle the heart."

34. Martha C. Nussbaum, *Poetic Justice: The Literary Imagination and Public Life* (Boston: Beacon, 1995), 80.

35. Michael Oakeshott, "The Voice of Poetry in the Conversation of Mankind," in *Rationalism in Politics, and Other Essays* (New York: Methuen, 1962), 197–247. Oakeshott's view of the poetic idiom stresses its leisurely contemplative nature more than its capacity to inspire actual democratic conversations. But his larger vision seems right: "Education, properly speaking, is an initiation into the skill and partnership of this conversation in which we learn to recognize the voices, to distinguish the proper occasions of utterance, and in which we acquire the intellectual and moral habits appropriate to conversation" (199).

36. Breyten Breytenbach, "Fumbling Reflections on the Freedom of the Word and the Responsibility of the Author," in *End Papers: Essays, Letters, Articles of Faith, Workbook Notes* (New York: Farrar, Straus and Giroux, 1986), 144.

Carolyn Forché, whose poetry I will examine in more detail below, expands Breytenbach's characterization of the artist's responsibility. All of us, not just the artist, have a positive responsibility for the words we use. They are not just technical instruments; they shape us as we use them to shape the world around us. Let me quote once again Forché's formulation: "We are responsible for the quality of our vision; we have a say in the shaping of our sensibility. In the many thousand daily choices we make, we create ourselves and the voice with which we speak and work."[37] Responsibility extends beyond resistance to external forces. It includes the responsibility one has for one's own sensibilities, and these are shaped by "the many thousand daily choices we make." The admonition is especially important for writers, who will not be able to recognize the clichés that obscure their political responsibility for severe violence if they do not take care to choose their words carefully line by line.

Some poetry, in different ways and at different times, has enabled readers and listeners to appreciate the complex links between severe violence and their own acts and silences. With its sharp juxtaposition of opposites and incongruous details, poetry can prick us in a way that heartfelt testimony, clear arguments, and absorbing narratives do not. These other interpretations and reenactments of severe violence can render us sympathetic and strengthen our resolve to see justice done. Poetry pulls us into the picture in a very different sense. It moves us swiftly into a new space in which we can see from the inside this particular sector of the web of complicity, denial, and responsibility that sustains severe violence.

A striking example of poetry's power to use clear images to illuminate a place for the reader or listener can be found in a poem at the beginning of the trilogy *Auschwitz and After* by survivor Charlotte Delbo:

> O you who know
> did you know that hunger makes the eyes sparkle that thirst dims
> them
> O you who know
> did you know that you can see your mother dead
> and not shed a tear[38]

Eyes sparkling with hunger, sadness beyond tears: Delbo captures in this stanza the emaciated condition of the prisoner no longer capable of the suffering that

---

37. Carolyn Forché, "Sensibility and Responsibility," in *The Writer and Human Rights,* ed. Toronto Arts Group for Human Rights (Garden City, N.Y.: Anchor Press, 1983), 25.

38. Charlotte Delbo, *Auschwitz and After,* trans. Rosette C. Lamont (New Haven: Yale University Press, 1995), 11.

we (who think we know) identify with imprisonment. Take a close look, she says. Try to see your mother dead and think about how it might feel not to shed a tear. Delbo's words have a certain immediacy. Otherwise unimaginable moments of suffering seem to be staring us in the face. It is not vicarious; we know we are not going through what Delbo went through. It is not self-absorbed; we do not fixate on how badly we feel about another's suffering. It is a moment of humility as we recognize that our imagination has failed us up to this point and we are standing on the edge of a new domain, about to witness a new truth about human cruelty and suffering.

The Polish poet Wisława Szymborska enables us to glimpse hunger in the same concrete way even when we have not experienced it ourselves. In the middle of the last stanza of "Starvation Camp at Jaslo," she writes:

> It became flesh right here, on this meadow.
> But the meadow's silent, like a witness who's been bought.
> Sunny. Green. A forest close at hand,
> with wood to chew on, drops beneath the bark to drink—
> a view served round the clock,
> until you go blind. Above, a bird
> whose shadow flicked its nourishing wings
> across their lips. Jaws dropped,
> teeth clattered.
>
> At night a sickle glistened in the sky
> and reaped the dark for dreamed-of loaves.
> Hands came flying from blackened icons,
> each holding an empty chalice.
> A man swayed
> on a grill of barbed wire.
> Some sang, with dirt in their mouths.[39]

Szymborska juxtaposes the present's silent meadow where the camp once stood, the ordinariness of the act of writing about it, and this nightmarish past. In this fleeting moment in which these contrasts pull us up short, we can imagine how strong the desire for food must be that we would fill our mouths with earth.

39. Wisława Szymborska, "Starvation Camp Near Jaslo," in *Poems, New and Collected, 1957–1997,* trans. Stanislaw Baranczak and Clare Cavanagh (New York: Harcourt, Brace, 1998), 42.

Poetic language like this is capable of framing severe violence in such a way that citizens who have benefited from this violence, and too often are insulated from the actual sites of violence, nevertheless can see themselves and others within this picture, not outside it as impartial observers or innocent bystanders. Delbo's poem does not target the complicity of the beneficiary, but rather the insufficient imagination of the compassionate commiserator.

Responding to the U.S.-led war against Iraq in a poem titled "Ogres," W. S. Merwin turns his own critical view of the war on himself in order to focus on the problem of complicity. Merwin's reverie, a metaphor for the complacency of those critics of war who consider themselves blameless, is interrupted by a rush of anger and the realization that the monstrous massacres conducted in his name are in part his own creations. He suddenly realizes that they are more than his responsibility in name only:

All night waking to the sound
of light rain falling softly
through the leaves in the quiet
valley below the window
and to Paula lying here
asleep beside me and to
the murmur beside the bed
of the dogs' snoring like small
waves coming ashore I
am amazed at the fortune
of this moment in the whole
of the dark this unspoken
favor while it is with us
this breathing peace and then I
think of the frauds in office
at this instant devising
their massacres in my name
what part of me could they have
come from were they made of my
loathing itself and dredged from
the bitter depths of my shame[40]

40. W. S. Merwin, "Ogres," in *Poets Against the War,* ed. Sam Hamill with Sally Anderson and others (New York: Thunder's Mouth Press/Nation Books, 2003), 137–38.

Merwin considers this war waged in his name wholly unjust and its leaders illegitimate usurpers of power. Even in this extraordinary situation in which a democratic society's highest political official has been appointed, not elected, Merwin suspects his own complicity, and by implication, ours. Has his "loathing" for "the frauds in office" somehow contributed to this loathsome campaign of violence? Is there a common source point, deep in the past, from which these massacres draw their energy?

Delbo and Merwin epitomize the poet who can face up to the present-tense consequences of severe violence. They describe the missing tears in the eyes of the survivors and the self-doubts visible only in the dark of night. They prompt us, we who think we know what we have seen and what we have stood for, to take a second look and one step forward into what was once a dark night.

Here are three other poems that attempt to heighten our awareness as everyday bystanders to severe violence in particularly difficult situations. The first, from Antjie Krog, stresses the way poetry can connect past severe violence with present political identity. Another poem by Szymborska helps us understand both what it takes to "put the past behind us and get on with building a new society" as well as who is responsible for this act of willful forgetting. The third poem, by Carolyn Forché, addresses the way in which the youth are exploited in wartime and how this complicates our feelings of political responsibility. All three, in different ways, illustrate how critical reenactments might adopt a poetic voice in order to capture the ambiguous responsibilities we create through our "many thousand daily choices."

One poetic element in critical reenactment involves making everyday bystanders more uncomfortable with the weight of the past and more aware of their ties to the complicity of their ancestors and predecessors. Feelings of political responsibility then may arise when we recognize how our place in the present depends on how we have benefited from past practices of severe violence. Consider these lines from the poem "litany" written by Antjie Krog in her book *Country of My Skull* about the South African Truth and Reconciliation Commission:

> here along the long white shadow
> where I thought where I thought I'd leave the litany of locust
> of locust and death I'll always hear the litany of sound

> here along the long white shadow
> where I grab luster grab honor that once was luster and white
> the truth I've heard and how to molest it

That I travel I travel along the corn and chaff of my past
that my past crawls forth on its deadly knees without once looking
up
that I claw on my knees claw to that place[41]

The "long white shadow" of apartheid hangs over Krog's country, and also over her own head as an Afrikaner who has turned against her kin and their past. But it is not a past that can be kept at arms length or repudiated; it continues to "crawl forth on its deadly knees."

The image of a long white shadow crawling forth on its deadly knees couldn't be more haunting. For Krog, who is appalled by the unrepentant cruelty of those who have "molest[ed] the truth," there is no comfort in reliving that past through the testimony of the TRC. Yet with this poetic imagery Krog points beyond the stalemate between those who celebrate forgiveness and those who mourn the loss of justice. The TRC has forced her to hear "the litany of the sound" of apartheid, watch as it crawls on "its deadly knees without looking up once," and begin to "claw" slowly forward herself. This is neither a cry for redemption nor the silence of defeat. It is a poetic refrain, reminding us of what it feels like to look on the macabre presence of the past. The poetic element in Krog's critical reenactment of the TRC, then, is to be found in poetic lines like these that make notions of a legacy or living history palpable. Krog's poetry neither convicts nor forgives the perpetrators. Instead, she turns the spotlight on her own (family's) complicity and attempts to trace the moving outline of their "long white shadow."

A second poetic element in the reenactment of severe violence is the way that language can be used to evoke how it feels when the meaning of the past has drifted away, like a cloud in the sky. The law can determine what perpetrators, bystanders, and beneficiaries are responsible for, but it cannot make time stand still. The carnage has to be removed and the land gradually returns to its former state, regardless of who else deserves to be punished, who owes what to whom, and who replaces those who have been displaced. Wisława Szymborska describes how this process might begin in her poem "The End and the Beginning":

After every war
someone has to tidy up.

41. Antjie Krog, "litany," in *Country of My Skull: Guilt, Sorrow, and the Limits of Forgiveness in the New South Africa* (New York: Times Books, 1999), 345.

Things won't pick
themselves up, after all.

Someone has to shove
the rubble to the roadsides
so the carts loaded with corpses can get by.

Someone has to trudge
through sludge and ashes,
through the sofa springs,
the shards of glass,
the bloody rags.

Someone has to lug the post
to prop the wall,
someone has to glaze the window,
set the door in its frame.

These are the concrete objects that someone must take care of in the wake of severe
violence. What distinguishes this process from cleaning up after a natural disaster
is the way it came into being and the way its origins get buried or carted off:

Someone, broom in hand,
still remembers how it was.
Someone else listens, nodding
his unshattered head.
But others are bound to be bustling nearby
who'll find all that
a little boring.

From time to time someone still must
dig up a rusted argument
from underneath a bush
and haul it off to the dump.

Those who knew
what this was all about
must make way for those

who know little.
And less than that.
And at last nothing less than nothing.[42]

As we clean up the "bloody rags" and "rusted argument," some will remember "what this was all about." Gradually, day by day, they "must make way" for those who remember nothing at all. Poetry like Krog's reminds us of the "long white shadow" of our past that stalks us. Szymborska's poem captures another side of the generational conflict. While Krog helps us put into words what it feels like to be responsible for the work of our ancestors, Szymborska wants us to feel what it is like to watch the next generation gradually forget what has happened and why. But, in the end, they too will lie flat on their back, mere ground cover:

Someone has to lie there
in the grass that covers up
the causes and effects
with a cornstalk in his teeth,
gawking at clouds.[43]

This feeling is not one of regret or sadness. We realize as we read these lines that the testimony of witnesses and victims, the rulings of judges, and the compassionate statements of commissioners that Krog replays are only possible because someone offstage has stopped listening and begun to clear away the rubble. Instead of helplessness or resentment, Szymborska offers another set of feelings to the everyday bystander to severe violence. As a witness to the "The End of the Beginning," we feel a mixture of resignation, relief, and regret. We wish we could do more to preserve the record of causes and effects, but then realize that "things won't pick up themselves."

The third poetic element in critical reenactment is its power to portray the fleeting experience of youth in severe violence. There are three sides to this, all involving some level of exploitation. The young, sometimes the very young, are bribed, tortured, or duped into committing severe violence.[44] Second, they can

42. Wisława Szymborska, "The End and the Beginning," in *View with a Grain of Sand*, trans. Stanisław Baranczak and Clare Cavanagh (New York: Harcourt, Brace, 1995), 178–80.

43. I am indebted to Anita Skeen for pointing out to me the ambiguity of the final stanza of this poem.

44. See United Nations secretary-general press release listing twenty-three parties to conflicts that use child soldiers, "Secretary-General's Report Lists Parties to Conflict Using Child Soldiers," SG/2082, HR/4635, http://www.un.org/News/Press/docs/2002/SG2082.doc.htm.

be manipulated more subtly and succumb to the ecstasy of severe violence.[45] Third, the young can be boxed in so that it appears to them that they have little choice under the circumstances. Poetry reveals the beauty and promise of youth at the same time that it reminds us of its vulnerability. Consider Forché's poem "Because One Is Always Forgotten" from her collection *The Country Between Us,* which was written in memory of José Rodolfo Viera, president of the National Union of Workers and Peasants in El Salvador, who was murdered by the Salvadoran secret police ("The White Glove") in 1981. Forché does not shy away from the brutalization of the "boy soldier," but the feeling the poem leaves us with is not one of horror:

> When Viera was buried we knew it had come to an end,
> his coffin rocking into the ground like a boat or a cradle.
>
> I could take my heart, he said, and give it to a *campesino*
> and he would cut it up and give it back:
>
> you can't eat heart in those four dark
> chambers where a man can be kept years.
>
> A boy soldier in the bone-hot sun works his knife
> to peel the face from a dead man
>
> and hang it from the branch of a tree
> flowering with such faces.
>
> The heart is the toughest part of the body.
> Tenderness is in the hands.[46]

The solidarity between Viera and the campesino is juxtaposed against the macabre image of the boy soldier artistically decorating a tree with human faces. What are we to make of this heartless boy soldier with tender hands? Youth, it seems, are capable of the most hideous cruelty; yet they are also capable of exhibiting unexpected artistry and even tenderness in the very act of violence.

45. On the ecstatic experience of soldiers in combat, see J. Glenn Gray, *The Warriors: Reflections on Men in Battle* (1959; repr., New York: Harper and Row, 1970), 30–39.

46. Carolyn Forché, "Because One Is Always Forgotten," in *The Country Between Us* (New York: Harper and Row, 1981), 23.

Like Krog's "country of my skull" and Szymborska's "unshattered head," these tender hands suggest the promise of rebirth and solidarity as well as brutality. Forché helps us see whom we must depend on to take responsibility for new acts of political courage despite their exploitation at the hands of others. There is still some tenderness left in the hands of these boy soldiers; there is still something to work with.[47]

Krog is haunted by the presence of a past in which the shattered skulls of the victims of apartheid compete with the crowning skull of a newborn country. Szymborska points us in another direction: we depend on those who are able to forget enough to do the cleanup. Forché's heartless "boy soldier" alongside his tree of dead faces combines tenderness, youthful innocence, and the grotesque. Poetry like this can help everyday bystanders feel more than just helplessness in the face of severe violence or resentment toward any insinuation that we have had any hand in such violence. What we feel, however, is hardly simple or sentimental. The global landscapes "between us" divide at the same time that they link us together. As everyday bystanders, we feel drawn toward those who suffer, frightened by their countenance, and repelled by our own silence. Unless we can recognize this complex of feelings as well as the web of benefits that generate severe violence, we will continue to be held fast by the rusting bonds of complicity.

Let me end this long chapter on reenactment with two counterexamples. The first is the series of photographs that Sabrina Harman took at Abu Ghraib. The second is a reenactment project produced by Amnesty International to dramatize the severe violence at Guantánamo Bay, Cuba.

The poetically interpreted images of artists such as Paul Taylor and Claude Lanzmann help everyday bystanders recognize how they have benefited from severe violence. The images that extraordinary bystanders such as Sabrina Harman remember from Abu Ghraib have none of the artistry and potential of Taylor's *Promethean Fire* or Lanzmann's portrait of Srebnik in front of the Chelmno cathedral. Harman's tableaux (described by other military personnel as "Charlie Foxtrot," a euphemism for the military slang term "clusterfuck," which means chaos and disorganization) has no equipoise or contrapuntal logic.

"It wasn't much of a pyramid," according to Peter Gourevitch and Errol Morris. "It was more of a dog pile, toppling this way and that, as the prisoners, unable to see, scrabbled for balance. . . . Harman turned on her smile for a

---

47. For an account of work done with children who have been kidnapped into the Lord's Resistance Army in Uganda, see the Web site for the 2006 documentary film *Lost Children,* directed by Ali Samadi Ahadi and Oliver Stolz, http://www.lost-children.de/en/home.htm.

Fig. 9   A "human pyramid" of prisoners at Abu Ghraib, including Sabrina Harman, the photographer of many of the images of torture by U.S. military personnel. AP Images.

photograph with [fellow officer Charles] Graner standing behind her, beaming, with his arms crossed over his chest, muscles flexed."[48] Harman may have thought that she was documenting her own complicity, and thereby lessening her culpability, when she photographed the torture perpetrated by others, but there is nothing excusable about her role in this "dog pile." There is no tenderness in her youthful hands, no matter how high up she might raise her thumbs in victory. This photograph of a pyramid of torture is a parody of a photovoice project in which a misguided attempt to project her own dissenting voice has been used by those up the chain of command to exculpate themselves and convict her.[49]

48. Peter Gourevitch and Errol Morris, *Standard Operating Procedure* (New York: Penguin, 2008), 194.

49. To paraphrase Caroline Wang, photovoice is a process by which people can identify, represent, and enhance their community through a specific photographic technique. It entrusts cameras to the hands of people to enable them to act as recorders in their own communities (as well a potential catalysts for social action and change). It uses the immediacy of the visual image and accompanying stories to furnish evidence and promote an effective, participatory means of sharing expertise in order to create healthful public policy. See "Photovoice, Social Change Through Photo-

Harman has lost her voice through this representation of severe violence. She has become a link in the chain.

One attempt to reenact, not just photographically freeze, similar U.S. acts of torture in Guantánamo Bay, Cuba, can be found among the Amnesty International's torture project photos on Flickr, the online image-hosting site. One photo set documents attempts to walk bystanders through a small torture cell, an exhibition that has traveled to cities such as Portland, Miami, and Washington, D.C. Passersby are invited to learn about the torture cell and to briefly experience what it feels like to be locked up and chained for twenty-three hours every day. In Washington the reenactment is more theatrical: AI protesters in orange prison suits and black hoods with their hands chained behind their backs are arranged on their knees as a speaker addresses the audience.[50] This reenactment is more like the video game *Darfur Is Dying*. It is didactic, not dialogical. It hopes to generate sympathetically the sensations, thoughts, and feelings that someone gagged or hooded might have in a claustrophobic prison cell. Bystanders and passersby do not find their own voice this way. The whole purpose of this reenactment is for them to feel what it is like to have their mouths taped shut so that they are unable to denounce torture. Like Harman, although not for the same self-serving reasons, this reenactment illustrates what it is like to lose one's voice in the face of severe violence, but does not teach us how to regain it.

---

graphy," Institute for Photographic Empowerment, June 19, 2008, http://joinipe.org /welcome /archives/405.

50. Amnesty International, "Cell Tour-Washington, DC-January 2007-13," http://www.flickr .com/photos/22837123@N05/2196071196/in/set-72157605466527128/.

9 DEMOCRATIC ACQUAINTANCESHIP

In 1776, in the very first number of *The American Crisis,* Tom Paine raised the issue of political responsibility. He was concerned that "summer soldiers" and "sunshine patriots" would not rise up against British tyranny: "Tyranny, like hell, is not easily conquered; yet we have this consolation with us, that the harder the conflict, the more glorious the triumph. What we obtain too cheap, we esteem too lightly:—'Tis dearness only that gives every thing its value. Heaven knows how to set a proper price upon its goods; and it would be strange indeed, if so celestial an article as FREEDOM should not be highly rated."[1] Paine mixed economic and religious metaphors haphazardly to rally his readers. His dutiful citizen-soldier is a calculating agent, on guard so as not to miss any comparative advantage. At the same time, this same citizen-soldier who is tempted to fight only during good times can be religiously inspired to protect his freedom during the harshest winter. It is no accident that in our time Paine's call to arms has been taken up by crusading antigovernment militia groups just as frequently as his faith in common sense has been invoked by populist movements. His model of the citizen-soldier appeals to both religious faith and economic self-interest.

There is another model of responsible citizenship that has existed in practice alongside the citizen-soldier but has never been as dominant. The vocation of the citizen-teacher is not to create economic wealth or deliver salvation, but rather to ensure that citizens have a practical understanding of democratic politics so that they can retain control over power and limit the effects of violence. The advocates of this model have been citizen-teachers themselves, just as Paine himself was a citizen-soldier, but they have not always been professional

1. Thomas Paine, *Collected Writings,* ed. Eric Foner (New York: Library of America, 1995), 91.

educators. Like Paine, they have not all held public office, although they have profoundly influenced social movements and through them electoral politics.

Today's citizen-teachers incorporate the lessons of critical reenactments (like those we have discussed) into experiments in political education for a broader audience. Some experiments focus on the bonds of complicity that link everyday bystanders to severe violence. Others have forged new bonds of acquaintance among erstwhile bystanders and others. Some are guided by allegories and stories; others are more stylized and poetic. Citizen-teachers can mediate between the work of artists and writers like Lanzmann, Szymborska, Forché, Kentridge, Krog, Sebald, and Jacobson and the larger body of everyday bystanders who are not yet familiar with these critical reenactments.

This chapter describes the concrete role of the citizen-teacher in the political education of students. It is the story of two projects in democratic political education in which I have been involved. These projects are not experiments in the scientific sense. No data were collected, and no one was systematically observed, recorded, or interviewed. The political education in question is the education of my own students, not the community partners with whom they worked.

25. Community Service-Learning

Public work, Harry Boyte and James Farr have argued, is not limited to the accomplishments of great political leaders and the ambitions of legendary founders: "Public work is the expenditure of visible efforts by ordinary citizens whose collective labors produce things or create processes of lasting civic value. Public work is work by ordinary citizens who build and sustain our basic public goods and resources. It solves common problems and creates common things."[2] It may seem odd to characterize schooling as public work in this sense. But Boyte and Farr argue that at its best, public education ought to be precisely this. They use the example of community service-learning to illustrate how this might occur:

> When thinking about service-learning, public work means the creation and sustenance of projects for which young people are taken and take

---

2. Harry C. Boyte and James Farr, "The Work of Citizenship and the Problem of Service-Learning," in *Experiencing Citizenship: Concepts and Models for Service-Learning in Political Science*, ed. Richard M. Battistoni and William E. Hudson (Washington, D.C.: American Association for Higher Education, 1997), 42–43.

themselves to be accountable, serious creators and producers. It also means that young people themselves identify the problems that they wish to set themselves to solve through their collective labors in and around their own spaces—whether schools, churches, or young group sites. Furthermore, for this form of self-consciously civic and work-oriented service-learning to contribute to generalized civic education, adults who work with young people in the field of youth development—including teachers, youth workers, counselors, clergy, and others—need to engage in public work with young people, both challenging and learning from them.[3]

Service-learning projects, such as clearing vacant lots and tutoring in after-school programs, can be public work. But public work should go beyond community service; it should prepare students and their community partners for participation in democratic political life.

This project began in 1996 in a course at Michigan State University on war and morality that focused on the stories of wartime veterans—soldiers, civilian workers, spouses, prisoners, and protestors.[4] Twenty college undergraduates (in a large class of approximately one hundred) helped twenty individual veterans write down their wartime memories and compile them in a small booklet, and then arranged to have selections performed in a readers' theater production for the class as a whole and interested community and family members at the end of the semester. The course culminated in this dramatic reenactment of the coauthored stories of students and veterans.

Some stories were clever and humorous, others tearful. Some lent themselves to dramatization, others were more declamatory. Some were pro-war, others anti-war. One value that both college students and community participants in the discussion after the performance identified was that the project enabled them to talk across a generation gap that they had been unable to bridge within their own families. Several of the older veterans noted that after this experience they felt they had the confidence to speak with their own grandchildren and children about the violence of war. One of the college students worked with her aging grandfather, an Italian immigrant who spoke little English. He had been conscripted to fight on the Fascist side in World War II and then deserted. She described the pleasure she felt in finally being able to communicate with a man she had lived with all her life but hardly knew. The story they wrote together

---

3. Ibid, 43.

4. I describe this first stage in "War, Political Violence, and Service-Learning," *Teaching Philosophy* 23, no. 3 (2000): 241–54.

about his life in hiding from the Germans made it possible, she said, to express her love for her grandfather and appreciate the hardships he went through when he was her age.

The more ambitious goal of the project was to help students think more concretely about the nature of violence through the study of war, but evidence of this did not surface in the comments of the students in the service-learning project or in evaluations done by the rest of the students in the course. Even though the main text for the course was J. Glenn Gray's *The Warriors,* a thinly veiled Heideggerian critique of modern technology, students ignored the frequent quotations from Nietzsche and Heidegger in this complex autobiography.

In the third year of the course I focused more exclusively on crimes of war and crimes against humanity. My hope was that by considering the roles of bystanders and beneficiaries in these situations, I would help students see how they are sometimes collectively responsible for certain aspects of violence although they are not individually guilty. Even though we addressed the issue of responsibility extensively, the students once again did not find many similarities between the various examples of severe violence they studied. They did, however, begin to speak in class more self-critically about their own responsibilities.

The course examined several cases of genocide (the Holocaust, Bosnia, and Rwanda) and the related case of apartheid in South Africa. Instead of a service-learning writing project with adult veterans and a readers' theater, I created a project with fifth-grade students at a nearby elementary school in which they and nine college students from a large class on genocide, justice, and reconciliation explored some of the themes of the course—in particular, the responsibilities of bystanders to violence and the effects of political violence on children. Three times over a three-year period, my college students and the fifth graders wrote their own short stories, read and discussed *The Diary of a Young Girl* by Anne Frank and then *Zlata's Diary* by the young Sarajevan girl Zlata Filipovic, kept their own journals modeled on Erin Gruwell's *Freedom Writers Diary,* and constructed a Web site to communicate with other students, parents, and refugee families in the area also concerned about the issue of responsibility and violence.[5] Together the college students and the fifth graders decided to call themselves the Truth Groupies.

Rereading parts of *Zlata's Diary,* hosting a visit to the school by Erin Gruwell, and listening to a presentation from a Bosnian refugee who works with a very

---

5. Zlata Filipovic, *Zlata's Diary: A Child's Life in Sarajevo,* trans. Christina Pribichevich-Zoric (New York: Penguin, 1994); and Erin Gruwell, *The Freedom Writers Diary* (New York: Main Street Books, 1999).

active local refugee services center, combined with an enthusiasm for using the web to "publish" the project, created an optimistic atmosphere among the college students in the project. To focus the project, the Truth Groupies concentrated on examining the situations of children who had been uprooted by severe violence. For example, they examined the experiences of the young Jewish children who were part of the Kindertransport to Britain in the early 1940s and compared them to the attempts to evacuate young children like Zlata by convoy out of Sarajevo in 1992. The fifth-grade students reenacted scenes from the films *Into the Arms of Strangers* and *Welcome to Sarajevo* to understand what it would be like to be separated from their parents and siblings under these conditions. The college students asked their fifth-grade students to think about what it was like for these Bosnian children and their families, some of whom now live in our community, to be separated. What responsibilities to assist in these rescue efforts do other countries feel? What responsibilities did the rescued children themselves feel for members of their families left behind? How have refugee families dealt with this experience, and what opportunities are there now to help them talk about the choices they made and the choices others who were bystanders to their lives made? Predictably, the brief reenactments did not capture the full brutality and fear of the actual evacuations. As one fifth grader put it, "Real bullies don't back down so easily."

In one of our final reflection sessions, the college students in the service-learning project were puzzling over what they wanted to say to the other college students in the larger genocide class about their work with the elementary school kids. Some wanted to show off their new website and invite their college classmates to e-mail the fifth-grade students. Some wanted to review what the fifth graders might have learned from reenacting the Kindertransport. Others were more impressed with what they had learned themselves. For one thing, they had not expected the fifth graders to take the subject so seriously. But, more surprising, the college students had not expected that they would begin to question their own roles as bystanders and beneficiaries. Was it enough, they wondered, just to try to open up a conversation with elementary school students on this difficult subject? Did they have a responsibility to follow up and do more?

At this point the reflection session began to drift in several directions. No one said that he or she realized that by bringing workers from the refugee center to class they had established a foundation for a more ongoing set of meetings between community groups. At the same time, there was none of the catharsis and pleasure, none of the patriotic pride that followed the dramatization of veterans' stories in the previous version of the class. Also, there was none of the satisfaction shown by the wartime veterans in previous years that now they could talk to their own family members about experiences that previously had been avoided or repressed. None of the college students imagined that he or she would suddenly be able to talk with a parent or grandparent who had been in war but had refused to talk to them about it heretofore. None of them vowed to talk candidly with their own future children about crimes of war.

The most common remark in their final reflection papers was the vague promise that by taking a small amount of responsibility to teach fifth graders about violence and the responsibilities of bystanders and beneficiaries, they had more confidence that they could continue to do this sort of thing later in life. Some were skeptical about how much their fifth-grade students had learned, others were impressed with the fifth graders' level of sophistication. It may be true that the inclination to do community service tends to rub off on service-learning students after they have finished a course or left college.[6] It is not clear, however, that the college students in this class had a clearer understanding of the bonds of complicity that make severe violence possible.

Several of the service-learning college students commented on the relevance that Primo Levi's poem "If This Is a Man" from *Survival in Auschwitz* had for them. Addressed to "You who live safe," this poem is a blinding reminder of the effects of human cruelty. "Consider if this is a man. . . . Consider if this is a woman," Levi writes, and then describes their diminished state. "Carve [these words] in your hearts," he warns us, and "repeat them to your children." And if you do not:

> . . . may your house fall apart,
> May illness impede you,
> May your children turn their faces from you.[7]

This passage came up repeatedly in their reflection papers. They noted the responsibility that they gradually came to feel toward the fifth-grade students. As one student put it, this was not a matter of simply feeling the responsibility to talk about genocide; it was a responsibility to discuss and decide among them what should be said and done to enable the fifth graders to actually consider what had happened. Other students were more cautious and less confident.

---

6. See Thomas Ehrlich, ed., *Civic Responsibility and Higher Education* (Phoenix: American Council on Education, Oryx Press, 2000).

7. Primo Levi, "If This Is a Man," in *Survival in Auschwitz*, trans. Stuart Woolf (1958; repr., New York: Touchstone, 1996), 11.

Another commented on what she learned about her own role as a bystander. In the process of teaching fifth graders about the extraordinary effort it can take to resist violence when it is directed at others, she said she was reminded of what she had felt at their age in the presence of playground bullies. She described her failure to intervene when a friend was being bullied, and compared it to Kindertransport stories the fifth graders had studied. Finally, one of the service-learning college students recalled the quotation from Carolyn Forché's essay "Sensibility and Responsibility" that we had discussed in class, stressing the need for taking responsibility every day, not just in crisis situations.[8]

As laudable as these thoughts are, they should not be taken at face value. There is undoubtedly a temptation for students to say what they think the instructor wants to hear. In this service-learning project some of the college students may not have progressed as far as they said they had, but they may have had a better sense of what it means to be a bystander and what questions they might have to face at some future time.

In the sixth year of the project, initially I hoped to find a sequel to the first two reenactments (the readers' theater and the Kindertransport) and control for some of the catharsis and exaggeration. Inspired by work done at the Jane Addams School for Democracy in St. Paul, Minnesota,[9] I hoped to combine the experience of wartime veterans and refugees with the curiosity and enthusiasm of our fifth-grade classrooms through some kind of intergenerational discussion group. Instead of asking wartime veterans simply to recall and reminisce in their own voices, I thought it would be valuable to use those voices to help a younger generation come to terms with the effects of severe violence on feelings of responsibility. Instead of a make-believe evacuation, I thought the fifth-grade students could capture in their own words the experiences of children in war. Similarly, instead of trying to coach a smaller number of veterans and refugees into writing

8. "We are responsible for the quality of our vision; we have a say in the shaping of our sensibility. In the many thousand daily choices we make, we create ourselves and the voice with which we speak and work." Carolyn Forché, "Sensibility and Responsibility," in *The Writer and Human Rights*, ed. Toronto Arts Group for Human Rights (Garden City, N.Y.: Anchor Press, 1983), 25.

9. The Jane Addams School for Democracy began in 1996, and it provides college students with an opportunity for community service-learning that extends well beyond a one-course, one-semester experience. For a short history of the school and its goals, see John Wallace, "The Problem of Time: Enabling Students to Make Long-Term Commitments to Community-Based Learning," *Michigan Journal of Community Service-Learning* 7, no. 1 (2000): 133–41. See also Nan Kari and Nan Skelton, eds., *Voices of Hope: The Story of the Jane Addams School for Democracy* (Dayton, Ohio: Kettering Foundation Press, 2007); and Nicholas V. Longo, *Why Community Matters: Connecting Education with Civic Life* (Albany: State University of New York Press, 2007).

their stories for their children and grandchildren, I thought the college students could serve as guides for the fifth graders.

One problem with this model, leaving aside the complex logistics and planning, is that it runs the risk of ignoring the political education of the college students. They would be facilitators for fifth graders and veterans rather than active partners in a reenactment of severe violence. Therefore, to involve the college students more actively, instead of pairing up wartime veterans and fifth-grade students, each of the eighteen college students worked as a mentor with two or three fifth graders. Two wartime veterans (a Bosnian refugee from the outskirts of Sarajevo and a former hidden child during the Holocaust) did present their stories in person to the fifth-grade students, but the focus of the project was on the creation of a dialogical journal that each fifth grader and mentor wrote together based on the texts we read and other special events. To prepare the fifth graders for a final reenactment project of their choice, the mentors had them rehearse and rephrase the published stories of children their own age during these earlier periods and the ongoing conflict in Iraq. The final projects varied considerably. Some were individual monologues; others were skits and dramatic presentations.

Once again, the semester began with *Zlata's Diary*. The fifth graders had specific historical questions, some of them too difficult for their mentors to answer. The college students had discussed Zlata's attempts to come to grips with the siege of Sarajevo through a variety of competing metaphors and her understanding of the relationship between war and politics. Given this large gap between fifth-grade questions and college classroom discussion, the first two meetings of mentors and mentees were guided by some relatively simple questions asked by the mentors: What questions would you ask Zlata or the characters in the other stories you have read? What advice would you give them, and why? Each fifth grader began a journal with answers to questions like these or simpler comments on the text, and each college mentor responded in the journal with leading questions and encouragement. The idea was to open up a dialogue about the wartime experiences of children and help the fifth graders understand what it is like for a child to be in such a situation. Throughout the term the fifth graders commented on how authentic Zlata's voice sounded to them and how they sometimes felt sad, angry, or frightened when Zlata expressed these emotions in her journal (which she addressed as "Mimi"). In fact, this was a small reenactment exercise for the fifth graders, but we did not make too much of this. That is, we did not call to their attention that they too were keeping a diary during wartime.

The next step was for the fifth graders to read one of the short stories in the collection *Shattered: Stories of Children and War,* edited by Jennifer Armstrong,[10] which is written at approximately the same level as *Zlata's Diary.* I chose a story about an Asian American teenager living with his family in Hawaii at the time of the bombing of Pearl Harbor. To my surprise, before the college students read this story by Graham Salisbury, "A Bad Day for Baseball," they were not all aware of the use of internment camps during World War II in the United States, and their own classroom discussion of this story became very animated. It also prompted several of them to worry about the way similar forms of detention have been used by the U.S. government since September 11, 2001. Some of the fifth graders responded well to this story and were able to comment on it in their journals. For others, writing about it was very difficult, not because of the content but because they did not have the confidence and skill as writers.

In response to this unanticipated challenge, the college students met twice with a pair of consultants from the university's Writing Resource Center to discuss strategies for encouraging students to write relevantly in their dialogical journals. The consultants suggested a poem, "In Response to Executive Order 9066," by Dwight Okita. Like the Salisbury short story, the Okita poem underscores the ethnic hatred that World War II elicited and its impact on the lives of children. From the mentors' perspective, this poem stood in sharp contrast to Zlata's impatient dismissal of Serbian politicians ("the kids") who promulgated an ideology of ethnic cleansing in Bosnia. The mentors noted a similar precocious attitude toward adults in Lore Segal's *Other People's Houses,* the story of a young girl rescued by the Kindertransport.[11]

The college students were again unaware of this chapter in the history of World War II. Their initial reaction to Segal's semiautobiographical novel—Segal was one of the rescued children featured in the film *Into the Arms of Strangers,* directed by Mark Harris—was surprise at her determination under such difficult circumstances and the overt nature of the social class distinctions she encountered. They did not immediately see the similarity to Zlata mentioned above. They did notice how in the book "Lore" became hardened by her lifelong journey that began with the Kindertransport and lasted thirteen years before she was able to establish a new, relatively stable home for herself in the United States. The fifth graders viewed a segment of the Harris film and read the corresponding

---

10. Jennifer Armstrong, ed., *Shattered: Stories of Children and War* (New York: Knopf, 2002).
11. Lore Segal, *Other People's Houses: A Novel* (1964; repr., New York: The New Press, 1994).

section in Segal's book that rehearses the scene in which the children are packing their small single suitcases and thinking about what they will be leaving behind. At the same time these children, Segal recalls, were often asked to do whatever would be necessary to get their parents and siblings out of Austria. Some literally went door to door in the small English village in which they lived asking for work and help in securing visas for the parents and siblings. Some succeeded; most did not. The fifth graders discussed these scenes and then wrote in their journals what they thought about this responsibility and what they would pack if they were asked by their parents to get the rest of their family out of Austria. The college mentors responded in writing with their own reflections on the same questions.

The next step in the process was the most difficult, both in form and content. The college mentors studied the graphic conditions of life in 1944 for Hungarian women who were enslaved, brutalized, and executed by the failing Nazi machine. In *Seed of Sarah* by Judith Magyar Isaacson,[12] the college students confronted for the first time someone who had survived the harshest kind of severe violence of the twentieth century. Astonishingly, many of them had no idea that this is what actually occurred in extermination and forced labor camps, and in discussing it they repeatedly expressed their shock and disbelief. On the other hand, they seemed less surprised by or skeptical of Isaacson's professed capacity for forgiveness at the end of the memoir.

Rather than take up this material directly with their fifth graders, however, the mentors addressed it through the recollections of a former hidden child, Miriam Winter, whose account of her experience in Poland they read and who presented her story in person to the fifth graders and their mentors.[13] Her story is one of identity crisis and recollection. As a young Jewish child she was hidden by a Catholic family and gradually adopted their religious identity; only much later in life did she begin to reclaim her original Jewish heritage.

Miriam Winter sometimes uses poetry and the image of trains to capture the rattling and disorienting experience of a young Jewish girl who adopts Catholicism as part of her strategy of survival. To prepare students for this story and for the violence facing hidden children like Miriam, I presented a poem to the fifth graders as a whole and asked them to think it through with me. Charles Simic's "Prodigy" juxtaposes the hunched-over image of a young

12. Judith Magyar Isaacson, *Seed of Sarah: Memoirs of a Survivor,* 2nd ed. (Urbana: University of Illinois Press, 1991).

13. Miriam Winter, *Trains: A Memoir of a Hidden Childhood During and After World War II* (Jackson, Mich.: Kelton Press, 1997).

chess prodigy against the image of the same child, whose mother wraps her overcoat around him so that he cannot see men hanging from telephone poles in 1944 in Belgrade, Yugoslavia. Later in life, the prodigy does not remember this experience, even though he is told about it by his mother. He does remember, however, how a retired professor of astronomy tells him that chess masters can play blindfolded against common opponents.[14]

The first time around, the fifth graders were not able to make too much of the parallel between war and chess. Nor did they see how hidden or covered or blindfolded children can navigate the horrors of war, forget what they have seen, and then be reminded of the forgotten image by the pieces of a chess set. They were introduced to a difficult image—a child "blindfolded" so that he couldn't see men hanging from telephone poles—in a poem that was couched in the more familiar language of a game of chess. Gradually, however, they began to talk about the image of severe violence by searching for similarities between being a blindfolded chess master and being a young child sheltered from the images of violence in wartime. With this poem in mind, they listened to Miriam describe what it was like to be hidden, change one's name to Maria, and pretend to be Catholic in order to survive.

Miriam asked to be introduced as Maria Orłowski, the name she took in hiding. Today a professor of theater, she was currently teaching at a nearby community college and had no trouble stepping into character. She explained how she was given up by her parents, told to never speak her real name again, and told to memorize the Lord's Prayer so that whenever she was asked a question by a stranger she could dispel any suspicion that she might be Jewish simply by reciting this prayer. The fifth-grade students wanted to know when Maria became Miriam again, when she told her own children this story, and how many, if any, of the rest of her family survived. None had. The mentors were more puzzled about Miriam's religious identity and whether she had become an observant Jew. She said that slowly she has returned to Judaism.

Miriam's story is engaging, in part because it is one of survival and religious rebirth. Her resilience as a child seems to be reflected in her energetic and compassionate adult persona. If Miriam compromised her religious beliefs by holding onto Maria a little longer than one might have thought, it hardly seems to be anything that rises to the level of complicity or collaboration. Hidden children like Miriam do not run that risk. In the next set of stories, however, the decisions that children had to make to survive genocide did involve these higher stakes.

14. Charles Simic, "Prodigy," in *Against Forgetting: Twentieth-Century Poetry of Witness*, ed. Carolyn Forché (New York: Norton, 1995), 353–54.

What is the difference between collaboration and complicity? I tried to raise this question in the college classroom through two very different accounts of survival, Primo Levi's *Survival in Auschwitz* and Imre Kertesz's *Fateless*.[15] These stories do not deal with the forgiveness and responsibility that Judith Isaacson faced. Nor do they raise the question of what is entailed when one must masquerade under a false religious identity. Instead, Levi and Kertesz deal with the numbness that can overcome young prisoners subjected to severe violence, as well as the more compromised roles that youth play in severe violence. The main characters in these two books, both young men, find ways to survive, but not through staunch acts of resistance like those demonstrated by Isaacson. The main characters in Levi's and Kertesz's books are much more ambiguous and are in no position to forgive themselves or others. They epitomize the kind of complicity that made survival possible for many of those who endured the harshest forms of severe violence during the Holocaust. These were the stories that the college mentors had in mind as they began to discuss these grimmer facts of severe violence with their fifth-grade mentees.

At this point in the semester the war against Iraq officially began. As the college students read Henri Raczymow's intricate novel *Writing the Book of Esther*,[16] we asked the fifth graders if they had any questions about the current war, especially about the lives of children caught up in it: now that you know about how children are hidden and rescued, how they learn how to survive on the street, how they change their names and their religions, how they sometimes get caught up in the war machine and do not escape, what questions do you have about children in this war? Fearful that some students might be unable to cope with such a discussion, the public school district had instructed its elementary and middle school teachers not to bring up the Iraq war with students. Our two fifth-grade instructors reluctantly had complied with this policy. When students mentioned the war, the teachers had acknowledged its seriousness without encouraging further discussion, and they did not bring it up themselves. But when the mentors explicitly asked students what they thought, the fifth graders reacted immediately with more animated conversation and more enthusiasm for writing in their journals. Some fifth graders seemed mesmerized by television images of the bombing of Baghdad. A few echoed the pervasive patriotic slogans

---

15. Imre Kertész, *Fateless*, trans. Christopher C. Wilson and Katharina M. Wilson (Evanston: Northwestern University Press, 1992).

16. Henri Raczymow, *Writing the Book of Esther: A Novel*, trans. Dori Katz (New York: Holmes and Meier, 1995).

in the American media. A few others, however, seemed to have been listening more carefully; of course, in such a short span of time it is difficult to say whether the arguments they made were their own or they were simply exposed to them more frequently at home.

I had planned to pursue the themes of responsibility, complicity, and forgiveness, but this intense interest in the war in Iraq that appeared to have been bottled up now began to drive the fifth graders' journal entries. The fifth graders wrote more, talked more about what they wrote, and seemed to respond more clearly to the comments in their journals from their mentors. In the context of this new-found energy for writing and comparing the current war to the war in Bosnia and World War II, I decided to devote the last two meetings with the fifth graders to a more open-ended project. Mentors and fifth-grade students designed an individual presentation or group project, rehearsed it one week, and performed it for the two assembled classes in the last week. Some students read a poem they wrote, other groups as large as five or six students performed a skit dramatizing a siege, a child transport, or a midnight raid. The performances themselves were not notable as dramatic reenactments; more revealing were the reflections of the college mentors. One, in particular, was stunned by the question posed to her Asian American mentee by another fifth-grade student: "What's your American name?" The mentor was saddened as well as surprised that something like this could happen at the end of the semester. This is the kind of political education I had hoped the mentors in this project would experience, but it did not result from a climactic analysis of the concepts of responsibility, complicity, and violence.

In the winter of 2003 history caught up with this experiment in political education. The memoirs, stories, poems, and museum exhibits on the fate of children during the Holocaust and ethnic cleansing in Bosnia could no longer be safely confined to the past. Now there were Kurdish and Iraqi children similarly trapped and suddenly visible to students a world away.

26. Study Abroad

The second example also comes from my own experience, this time as a coleader of a study abroad program in Mali in the summer of 2006. Like the community service-learning project described above, this experience is far from conclusive. It illustrates another way in which a citizen-teacher might interpret critical reenactments of severe violence, in this case the reenactment of violence that is inscribed in the traditional *bogolan* made in the Beledougou region of Mali. The meanings of these textiles are not reducible to their abstract iconography. As texts, their meanings depend on a complex contemporary local and global context.[17] This is the story of one set of texts produced by the traditional bogolan artist Nakunte Diarra and her son Bindé Traoré.

On their visit to the National Museum of Mali, our students discussed with museum director Samuel Sidibé the importance of the museum as a site for public education. Although he considered this the institution's primary function, Sidibé was fairly blunt about its limits in this regard. He realized that only tourists and a small middle-class audience who lived in the national capital, Bamako, ever visited the museum's collection of archaeological artifacts, textiles, and sculptures. He hoped that as the museum gradually increased its collection, it would be able to share it with other museums internationally and also bring some of the nation's own artwork back to Mali for temporary exhibitions.

Several students took an interest in the handmade textiles in the National Museum, in particular the bogolan, or mud cloth, of Nakunte Diarra. Her work has been displayed in major museums in Europe and North America, and several art historians have chronicled her life in a small village not far from Bamako.[18] One week after our discussion with Sidibé, we spent a day with Nakunte and her family in their compound in the small town of Kolokani.

Our contact was Bindé, a textile artist himself who had taken on the role of family business manager. Bindé traveled regularly to the capital city to negotiate commissions from the National Museum, the few expensive tourist shops in town, and private collectors. While the family had a small plot of land that they farmed on the edge of their village, their primary source of income was the sale of traditional textiles made by Nakunte and the other members of the family (who were, in effect, her apprentices).

The family compound is approximately five hundred square feet, surrounded by a four-foot-high mud-brick wall. There is a large shade tree in the middle of the compound against which Nakunte sits every day doing her work. Several adult women (possibly cousins), two high-school-aged grandchildren (Salif and Yaoussou), and almost a dozen other grandchildren from the extended

17. See Aïssata G. Sidikou, *Recreating Words, Reshaping Worlds: The Verbal Art of Women from Niger, Mali, and Senegal* (Trenton, N.J.: Africa World Press, 2001); and Christine Mullen Kreamer and others, eds., *Inscribing Meaning: Writing and Graphic Systems in African Art* (Washington, D.C.: Smithsonian, National Museum of African Art, 2007).

18. For example, see Tavy D. Aherne, *Nakunte Diarra: Bogolanfini Artist of the Beledougou* (Bloomington: Indiana University Museum of Art, 1992).

family socialize and play within the compound. There is a small one-story, three-room, mud-brick hut in one corner where the family sleeps, and a separate mud-brick outhouse without a roof in another corner. Cooking is done over an open fire surrounded by several bamboo chairs and small wooden benches.

Despite these modest surroundings, one might describe Nakunte as an international figure in bogolan art. Her two-week visit to Washington, D.C., to participate in the Smithsonian Folklife Festival in 2003 is something she fondly remembers. Each day she sat cross-legged under a small canopy on the National Mall, displaying her bogolan and answering questions through translators. Her work now is part of the permanent exhibition "African Voices" in the Smithsonian's National Museum of Natural History.

We arrived at 10:00 A.M. at the Diarra family compound on a hot sunny day. The extended family turned out to welcome us. Before we began the workshop for our students in Kolokani, Nakunte gave each student a new name in her native language. Then, she and Bindé demonstrated their traditional bogolan techniques, which include dying cotton cloth and painting it with a special mud paste. The figures they paint in the negative are abstract symbols that refer to various family and village social relations. Nakunte's bogolan is organized according to aesthetic conventions and social norms. It is proverbial knowledge (e.g., jagged teeth symbolizing a jealous husband, a dot with a circle around it symbolizing the value of spending time together as a family). When these symbols are truncated and arranged for a more dramatic visual effect by other contemporary artists, the text becomes incoherent and the story is lost. Contemporary art and fashion that selectively mine Nakunte's lexicon can be visually beautiful, but they are not historical reenactments. Nakunte stressed to the students that they do not tell the story of family struggles and village politics, and most important, they do not offer advice on how to meet one's responsibilities.[19]

The students were given ten square feet of treated cloth and photocopies of this lexicon, which researchers had already assembled. With the help of the children and grandchildren, they began to design and paint their own patterns. The painting and drying process took four hours. While the students worked, I spoke with Bindé. At age fifty-seven, Nakunte's eyesight and stamina were beginning to decline, and she was no longer able to produce many museum-quality textiles. Bindé is a skilled artist, but he is not sure that his work will command the same critical attention as Nakunte's. Hence, he has begun to expand his search

19. Victoria L. Rovine, *Bogolan: Shaping Culture Through Cloth in Contemporary Mali* (Washington, D.C.: Smithsonian Institution Press, 2001), 22–23.

for customers. Nakunte has always worked with individual clients to design textiles, not a general tourist market (which is how the bogolan from the San region of Mali is produced). Bindé has continued to take individual orders on commission, but he is feeling new pressures to expand his sales. He confided that his niece Yaoussa was having difficulty in school and also seemed to be losing interest in bogolan. Bindé was worried that without her help, he could not continue to produce enough quality bogolan. He mentioned that his brother, who had moved to Ivory Coast several years before to work on the docks unloading containers, had returned to the village because of the violence there. Soon thereafter he had become mentally ill and unable to care for himself.

At this point in the conversation, the students finished their work and began to ask if there were some finished pieces they could buy. Bindé ushered them into the front room of the three-room family home, which had been cleared of mattresses and furniture. The family's finished artwork was on display from wall to wall, and Bindé stood poised with his spiral notebook and ballpoint pen ready to sell. The students, however, did not want to buy the pieces on display. Some wanted a darker color or a different size. Some wanted something more practical like a set of place mats or napkins in the style of one of the wall hangings on display. Some wanted a shirt or small jacket in the traditional bogolan style.

Bindé was initially unsure what to do. He would need money up front to buy the cotton fabric for these new orders. He would also need time to organize the family so that they could produce the special orders before the students left Mali in three weeks. He knew he did not have the money, and he feared that Yaoussa would not be able to work overtime to fill the order on time. He was unsure whether to try to persuade the students to buy what was on display—as they might in a museum gift shop—or try to raise the prices of the special orders to cover his new costs and hire an extra worker. But if he raised them too high, he feared that the students might change their minds. As he stood there mulling this over, the rest of the family, including Nakunte, took a strong interest in the conversation. They seemed to sense what was at stake.

As I watched this scene unfold, I realized that I had a responsibility to advise our students or at least make them aware of Bindé's dilemma. I had decided to focus the study abroad program on cotton as the thread that runs through the development process in Mali, and here we were pulling on the thread and testing its strength.

Cotton is the only export crop produced by mostly small farmers in Mali, and in part because of subsidies provided to farmers in richer countries, including the United States, the market price has dropped considerably in the last few years. The United States and the World Bank have urged Malian farmers to both increase productivity through the use of Bt cotton and diversify in order to offset the effects of the subsidy program and other cheaper cotton imports. But reducing production costs by using Bt cotton to reduce the costs of pesticides is politically unlikely in Mali. Few finished cotton fabrics are manufactured domestically, and that too is unlikely to change given the high costs of energy and the unreliability of the transportation system. While hardly a panacea, one way to increase exports would be to produce and market handicrafts based on distinctive traditional fabric art, such as Nakunte's, that is known worldwide. Without a more diversified agricultural export sector based on higher productivity among small landholders, of course, this would not be enough. But it could be one part of a more general response to the current problems our students were witnessing.[20]

From the perspective of the study abroad course, it appears that Bindé should continue to move toward a more commercial model. He may have to hire other apprentices rather than depend on family members. He may have to move to Bamako to avoid transportation problems. He may have to find ways of branding Nakunte's symbols and designs. Other artists have done this, and he may be able to secure enough credit to start the process. In other words, our students were asking Bindé to do just what we had discussed in class should be done.

From Bindé's perspective, however, other questions were just as important as the ones posed to our students. Would the revenues from a more commercial business be enough to cover the costs of Yaoussa's technical education in Bamako and his brother's medical care? Would it preserve Nakunte's work more effectively? One of my responsibilities was to convey to our students that their decisions to place orders with Bindé would have social implications for his family not immediately obvious from the perspective of institutions like the World Bank or groups like the U.S. cotton lobby. The bargain they would strike with Bindé would not be just a matter of negotiating a fair price.

20. On the colonial history of cotton production in West Africa, see Richard L. Roberts, *Two Worlds of Cotton: Colonialism and the Regional Economy in the French Soudan, 1800–1946* (Stanford: Stanford University Press, 1996). See also Erik Orsenna, *Voyage aux pays du coton: Petit précis de mondialisation* (Paris: Fayard, 2006); and Pietra Rivoli, *The Travels of a T-Shirt in the Global Economy: An Economist Examines the Markets, Power, and Politics of World Trade* (Hoboken, N.J.: John Wiley, 2005). For a detailed analysis of what agriculture-led economic development would require in Mali and throughout the region, see John M. Staatz and Niama Nango Dembélé, "Agriculture for Development in Sub-Saharan Africa" (background paper for the *World Development Report, 2008*, World Bank, Washington, D.C.), http://siteresources.worldbank.org/INTWDR2008/Resources/2795087-1191427986785/StaatzJ&DembeleN_AgriForDevtInSSA_ve19.pdf.

If cotton is to play a more positive role in Mali's political and economic development, then artists like Nakunte Diarra and Bindé Traoré will have to make some difficult choices. So will students in our study abroad program, and so will citizen-teachers leading programs like this one. These choices cannot be made in an institutional vacuum. They depend on factors as different as the educational opportunities available to Nakunte's children and grandchildren, the shared control of family resources between Nakunte and Bindé, the health-care available to their brothers and sisters, the regional regulatory framework developed for transgenic crops, and the interpretations of bogolan promulgated by professors, curators, journalists, and other citizen-teachers. While some Malians will have an important say in these matters, so will other individuals outside Mali, as will groups and institutions whose political and economic power cut across Mali's national boundaries. The push from companies that favor transgenic crops (such as Syngenta and Monsanto) will be significant. The linkage agreement between Michigan State University and the University of Bamako will also have an effect on how this facet of cotton production proceeds. Finally, the empathy of students who have become acquainted with the work of Nakunte and Bindé may also play a role in this unfolding story. It is this pattern of connections for which those of us who are citizen-teachers have a shared political responsibility.[21]

21. In summer 2008 we visited Nakunte and Bindé for a third time. Nakunte had been hospitalized recently, and the costs of her medication had forced Bindé to sell the small motorcycle he used to market his products. Yaoussa had left the compound in Kolokani to attend the University of Bamako. Bindé had been forced to borrow money from neighbors in order to produce the bogolan he hoped to sell to our students on this visit. The sales he made to them just covered these outstanding debts.

CONCLUSION

I began with my own experience as a teacher uncomfortable using liberal and neoliberal maps to make sense out of a world rife with severe violence and dominated by a hopscotching global culture of simulation. This led to a search for help with my own teaching and thinking about political responsibility, first in eastern Europe and then in West Africa. The experiments in political education described in chapter 9 have not solved that problem. The old maps are heavily marked up but still on the wall, and my political responsibilities as an everyday bystander are still largely unmet. But some things have changed.

Working with former hidden children like Miriam Winter and artists like Nakunte Diarra has helped me see what parts of our world my students and I share with these people. Working with younger students who do not understand what it is to demand "What's your American name?" or who do not know how to answer this hurtful question, teaches us what it sounds like to be disenfranchised. One change that has occurred over the course of this modest odyssey is that I am not as "coolly accustomed to" severe violence as I once was.[1] Discussing the reenactments of Lanzmann, Kentridge, and Jacobson, and the poetic language of Szymborska, Merwin, Forché, Simic, Krog, and Delbo has made me and possibly my students (like the one who sent me the e-mail about her Latino family's complicity in the internment of Japanese Americans) better listeners in this sense.

There are other ways besides reenactment to get a bystander's attention. Simulations of severe violence can do this, but I have argued that they tend to have

---

1. Jean Drèze and Amartya K. Sen, *Hunger and Public Action* (1989), reprinted in *The Amartya Sen and Jean Drèze Omnibus* (New York: Oxford University Press, 1999), 275–76.

a very different political effect. At best they create sympathetic observers, not empathetic acquaintances. Other ways of representing severe violence that evoke sympathy need not have the same unwanted political effect as simulations.

For example, Sebastião Salgado's photographic essays, which I discussed in §14, are not sensational and horrific. They do not leave us tearful or speechless. Even under the best interpretive light, however, they do not weave new bonds of acquaintance among bystanders and victims of severe violence. They are allegories of rescue, not stories of responsibility. Salgado's *Sahel: The End of the Road,* originally published in France after the devastating 1984–85 famine in West Africa, was composed to raise money for Médecins Sans Frontièères (MSF).[2] Recently translated into English, this collection once again brings us face-to-face with those the reviewer Christopher Morton calls "residents of a world in perpetual twilight." As "beautiful, beguiling, and visceral" as these portraits are, however, Morton correctly calls our attention to their "anonymity."[3] One issue that this silence obscures is the relationship between emergency aid like that provided by MSF and the plight of those who suffer. This is a complicated story about food security, long-term development, and carefully planned aid.[4] MSF has played a constructive role, but it is not an unambiguously beneficent one.[5] The story of hunger that links famine and war together cannot be deduced from the faces in *Sahel.*[6] It must be told by the small farmers, herders, traders, refugees, displaced persons, humanitarian organizations, government agencies, and private corporations who live this complicated existence. Everyday bystanders have to learn how to listen to these voices before they respond viscerally out of sympathy. This is the purpose of a critical, responsible, and democratic political education.

What separates Salgado's representations of severe violence from critical reenactments such as Lanzmann's, Krog's, and Kentridge's is the power of critical reenactments to prepare bystanders to listen more closely to their own voices

2. Sebastião Salgado, *Sahel: The End of the Road* (Berkeley and Los Angeles: University of California Press, 2004).

3. Christopher Morton, review of *Sahel: The End of the Road,* by Sebastião Salgado, *Anthropological Quarterly* 79, no. 1 (2006): 177.

4. Nancy Birdsall, Dani Rodrik, and Arvind Subramanian, "Getting Development Right," *Foreign Affairs* 84, no. 4 (2005): 136–52.

5. On the dilemmas facing international nongovernmental organizations like MSF, Amnesty International, and Habitat for Humanity, see Daniel A. Bell and Joseph H. Carens, "The Ethical Dilemmas of International Human Rights and Humanitarian NGOs: Reflections on a Dialogue Between Practitioners and Theorists," *Human Rights Quarterly* 26, no. 2 (2004): 300–329.

6. Alex de Waal, *Famine Crimes: Politics and the Disaster Relief Industry in Africa* (Bloomington: Indiana University Press, 1998).

and the voices of others entwined in global and local structures of power. This ability to hear orchestral voices is also what Jim lacks in the story of "Ousmane at the Crossroads." In contrast, William Kentridge's implicit conversations between his two alter egos, Felix and Soho, and Antjie Krog's dialogues with her family and fellow citizens illustrate how an exploration of complicity can compose new acquaintanceships for bystanders. As I suggested in §15, the most powerful figures in *Ubu and the Truth Commission* are the puppets, whose silent testimony is so riveting. Their gestures and deeply lined faces represent the suffering that comes with acquiescence and humiliation. The puppeteers in *Ubu* have close everyday contact with these impoverished providers, but they do not yet hear their voices. Kentridge suggests that only through something like two-track stereoscopic listening in *History of the Main Complaint* (in which the doctor hears the inner voices of the patient at the same time the audience sees the repressed memories of the doctor) can we hear and see these conflicting voices—what Bakhtin called double-voicedness.[7]

Democratic acquaintanceships like those that Soho and Felix struggle to make with the seemingly silent victims of apartheid have to be developed slowly. They cannot be fused together with shocking images. Like Kentridge, Lanzmann does not rely on documentary footage of severe violence for this reason. Instead, he tries to show us what it is like to listen carefully to and speak with complicit bystanders as they tentatively walk across now-empty fields. He certainly asks probing questions; sometimes he pushes too hard ("You must go on," he tells Abraham Bomba, one of the barbers in Treblinka, as Bomba reenacts in a staged Jerusalem barber shop the painful scene in which he prepared women he knew from his village for the gas chambers). But other times he finds just the right voice. In scenes like the reenactment of the crucifixion in front of the cathedral in Chelmno, Srebnik is not merely incredulous. Lanzmann positions Srebnik so that he can see what it feels like to be treated as if he weren't there by a group of bystanders. He has been displaced by the abstract category "Jews who had been held in the Chelmno cathedral." In terms of the distinction I have drawn between sympathy and empathy, Lanzmann does not invite us to sympathetically stand in Srebnik's shoes. Instead, Lanzmann engages Srebnik in a silent dialogue that sets the stage for a much more difficult conversation with the film audience about the shared political responsibilities of bystanders and the institutional responsibilities of the Catholic Church, corporations, and even Jewish community organizations.

---

7. M. M. Bakhtin, *Speech Genres, and Other Late Essays*, trans. Vern W. McGee (Austin: University of Texas Press, 1986), 110.

In §6 I likened the process of democratic political education to a tour through what W. G. Sebald has called an "alternative Holocaust museum." Lanzmann's reenactments are artifacts in this fictional museum. More successfully than Daniel Libeskind's actual Jewish Museum Berlin,[8] Sebald's alternative Holocaust museum enables us to retrace the steps of ordinary people caught up in unimaginable circumstances and still struggling to make their way, one day at a time. The names and captionless pictures are connected in subterranean ways to other persons across national political borders and generations. Stories told in this embodied way may help us keep our balance when we face situations, such as the one Srebnik faced in front of the Chelmno cathedral. But it is very difficult to navigate these waters alone. Citizen-teachers can serve as guides or docents.

I have used Sebald's "Paul Bereyter" in *The Emigrants* to illustrate two virtues of the citizen-teacher. Sebald's method of interview and narration in his final novel, *Austerlitz* (2001), provides a more complete model. Like the other artists, filmmakers, and poets I described in chapter 9, Sebald structures his stories as critical reenactments. These reenactments are not writ large like Arendt's reenactment of the Eichmann trial or Kentridge's reenactment of the TRC. They are reenactments of the lives of minor characters, even if their names recall famous battles; what makes them valuable as instances of political education is the cautionary note they sound.

Consider Sebald's title character Jacques Austerlitz, a scholar whose interests run from architecture, especially train stations and libraries, to entomology. Among the many fragments of his life that he pieces together during his interviews with Sebald's narrator in *Austerlitz* is an early recollection of a boarding school teacher, André Hilary, an expert on the history of the Napoleonic era: "Hilary brought it all vividly to life for us, partly by recounting the course of these events, often passing from plain narrative to dramatic descriptions and then on to a kind of impromptu performance distributed among several roles, from one to another of which he switched back and forth with astonishing virtuosity,

8. See the Jewish Museum Berlin Web site, http://www.juedisches-museum-berlin.de/site/EN /05-About-The-Museum/03-Libeskind-Building/01-Groundplan/groundplan.php. There are three axes in Libeskind's museum: Continuity, Emigration, and Holocaust. After traversing these three intersecting axes, retracing the paths of German Jews, one then follows a zigzag of exhibits that periodically, at different levels of the building, provide a difficult angle of vision on five vertical voids that symbolize the unspeakable truth of the Holocaust. For an interpretation of Libeskind's attempt to represent the void left by the extermination of Berlin's Jewish community, see James E. Young, "Daniel Libeskind's Jewish Museum in Berlin: The Uncanny Arts of Memorial Architecture," *Jewish Social Studies* 6, no. 2 (2002): 1–23. I am indebted to Carolyn Loeb and Richard Peterson for a tour of this museum and the benefit of their extensive knowledge of Berlin and its built environment.

and partly by studying the gambits of Napoleon and his opponents with the cold intelligence of a nonpartisan strategist, surveying the entire landscape of those years from above with an eagle eye, as he once and not without pride remarked."[9] These critical reenactments of Hilary's were all the more impressive, according to Austerlitz, because due to his bad back he would often have to deliver them lying on the floor.[10]

The effects on Jacques Austerlitz were profound. Hilary's pièce de résistance was his critical reenactment of the Battle of Austerlitz. Young Jacques's original name (Dafydd Elias) and the one he was still known by at the boarding school, according to the boarding school headmaster, had to be officially replaced by "Austerlitz" on Dafydd's examination papers. The reasoning was obscure, and Jacques was told that it had something to do with his adoption by the Eliases through the Kindertransport.[11] At any rate, the name "Austerlitz" meant nothing to Dafydd until Hilary brought it to life: "The more often Hilary mentioned the word Austerlitz in front of the class, the more it really did become my own name, and the more clearly I thought I saw that what had at first seemed like an ignominious flaw was changing into a bright light always hovering before me, as promising as the sun of Austerlitz itself when it rose over the December mists. All that school year I felt as if I had been chosen, and although, as I also knew, such a belief in no way matched my uncertain status, I have held fast to it almost my whole life."[12] This personal transformation was coupled with a more lasting intellectual revelation that Austerlitz refers to as "Hilary's thesis" of the limits of our historical imagination:

9. W. G. Sebald, *Austerlitz,* trans. Anthea Bell (New York: Random House, 2001), 70.

10. We find the same synoptic vision in Sebald's controversial description of the Allied bombing in World War II in his essays in *On the Natural History of Destruction,* trans. Anthea Bell (New York: Random House, 2003). According to Todd Samuel Presner, "What is remarkable about Sebald's description of the fire-bombing of Hamburg is that no eyewitness could have possibly seen or experienced it in this way. In a single 'synoptic' view Sebald has spliced together information and experiences culled from a multiplicity of perspectives: the U.S. Air Force and the RAF, the bomber pilots in the planes, eyewitnesses on the ground, as well as meteorologists, police, survivors, punishment battalions, and historians. His description oscillates between global and local views, perspectives from above and below, points of view within and external to the bombing, and finally knowledge gained before, during, and after the catastrophe. No one who was there could have seen what he describes, and yet—for exactly this reason—it is strikingly real." Presner, "What a Synoptic and Artificial View Reveals: Extreme History and the Modernism of W. G. Sebald's Realism," *Criticism* 46, no. 3 (2004): 353.

11. It is no accident, commentators have observed, that Sebald chose the name Elias. He admired the work of Elias Canetti, who argued that is very easy for us to join the crowd of bystanders when we have not thought about responsibility in advance. See Elias Canetti, *Crowds and Power,* trans. Carol Stewart (1962; repr., New York: Farrar, Straus and Giroux, 1984), 75–80.

12. Sebald, *Austerlitz,* 72–73.

All of us, even when we think we have noted every tiny detail, resort to set pieces which have already been staged often enough by others. We try to reproduce the reality, but the harder we try, the more we find the pictures that make up the stock-in-trade of the spectacle of history forcing themselves upon us: the fallen drummer boy, the infantryman shown in the act of stabbing another, the horse's eye staring from its socket, the invulnerable Emperor surrounded by his generals, a moment frozen still amidst the turmoil of battle. Our concern with history, so Hilary's thesis ran, is a concern with preformed images already imprinted on our brains, images at which we keep staring while the truth lies elsewhere, away from it all, somewhere as yet undiscovered.[13]

Despite his own painstaking work as a research scholar, Austerlitz confesses, he succumbs to this tendency to substitute "set pieces . . . staged often by others" for actual details.

After Austerlitz confided in Hilary that his name had been officially changed, the teacher seemed to take an even greater interest in his most promising student. As a tutor and friend, Hilary was responsible, according to Austerlitz, for his academic success and for making it possible for him to go on his "own way into freedom," or at least this is what Austerlitz "confidently thought at the time." In later interviews, we learn that this ominous foreshadowing was justified: Austerlitz's health declines, his relationships with others deteriorate, and by the end of his life, in the vicinity of the Gare d'Austerlitz in Paris, his search for his own father's story and possible remains ends inconclusively. The narrator of *Austerlitz* slips effortlessly back into the "set pieces" left to him by others.

If, as citizen-teachers, we are searching for lessons from this small reenactment, let me suggest two, both of which bear on the capacity of citizen-teachers to somehow make us more aware of our past complicity in and potential political responsibility for severe violence. The first is that teachers like Paul Bereyter and André Hilary indeed can give students the confidence to ask what their real name means and who should be responsible for the world they have inherited. Without Hilary's synoptic vision of history and his skepticism toward detailed historical accuracy, Austerlitz would not have been able to embark on his journey.

The second lesson is that this journey can become an individualistic obsession and eventually suffocate us, as it did Austerlitz. The more we rely on set pieces

13. Ibid., 71–72.

staged by others to interpret historical spectacles, the more frustrated and morbid we will become. The alternative is not to try quixotically to write our own stories from the ground up, but to make the acquaintance of others so that we can compare notes. In the end Sebald's narrator may be too passive. Unlike Lanzmann, he never steps forward in front of the camera to press his informants for more clarity and detail.[14] *Austerlitz* is a valuable example of a critical reenactment, but Hilary, like Paul Bereyter, is not an ideal citizen-teacher.[15]

Do these stories and claims about the motivational force of critical reenactment add up to a theory of democratic political education? If we mean a systematic account of otherwise disparate intuitions and observations, then there is certainly no theory here. Perhaps, however, a theory of this sort is not exactly what is needed to prompt everyday bystanders to recognize their shared political responsibilities for severe violence.

My goal has been to use other theories to move my argument about democratic political education forward where possible and to break with some theories when they point in directions that seem inappropriate. One debt is to the human capability approach of Amartya Sen and Martha Nussbaum. Sen and Nussbaum have argued that standard measures of development, especially those that reduce well-being to per capita income, are misleading. Human capabilities and the freedom to choose among them are much more complicated than this, and democratic freedoms are among the most important for helping us sort out what our development priorities ought to be. The emphasis I have placed on democratic political education is consistent with this view of "development as freedom," to use Sen's preferred language.[16] I have argued that one of the key human capabilities that is both a means to and an end of the capability conception of human development is empathy—that is, the capacity for critical discursive engagement over the causes and allocation of benefits of severe violence. Despite my

14. But see Mark M. Anderson, "The Edge of Darkness: On W. G. Sebald," *October* 106 (Fall 2003): 107. Anderson argues that like Lanzmann in *Shoah*, Sebald's narrator "is the secret center, the thread that holds these narrations together in an implicit gesture of solidarity and identification that is all the more effective for being unstated."

15. Their flaws may have more to do with Sebald's own autobiographical struggle than the role that citizen-teachers might play in a search for shared and institutional responsibility. In his own life, Sebald has suggested, the details of both the Holocaust and the Allied war against Germany were suppressed until he reached college age. See W. G. Sebald, "Recovered Memories: Interview with Maya Jaggi," *Guardian*, September 22, 2001; and "The Last Word: Interview with Maya Jaggi," *Guardian*, December 21, 2001.

16. Amartya Sen, *Development as Freedom* (New York: Knopf, 1999).

criticisms of Sen's allegorical moral reasoning and Nussbaum's treatment of poetry, I believe that democratic political education is essential for cultivating the political virtue of empathy, and that empathy is a key capability in human development.[17]

I have already mentioned (§8) how feminist ethics of care (including Nussbaum's own work[18] have helped me understand the importance of social relations, and particularly how to describe individual political responsibility within its institutional context. There are two other elements of feminist writings that are equally important for my understanding of democratic political education. One is the emphasis on responsibilities rather than rights; the second is the emphasis on human needs. Onora O'Neill's work has been the most helpful with regard to the former.[19] Practitioners of the capability approach, at least as Sen, Nussbaum, and many of their colleagues have advanced it, seem to be skeptical of the idea of giving responsibilities some kind of conceptual priority over rights.[20] Capability theorists prefer the priority of human rights, despite the selective way that it has been used in the past.[21] They also resist the argument that "basic needs" is a more important category than human capability for measuring human development.[22]

I am inclined to heed O'Neill's warning about the past use of human rights, although I do not think human rights are inherently flawed.[23] I'm less sure about the relationship between a capability approach and a basic needs approach, but it seems clear that the capability approach has not paid adequate attention to the question of where needs come from. Simply criticizing adaptive preferences, as Sen and Nussbaum do, does not fully address the problem of more deeply rooted cultural needs. What is most valuable about O'Neill's approach, as I mentioned

17. For relevant criticisms of Sen's capability approach, see Stephen L. Esquith and Fred Gifford, eds., *Capabilities, Power, and Institutions: Toward a More Critical Development Ethics* (University Park: Pennsylvania State University Press, 2010).

18. Martha C. Nussbaum, *Women and Human Development: The Capabilities Approach* (New York: Cambridge University Press, 2000).

19. On the priority of duties and responsibilities, see Onora O'Neill, *Towards Justice and Virtue: A Constructive Account of Practical Reason* (New York: Cambridge University Press, 1996).

20. Martha C. Nussbaum, *Frontiers of Justice: Disability, Nationality, Species Membership* (Cambridge, Mass.: Belknap Press, 2006), 271–83.

21. Amartya Sen, "Elements of a Theory of Human Rights," *Philosophy and Public Affairs* 32, no. 4 (2004): 315–56.

22. See Soran Reader, "Does a Basic Needs Approach Need Capabilities?" *Journal of Political Philosophy* 14, no. 3 (2006): 337–50; and in defense of the capability approach, Sabina Alkire, "Needs and Capabilities," in *The Philosophy of Need*, ed. Soran Reader (New York: Cambridge University Press, 2005), 229–51.

23. Onora O'Neill, "The Dark Side of Human Rights," *International Affairs* 81, no. 2 (2005): 427–39. For an acute critique of this argument, see Charles R. Beitz, *The Idea of Human Rights* (New York: Oxford University Press, 2009), 164–66.

in §12, is the emphasis she places on our moral and political expectations of others that are embedded in our practical dealings with them and their institutions.[24] Human needs are equally embedded in dominant institutions and practices, but this is another story for another time.

Another important debt that I have incurred is to democratic theory. I began this book by distinguishing my conception of citizen-teachers from Michael Walzer's theory of social criticism and the figure of the connected social critic that he extols. Despite this difference, it should be clear that like Walzer I am skeptical of universalistic theories of justice. "The crucial commonality of the human race," he argues, "is particularism."[25] I share his view that we can only approach political values such as justice, fairness, and toleration imperfectly, one experiment at a time. The experiments he discusses are guided by the values of "territorial integrity and communal identity."[26] I agree with Walzer that the postmodern thesis that we live in a world in which no one is a stranger anymore is false.[27] But territorial integrity and communal identity do not seem to be adequate guides for solving many of our global problems. For example, should refugees who have fled severe violence be prohibited from bringing other members of their family with them when their marital practices do not conform to the laws of the immigrant-receiving country? An answer cannot be guided by Walzer's ideal of communal identity unless we are willing to say that the protection of young children in polygamous families is not a part of the communal identity of predominantly monogamous societies.

Then how should responsible bystanders settle their differences with refugees like these or others in need of assistance? Recognizing their responsibilities is an important first step for everyday bystanders, but there is no reason to think that these responsibilities will never conflict or that there will be adequate resources available to meet all of them. In the case of polygamy, should concern for the women who must endure this patriarchal practice override the concern one might have for those children in the family who may be left behind in poverty because of prohibitions against entry by polygamous families?

24. For a response to O'Neill's critique of basic needs, see Bill Wringe, "Needs, Rights, and Collective Obligations," in Reader, *Philosophy of Need*, 187–207.

25. Michael Walzer, *Thick and Thin: Moral Argument at Home and Abroad* (Notre Dame: Notre Dame University Press, 1994), 83.

26. Ibid., 75.

27. He has in mind Julia Kristeva's postmodernist view of "polyvalent communities . . . a world without foreigners." See Michael Walzer, *On Toleration* (New Haven: Yale University Press, 1997), 90.

This is only one instance of a more general question. Once everyday bystanders recognize their complicity in severe violence, what are they supposed to do? Political responsibilities often will conflict. Should everyday bystanders support reparations, reform immigration laws, or increase foreign aid and charitable giving? What I have suggested is that none of these competing issues, as important as they are, will be addressed and resolved until everyday bystanders feel responsible for participating in democratic conversations about them. My argument does draw on democratic theory, but it is neither exclusively communitarian nor cosmopolitan. It is an argument about how to build democratic acquaintanceships within and across heterogeneous local and global communities.[28] Once everyday bystanders to severe violence can hear the voices of those who suffer in silence, and can see how they benefit from this suffering, the chances of addressing these divisive issues may increase.

This leads to my last and greatest debt. I have chosen to approach the problem of severe violence from what may appear to be an unusual angle: democratic political education. Why focus on this downstream question? Why not dig deeper upstream, pin the blame on the real culprits, and expose the worst collaborators? Everyday bystanders, a skeptic might say, are not going to solve this problem no matter how much more clearly they can recognize themselves through critical reenactments as the beneficiaries of severe violence. If they are complicit but not to blame, they are not likely to be persuaded to contribute to solving the problem.

On the contrary, I believe that until everyday bystanders get more involved as democratic citizens, as flexible as the concept of citizenship may be today, there will be little effective agreement about who are the real culprits and the worst collaborators, and inadequate pressure to bring them to justice. As Sheldon S. Wolin has argued repeatedly, democracy is a formative concept, not a fixed ideal arrangement to be imposed or mimicked. Critics such as Plato and Tocqueville understood the importance of this link between democracy and education, as have reformers such as Addams and Dewey. In recent years, Wolin notes, those

---

28. Some democratic theorists have argued that without trust, democratic acquaintanceships like these will not form. Experiments with deliberative democracy, for example, have sought to establish some preliminary trust through small-group discussions and expert tutoring before rushing individuals to a vote on particular issues. For example, James S. Fishkin, *Deliberative Polling®: Toward a Better-Informed Democracy* (Stanford, Calif.: Center for Deliberative Democracy, Stanford University, 2002), http://cdd.stanford.edu/polls/docs/summary/. But these artificial experiments do not address more deep-seated suspicions and conflicts in the way that Addams's Hull-House and other Progressive Era experiments sometimes did. See Kevin Mattson, *Creating a Democratic Public: The Struggle for Urban Participatory Democracy During the Progressive Era* (University Park: Pennsylvania State University Press, 1998).

hostile to democracy have grasped this connection between education and democracy more fully than its defenders. "Democracy," he writes, "is ultimately dependent on the quality and accessibility of public education," and it is no accident that elite support for public education has declined precipitously at the same time that democratic practices and institutions have eroded.[29] In the riparian terms in which I began, opening up new channels of democratic political education downstream, so that the responsibilities of everyday bystanders are not hidden, can reveal the flow of power and the depths of severe violence upstream.

29. Sheldon S. Wolin, *Democracy Incorporated: Managed Democracy and the Specter of Inverted Totalitarianism* (Princeton: Princeton University Press, 2008), 161.

BIBLIOGRAPHY

Ackerly, Brooke A. *Political Theory and Feminist Social Criticism.* New York: Cambridge University Press, 2000.

Addams, Jane. *Democracy and Social Ethics.* 1902. Reprint, Urbana: University of Illinois Press, 2002.

————. *A New Conscience and an Ancient Evil.* New York: Macmillan, 1912.

————. *Twenty Years at Hull-House.* 1910. Reprint, New York: New American Library, 1981.

Aeschylus. *Prometheus Bound.* Translated by George Thomson. New York: Dover, 1995.

Agamben, Giorgio. *Remnants of Auschwitz: The Witness and the Archive.* Translated by Daniel Heller-Roazen. New York: Zone Books, 2002.

Agee, James, and Walker Evans. *Let Us Now Praise Famous Men.* 1941. Reprint, Boston: Houghton Mifflin, 1969.

Agreement Between the Government of the United States of America and the Government of the Federal Republic of Germany Concerning the Foundation "Remembrance, Responsibility, and the Future." Berlin, Germany, July 17, 2000. http://germany .usembassy.gov/germany/img/assets/8497/agreement.pdf.

Aherne, Tavy D. *Nakunte Diarra: Bogolanfini Artist of the Beledougou.* Bloomington: Indiana University Museum of Art, 1992.

Alkire, Sabina. "Needs and Capabilities." In *The Philosophy of Need,* edited by Soran Reader, 229–51. New York: Cambridge University Press, 2005.

Allen, James, and John Littlefield. *Without Sanctuary: Lynching Photography in America.* Santa Fe, N.Mex.: Twin Palms, 2000.

Aly, Göötz. *Hitler's Beneficiaries: Plunder, Racial War, and the Nazi Welfare State.* Translated by Jefferson Chase. New York: Henry Holt, 2005.

Amnesty International. "Cell Tour-Washington, DC-January 2007-13." http://www.flickr .com/photos/22837123@N05/2196071196/in/set-72157605466527128/.

Anderson, Mark M. "The Edge of Darkness: On W. G. Sebald." *October* 106 (Fall 2003): 102–21.

Archibugi, Daniele. *The Global Commonwealth of Citizens: Toward Cosmopolitan Democracy.* Princeton: Princeton University Press, 2008.

Arendt, Hannah. *Eichmann in Jerusalem: A Report on the Banality of Evil.* Rev. ed. New York: Viking, 1965.

————. *The Origins of Totalitarianism.* New York: Harcourt, Brace, 1951.

————. *Responsibility and Judgment.* Edited by Jerome Kohn. New York: Schocken Books, 2003.

Armstrong, Jennifer, ed. *Shattered: Stories of Children and War.* New York: Knopf, 2002.

Arneson, Richard J. "Moral Limits on the Demands of Beneficence." In *The Ethics of Assistance: Morality and the Distant Needy,* edited by Deen K. Chatterjee, 33–58. New York: Cambridge University Press, 2004.

Ashford, Elizabeth. "The Alleged Dichotomy Between Positive and Negative Rights and Duties." In *Global Basic Rights,* edited by Charles R. Beitz and Robert E. Goodin, 92–112. New York: Oxford University Press, 2009.

Baier, Annette C. *The Commons of the Mind.* Chicago: Open Court, 1997.

Baier, Kurt. "Moral, Legal, and Social Responsibility." In *Shame, Responsibility, and the Corporation,* edited by Hugh Cutler, 183–95. New York: Haven, 1986.

Bakhtin, M. M. *Speech Genres, and Other Late Essays.* Translated by Vern W. McGee. Austin: University of Texas Press, 1986.

Bakker, Egbert J. "Mimesis as Performance: Rereading Auerbach's First Chapter." *Poetics Today* 20, no. 1 (2001): 11–26.

Barnett, Victoria J. *Bystanders: Conscience and Complicity During the Holocaust.* Westport, Conn.: Greenwood, 1999.

Barney, Darin. *Prometheus Wired: The Hope for Democracy in the Age of Network Technology.* Chicago: University of Chicago Press, 2001.

Barry, Christian. "Applying the Contribution Principle." In *Global Institutions and Responsibilities: Achieving Global Justice,* edited by Christian Barry and Thomas W. Pogge, 281–97. Malden, Mass.: Blackwell, 2005.

Bassler, William G. *In re: Nazi Era Cases Against German Defendants Litigation,* 198 F.R.D. 448 (D.N.J. 2000).

Baudrillard, Jean. *Simulations.* Translated by Paul Foss, Paul Patton, and Philip Beitchman. New York: Semiotext(e), 1983.

Beitz, Charles R. *The Idea of Human Rights.* New York: Oxford University Press, 2009.

————. *Political Theory and International Relations.* Rev. ed. Princeton: Princeton University Press, 1979.

Beitz, Charles R., and Robert E. Goodin, eds. *Global Basic Rights.* New York: Oxford University Press, 2009.

Bell, Daniel A., and Joseph H. Carens. "The Ethical Dilemmas of International Human Rights and Humanitarian NGOs: Reflections on a Dialogue Between Practitioners and Theorists." *Human Rights Quarterly* 26, no. 2 (2004): 300–329.

Benhabib, Seyla. "Democratic Citizens and the Crisis of Territoriality." *PS: Political Science and Politics* 38, no. 4 (2005): 674–75.

————. *The Rights of Others: Aliens, Residents, and Citizens.* New York: Cambridge University Press, 2004.

Bilefsky, Dan. "Hurdles in Eastern Europe Thwart Restitution Claims: Reluctance to Act on Holocaust Seizures." *New York Times,* August 2, 2009.

Birdsall, Nancy, Dani Rodrik, and Arvind Subramanian. "Getting Development Right." *Foreign Affairs* 84, no. 4 (2005): 136–52.

Blackmon, Douglas A. "From Alabama's Past, Capitalism and Racism in a Cruel Partnership." *Wall Street Journal,* July 16, 2001.

————. *Slavery by Another Name: The Re-enslavement of Black Americans from the Civil War to World War II.* New York: Doubleday, 2008.

Bloński, Jan. "The Poor Poles Look at the Ghetto." In *Four Decades of Polish Essays*, edited by Jan Kott, 222–35. Evanston: Northwestern University Press, 1990.

Bobbitt, Philip. *Terror and Consent: The Wars for the Twenty-first Century*. New York: Knopf, 2008.

Bock, Greg, and Jamie Good, eds. *Empathy and Fairness*. Novartis Foundation Symposium 278. Hoboken, N.J.: John Wiley, 2006.

Borkin, Joseph. *The Crime and Punishment of I. G. Farben*. New York: Free Press, 1978.

Bourdieu, Pierre. *Practical Reason: On the Theory of Action*. Translated by Randall Johnson. Stanford: Stanford University Press, 1998.

Boyte, Harry C., and James Farr. "The Work of Citizenship and the Problem of Service-Learning." In *Experiencing Citizenship: Concepts and Models for Service-Learning in Political Science*, edited by Richard M. Battistoni and William E. Hudson, 35–48. Washington, D.C.: American Association for Higher Education, 1997.

Braziel, Jana Evans, and Anita Mammy, eds. *Theorizing Diaspora: A Reader*. Oxford: Blackwell, 2003.

Brecht, Bertolt. "Conversation About Being Forced into Empathy." In *Brecht on Theatre: The Development of an Aesthetic*, edited and translated by John Willett, 270–71. New York: Hill and Wang, 1964.

Breytenbach, Breyten. "Fumbling Reflections on the Freedom of the Word and the Responsibility of the Author." In *End Papers: Essays, Letters, Articles of Faith, Workbook Notes*. New York: Farrar, Straus and Giroux, 1986.

Brooks, Rodney A. *Flesh and Machines: How Robots Will Change Us*. New York: Pantheon, 2002.

Brown, Derek. "Litigating the Holocaust: A Consistent Theory in Tort for the Private Enforcement of Human Rights Violations." *Pepperdine Law Review* 27, no. 3 (2000): 553–90.

Brummer, James J. *Corporate Responsibility and Legitimacy: An Interdisciplinary Analysis*. New York: Greenwood, 1991.

Burger-Fischer v. Degussa AG, 65 F. Supp. 2d 248 (D.N.J. 1999).

Burkett, Paul. *Marx and Nature*. New York: St. Martin's Press, 1999.

Buscher, Frank M. *The U.S. War Crimes Trial Program in Germany, 1946–1955*. New York: Greenwood, 1989.

Butt, Daniel. "On Benefiting from Injustice." *Canadian Journal of Philosophy* 57, no. 1 (2007): 129–52.

Callan, Eamonn. *Creating Citizens: Political Education and Liberal Democracy*. New York: Oxford University Press, 1997.

Calling the Ghosts. Directed by Mandy Jacobsen and produced by Bowery Productions in association with Julia Ormond and Indican Productions. Cinemax, 1997.

Canetti, Elias. *Crowds and Power*. Translated by Carol Stewart. 1962. Reprint, New York: Farrar, Straus and Giroux, 1984.

Carothers, Thomas. "The End of the Transition Paradigm." *Journal of Democracy* 13, no. 1 (2002): 5–21.

Carr, Edward R. "Millennium Village Project and African Development: Problems and Potentials." *Progress in Development Studies* 8, no. 4 (2008): 333–44.

Chatterjee, Deen K., ed., *The Ethics of Assistance: Morality and the Distant Needy*. New York: Cambridge University Press, 2004.

Cheadle, Don, and John Prendergast. *Not on Our Watch: The Mission to End Genocide in Darfur and Beyond*. New York: Hyperion Books, 2007.

Chronic Poverty Research Centre. *Chronic Poverty Report, 2008–09: Escaping Poverty Traps.* Manchester, UK: Chronic Poverty Research Centre, University of Manchester, 2009. http://www.chronicpoverty.org/cpra-report-0809.php.

Cioran, E. M. *On the Heights of Despair.* Translated by Ilinca Zarifopol-Johnson. Chicago: University of Chicago Press, 1992.

Coady, C. A. J. "The Idea of Violence." *Journal of Applied Philosophy* 3, no. 1 (1986): 3–19.

Coetzee, J. M. "History of the Main Complaint." In *William Kentridge,* ed. Dan Cameron, Carolyn Christov-Bakargiev, and J. M. Coetzee, 82–93. New York: Phaidon, 1999.

Cohen, Roger. "Last Chapter: Berlin to Pay Slave Workers Held by Nazis." *New York Times,* May 31, 2001.

Coles, Robert. *Doing Documentary Work.* New York: Oxford University Press, 1997.

Collier, Paul. *The Bottom Billion: Why the Poorest Countries Are Failing and What Can Be Done About It.* New York: Oxford University Press, 2007.

————. *Breaking the Conflict Trap: Civil War and Development Policy.* Washington, D.C.: Oxford University Press and the World Bank, 2003.

Collins, Daryl, Jonathan Morduch, Stuart Rutherford, and Orlanda Ruthven. *Portfolios of the Poor: How the World's Poor Live on $2 a Day.* Princeton: Princeton University Press, 2009.

"Come Clean 4 Congo." Enough Project/YouTube. http://www.youtube.com/enough project/.

Commission on Wartime Relocation and Internment of Civilians. *Personal Justice Denied.* Washington, D.C.: National Park Service, 1982. http://www.nps.gov/history/history /online_books/personal_justice_denied/.

Cronin, Michael. *Translation and Globalization.* New York: Routledge, 2003.

Dan-Cohen, Meir. *Rights, Persons, and Organizations.* Berkeley and Los Angeles: University of California Press, 1986.

Danner, Mark. "The Red Cross Torture Report: What It Means." *New York Review of Books,* April 30, 2009, http://www.nybooks.com/articles/22614.

————. *Torture and Truth: America, Abu Ghraib, and the War on Terror.* New York: New York Review of Books, 2004.

————. "U.S. Torture: Voices from the Black Sites." *New York Review of Books,* April 9, 2009, http://www.nybooks.com/articles/22530.

Darfur Is Dying. Reebok Human Rights Foundation/International Crisis Group/mtvU. Darfur Digital Activist Context. http://www.darfurisdying.com/aboutgame.html.

Das, Veena, Arthur Kleinman, Margaret Lock, Mamphela Ramphele, and Pamela Reynolds. *Remaking a World: Violence, Social Suffering, and Recovery.* Berkeley and Los Angeles: University of California Press, 2001.

Davies, Ian, Mark Evans, and Alan Reid. "Globalising Citizenship Education? A Critique of 'Global Education' and 'Citizenship Education.'" *British Journal of Educational Studies* 53, no. 1 (2005): 66–89.

Davis, Mike. *Late Victorian Holocausts: El Niño Famines and the Making of the Third World.* New York: Verso, 2001.

Dawes, James. *That the World May Know: Bearing Witness to Atrocity.* Cambridge: Harvard University Press, 2007.

The Day After Trinity: J. Robert Oppenheimer and the Atomic Bomb. Directed by John Else. Image Entertainment, 1981.

Delbo, Charlotte. *Auschwitz and After.* Translated by Rosette C. Lamont. New Haven: Yale University Press, 1995.

DeLue, Steven M. *Political Obligation in a Liberal State.* Albany: State University of New York Press, 1989.

de Man, Paul. *Allegories of Reading: Figural Language in Rousseau, Nietzsche, Rilke, and Proust.* New ed. New Haven: Yale University Press, 1982.

de Waal, Alex. *Famine Crimes: Politics and the Disaster Relief Industry in Africa.* Bloomington: Indiana University Press, 1998.

Dewey, John. *Lectures on the Sociology of Ethics.* Lecture 22, November 19, 1902. Center for Dewey Studies, Southern Illinois University, Carbondale, Ill.

Dolan, Frederick M. *Allegories of America.* Ithaca: Cornell University Press, 1994.

Douglas, Lawrence. *The Memory of Judgment: Making Law and History in the Trials of the Holocaust.* New Haven: Yale University Press, 2001.

Dower, Nigel. *An Introduction to Global Citizenship.* Edinburgh: Edinburgh University Press, 2003.

Drakulić, Slavenka. *They Would Never Hurt a Fly: War Criminals on Trial in The Hague.* New York: Penguin, 2004.

Drèze, Jean, and Amartya K. Sen. *Hunger and Public Action.* 1989. Reprinted in *The Amartya Sen and Jean Drèèze Omnibus,* 1–373. New York: Oxford University Press, 1999.

Drydyk, Jay. "Unequal Benefits: The Ethics of Development-Induced Displacement." *Georgetown Journal of International Affairs* 8, no. 1 (2007): 105–13.

Dummett, Michael. *On Immigration and Refugees.* New York: Routledge, 2001.

Ehrlich, Thomas, ed. *Civic Responsibility and Higher Education.* Phoenix: American Council on Education, Oryx Press, 2000.

Elster, Jon. *Closing the Books: Transitional Justice in Historical Perspective.* New York: Cambridge University Press, 2004.

Enough Project. http://enoughproject.org/.

Eriksson, Joakim, Niclas Finne, and Sverker Janson. "Evolution of a Supply Chain Management Game for the Trading Agent Competition." *AI Communications* 19, no. 1 (2006): 1–12.

Esquith, Stephen L. "Corporate Responsibility for Reparations." *Global Virtue Ethics Review* 4, no. 2 (2003): 129–50.

———. "An Experiment in Democratic Political Education." *Polity* 36, no. 1 (2003): 73–90.

———. *Intimacy and Spectacle: Liberal Theory as Political Education.* Ithaca: Cornell University Press, 1994.

———. "Reenacting Mass Violence." *Polity* 35, no. 4 (2003): 513–34.

———. "Toward a Democratic Rule of Law: East and West." *Political Theory* 27, no. 3 (1999): 334–56.

———. "War, Political Violence, and Service-Learning." *Teaching Philosophy* 23, no. 3 (2000): 241–54.

Esquith, Stephen L., and Fred Gifford, eds. *Capabilities, Power, and Institutions: Toward a More Critical Development Ethics.* University Park: Pennsylvania State University Press, 2010.

Evans, Gareth. *The Responsibility to Protect: Ending Mass Atrocity Crimes Once and for All.* Washington, D.C.: Brookings Institution Press, 2008.

Facing History and Ourselves: Helping Classrooms and Communities Worldwide Link the Past to Moral Choices Today. Brookline, Mass. http://www.facinghistory.org/.

Farr, James. "Hume, Hermeneutics, and History: A Sympathetic Account." *History and Theory* 17, no. 3 (1978): 285–310.

Fears, Darryl. "House Issues an Apology for Slavery." *Washington Post,* July 30, 2008.

Feinberg, Joel. "Collective Responsibility." *Journal of Philosophy* 65, no. 21 (1968): 674–88.

———. *Doing and Deserving.* Princeton: Princeton University Press, 1970.

Fesmire, Steven. *John Dewey and Moral Imagination: Pragmatism in Ethics.* Bloomington: Indiana University Press, 2003.

Filipovic, Zlata. *Zlata's Diary: A Child's Life in Sarajevo.* Translated by Christina Pribichevich-Zoric. New York: Penguin, 1994.

Fishkin. James S. *Deliberative Polling®®: Toward a Better-Informed Democracy.* Stanford, Calif.: Center for Deliberative Democracy, Stanford University, 2002. http://cdd.stanford.edu/polls/docs/summary/.

Fogel, William, and Stanley L. Engerman. *Time on the Cross: The Economics of American Negro Slavery.* Boston: Little, Brown, 1974.

Food Force. United Nations World Food Programme. http://www.food-force.com/.

Forché, Carolyn. *The Country Between Us.* New York: Harper and Row, 1981.

———. "Sensibility and Responsibility." In *The Writer and Human Rights,* edited by the Toronto Arts Group for Human Rights, 23–25. Garden City, N.Y.: Anchor, 1983.

Foster, John Bellamy. *Marx's Ecology: Materialism and Nature.* New York: Monthly Review Press, 2000.

French, Howard W. *A Continent for the Taking: The Tragedy and Hope of Africa.* New York: Vintage Books, 2005.

French, Peter A. *Collective and Corporate Responsibility.* New York: Columbia University Press, 1984.

———, ed. *Individual and Collective Responsibility: The My Lai Massacre.* Cambridge, Mass.: Schenkman, 1972.

———. *Responsibility Matters.* Lawrence: University Press of Kansas, 1992.

Frey, Bruno S. "Flexible Citizenship for a Global Society." *Politics, Philosophy, and Economics* 2, no. 1 (2003): 93–114.

Frohardt, Mark. "Justice After Genocide: Rwanda." Speech delivered at U.S. Holocaust Memorial Museum, Washington, D.C., January 29, 2002. http://www.ushmm.org/genocide/analysis/details.php?content=2002-01-29.

Galbraith, John Kenneth. *The Affluent Society.* 1958. Reprint, New York: Houghton Mifflin, 1998.

Galtung, Johan. "Violence, Peace, and Peace Research." *Journal of Peace Research* 6, no. 3 (1969): 167–91.

Gellately, Robert, and Ben Kiernan, eds. *The Specter of Genocide: Mass Murder in Historical Perspective.* New York: Cambridge University Press, 2003.

Geras, Norman. *The Contract of Mutual Indifference: Political Philosophy After the Holocaust.* New York: Verso, 1998.

Gettleman, Jeffrey. "Rape Epidemic Raises Trauma of Congo." *New York Times,* October 7, 2007.

———. "Touring a Camp's Circles of Loss." *New York Times,* November 5, 2006.

Gilbert, Margaret. *A Theory of Political Obligation: Membership, Commitment, and the Bonds of Society.* New York: Oxford University Press, 2006.

Global Partnership for the Prevention of Armed Conflict. "Genocide on Trial: Arusha Video Project." http://www.gppac.net/documents/Media_book_nieuw /p2_11_rwanda.htm.

Goldman, Alvin I. *Simulating Minds: The Philosophy, Psychology, and Neuroscience of Mindreading.* New York: Oxford University Press, 2006.

Goodin, Robert E. *Motivating Political Morality.* Cambridge, Mass.: Blackwell, 1992.

Gourevitch, Philip. "The Life After: Fifteen Years After the Genocide in Rwanda, the Reconciliation Defies Expectations." *New Yorker*, May 4, 2009, 36–49.

Gourevitch, Philip, and Errol Morris. *Standard Operating Procedure.* New York: Penguin, 2008.

———. Video recording from *New Yorker* 2007 Film Festival. http://www.newyorker .com/online/video/festival/2007/MorrisGourevitch.

Graham, Gordon. *The Internet: A Philosophical Inquiry.* New York: Routledge, 1999.

Gray, J. Glenn. *The Warriors: Reflections on Men in Battle.* 1959. Reprint, New York: Harper and Row, 1970.

Green, Michael. "Institutional Responsibility for Moral Problems." In *Global Responsibilities: Who Must Deliver on Human Rights?* edited by Andrew Kuper, 117–34. New York: Routledge, 2005.

Grey, Stephen. *Ghost Plane: The True Story of the CIA Torture Program.* New York: St. Martin's Press, 2006.

Gruwell, Erin. *The Freedom Writers Diary.* New York: Main Street Books, 1999.

GuelphQuest Online. City of Guelph, Ontario. http://guelph.ca/living.cfm?SubCatId =1615&smocid=2193.

Guibert, Emmanuel, Didier Lefèèvre, and Frédéric Lemercier. *The Photographer.* Translated by Alexis Siegel. New York: First Second, 2006.

Gungwu, Wang, ed. *Global History and Migrations.* Boulder, Colo.: Westview, 1997.

Gutman, Roy. *A Witness to Genocide.* New York: Macmillan, 1993.

Hall, Edith. "Tony Harrison's *Prometheus*: A View from the Left." Review of *Prometheus,* by Tony Harrison. *Arion,* 3rd ser., 10, no. 1 (2002): 129–40.

Hallie, Philip. *Lest Innocent Blood Be Shed.* New York: Harper Colophon, 1980.

———. *The Paradox of Cruelty.* Middleton: Wesleyan University Press, 1969.

Hamington, Maurice. *Embodied Care: Jane Addams, Maurice Merleau-Ponty, and Feminist Ethics.* Urbana: University of Illinois Press, 2004.

Hamington, Maurice, and Dorothy C. Miller, eds. *Socializing Care: Feminist Ethics and Public Issues.* Lanham, Md.: Rowman and Littlefield, 2006.

Handspring Puppet Company. Cape Town, South Africa. http://www.handspringpuppet .co.za/.

Harris, John. *Violence and Responsibility.* London: Routledge and Kegan Paul, 1980.

Harrison, Tony. *Prometheus.* London: Faber and Faber, 1998.

Hauser, Marc. *Moral Minds: The Unconscious Voice of Right and Wrong.* New York: HarperCollins, 2007.

Hayles, N. Katherine. "The Condition of Virtuality." In *The Digital Dialectic: New Essays on New Media,* edited by Peter Lunenfeld, 68–95. Cambridge, Mass.: MIT Press, 1999.

Hayward, Clarissa Rile. "Binding Problems, Boundary Problems: The Trouble with 'Democratic Citizenship.'" In *Identities, Affiliations, and Allegiances,* edited by Seyla Benhabib, Ian Shapiro, and Danilo Petranoviç_, 181–205. New York: Cambridge University Press, 2007.

Held, Virginia. *The Ethics of Care: Personal, Political, and Global.* New York: Oxford University Press, 2006.

———. "Group Responsibility for Ethnic Violence." *Journal of Ethics* 6, no. 2 (2002): 157–78.

Herman, Barbara. *Moral Literacy.* Cambridge: Harvard University Press, 2007.

Hersh, Seymour M. *Chain of Command: The Road from 9/11 to Abu Ghraib.* New York: HarperCollins, 2004.

Hoffman, Martin L. *Empathy and Moral Development: Implications for Caring and Justice.* New York: Cambridge University Press, 2000.

Holzgrefe, J. L., and Robert O. Keohane, eds. *Humanitarian Intervention: Ethical, Legal, and Political Dilemmas.* New York: Cambridge University Press, 2003.

Horton, Myles. *The Long Haul: An Autobiography.* New York: Teachers College Press, 1998.

Horwitz, Tony. *Confederates in the Attic: Dispatches from the Unfinished Civil War.* New York: Pantheon, 1998.

Howard, Julie. "Partnership to Cut Hunger and Poverty in Africa." Speech delivered at United Nations Economic and Social Council Special Event on Food Crisis in Africa, New York, October 27, 2005. http://www.un.org/docs/ecosoc/meetings/2005/docs/Howard%20Speech-%20Food%20Crises-%2027%20October%202005.pdf.

Howard-Hassmann, Rhoda. "Genocide and State-Induced Famine: Global Ethics and Western Responsibility for Mass Atrocities in Africa." *Perspectives on Global Development and Technology* 4, nos. 3–5 (2005): 487–516.

Human Security Report Project. *Human Security Brief, 2006.* Vancouver: Human Security Centre, University of British Columbia. http://www.humansecuritybrief.info/2006/index.html.

"Hurricane Pam Exercise Concludes." FEMA news release, July 23, 2004. http://www.fema.gov/news/newsrelease.fema?id=13051.

International Comparison Program. *Global Purchasing Power Parities and Real Expenditures.* Washington, D.C.: International Bank for Reconstruction and Development, 2008.

Isaacson, Judith Magyar. *Seed of Sarah: Memoirs of a Survivor.* 2nd ed. Urbana: University of Illinois Press, 1991.

Jaar, Alfredo. http://www.alfredojaar.net/.

Jackson, William A. "Capabilities, Culture, and Social Structure." *Review of Social Economy* 63, no. 1 (2005): 101–24.

Jaspers, Karl. *The Question of German Guilt.* Translated by E. B. Ashton. 1947. Reprint, New York: Fordham University Press, 2000.

Jefferson, Thomas, to Samuel Kercheval. Letter, July 12, 1816. In *The Portable Jefferson,* edited by Merrill D. Peterson, 560. New York: Penguin, 1979.

Jewish Museum Berlin. Libeskind Building, "Between the Lines." http://www.juedisches-museum-berlin.de/site/EN/05-About-The-Museum/03-Libeskind-Building/01-Groundplan/groundplan.php.

Jones, David H. *Moral Responsibility in the Holocaust: A Study in the Ethics of Character.* Lanham, Md.: Rowman and Littlefield, 1999.

"JPMorgan Chase Slavery Apology to Be Challenged at Company's Annual Meeting." National Legal and Policy Center press release, May 14, 2007. http://www .prnewswire.com/news-releases/jpmorgan-chase-slavery-apology-to-be-challenged-at-companys-annual-meeting-nlpc-shareholder-proposal-says-bank-opens-itself-to-slave-reparations-liability-58124352.html.

Jul-Larsen, Eyolf, Bréhima Kassibo, Siri Lange, and Ingrid Samset. *Socio-economic Effects of Gold Mining in Mali: A Study of the Sadiola and Morila Mining Operations.* Bergen, Norway: Chr. Michelsen Institute, 2006. http://www.cmi.no/publications/file/2340-socio-economic-effects-of-gold-mining-in-mali.pdf.

Karakotios, Ken, and Michael Bremmer. *SimLife: The Official Strategy Guide.* Roseville, Calif.: Prima, 2003.

Kari, Nan, and Nan Skelton, eds. *Voices of Hope: The Story of the Jane Addams School for Democracy.* Dayton, Ohio: Kettering Foundation Press, 2007.

Katz, Robert L. *Empathy: Its Nature and Uses.* New York: Free Press of Glencoe, 1963.

Kentridge, William. "The Crocodile's Mouth." In *William Kentridge,* ed. Dan Cameron, Carolyn Christov-Bakargiev, and J. M. Coetzee, 132–39. New York: Phaidon, 1999.

Keohane, Robert O. "Global Governance and Democratic Accountability." In *Taming Globalization: Frontiers of Governance,* edited by David Held and Mathias Koenig-Archibugi, 130–59. Oxford: Polity, 2003.

Kertész, Imre. *Fateless.* Translated by Christopher C. Wilson and Katharina M. Wilson. Evanston: Northwestern University Press, 1992.

Kidder, Tracy. *Mountains Beyond Mountains: The Quest of Dr. Paul Farmer, a Man Who Would Cure the World.* New York: Random House, 2003.

———. *Strength in What Remains.* New York: Random House, 2009.

Kiernan, Ben. *Blood and Soil: A World History of Genocide and Extermination from Sparta to Darfur.* New Haven: Yale University Press, 2007.

Kingsolver, Barbara. *High Tide in Tucson: Essays from Now and Never.* New York: Harper Perennial, 1996.

Kisselgoff, Anna. "Promethean Light Illuminates Hope." Review of *Promethean Fire,* by Paul Taylor Dance Company, New York. *New York Times,* June 10, 2002.

Klosko, George. *Political Obligations.* New York: Oxford University Press, 2005.

Kögler, Hans Herbert, and Karsten R. Stueber, eds. *Empathy and Agency: The Problem of Understanding in the Human Sciences.* Boulder, Colo.: Westview, 2000.

Kołakowski, Leszek. *Main Currents of Marxism.* New York: Oxford University Press, 1978.

Korsgaard, Christine M. "The Reasons We Can Share: An Attack on the Distinction Between Agent-Relative and Agent-Neutral Values." In *Creating the Kingdom of Ends.* New York: Cambridge University Press, 1996.

Kreamer, Christine Mullen, Mary Nooter Roberts, Elizabeth Harney, and Allyson Purpura, eds. *Inscribing Meaning: Writing and Graphic Systems in African Art.* Washington, D.C.: Smithsonian, National Museum of African Art, 2007.

Kristof, Nicholas D. "What to Do About Darfur." *New York Review of Books,* July 2, 2009, http://www.nybooks.com/articles/22771.

Krog, Antjie. *Country of My Skull: Guilt, Sorrow, and the Limits of Forgiveness in the New South Africa.* New York: Times Books, 1999.

Kurzweil Technologies Inc. "A Brief Career Summary of Ray Kurzweil." http://www.kurzweiltech.com/aboutray.html.

Kutz, Christopher. *Complicity: Ethics and Law for a Collective Age.* New York: Cambridge University Press, 2000.

Kymlicka, Will. *Multicultural Citizenship: A Liberal Theory of Minority Rights.* New York: Oxford University Press, 1996.

Ladd, John. "Corporate Mythology and Individual Responsibility." *International Journal of Applied Philosophy* 2, no. 1 (1984): 1–21.

———. "Morality and the Ideal of Rationality in Formal Organizations." *Monist* 54, no. 4 (1970): 488–516.

LaFollette, Hugh, and Larry May. "Suffer the Little Children." In *World Hunger and Morality,* edited by William Aiken and Hugh LaFollette, 70–84. Upper Saddle River, N.J.: Prentice Hall, 1996.

LaFraniere, Sharon. "Africa's World of Forced Labor in a 6-Year-Old's Eyes." *New York Times,* October 29, 2006.

Lassiter, Matthew D. *The Silent Majority: Suburban Politics in the Sunbelt South.* Princeton: Princeton University Press, 2006.

Lavin, Chad. *The Politics of Responsibility.* Urbana: University of Illinois Press, 2008.

Lester, Gideon. "Balm of Ancient Words." *ARTicles* 1, no. 2 (2002). http://www.american repertorytheater.org/inside/articles/articles-vol-1-i2-balm-ancient-words.

"Letters." *New York Times,* October 31, 2006.

Levi, Primo. *The Drowned and the Saved.* Translated by Raymond Rosenthal. 1988. Reprint, New York: Vintage, 1989.

———. "If This Is a Man." In *Survival in Auschwitz,* translated by Stuart Woolf, 11. 1958. Reprint, New York: Touchstone, 1996.

Longo, Nicholas V. *Why Community Matters: Connecting Education with Civic Life.* Albany: State University of New York Press, 2007.

Lost Children. Directed by Ali Samadi Ahadi and Oliver Stoltz. Dreamer Joint Venture, 2006. http://www.lost-children.de/en/home.htm.

Lyons, David. "Corrective Justice, Equal Opportunity, and the Legacy of Slavery and Jim Crow." *Boston University Law Review* 84 (December 2004): 1375–1404.

Macedo, Stephen, and Iris Marion Young, eds. *Moral and Political Education.* Nomos 43. New York: New York University Press, 2001.

MacLean, Ian, Alan Montefiore, and Peter Winch, eds. *The Political Responsibility of Intellectuals.* New York: Cambridge University Press, 1990.

Mamdani, Mahmood. *Saviors and Survivors: Darfur, Politics, and the War on Terror.* New York: Pantheon Books, 2009.

Mancini, Matthew J. *One Dies, Get Another: Convict Leasing in the American South, 1866-1928.* Columbia: University of South Carolina Press, 1996.

Mann, Michael. *The Dark Side of Democracy: Explaining Ethnic Cleansing.* New York: Cambridge University Press, 2005.

Marshall, Thomas H. *Class, Citizenship, and Social Development.* New York: Doubleday, 1965.

Mattson, Kevin. *Creating a Democratic Public: The Struggle for Urban Participatory Democracy During the Progressive Era.* University Park: Pennsylvania State University Press, 1998.

May, Larry. *The Morality of Groups: Collective Responsibility, Group-Based Harm, and Corporate Rights.* Notre Dame: University of Notre Dame Press, 1987.

———. *Sharing Responsibility.* Chicago: University of Chicago Press, 1992.

McCarthy, Thomas A. "Coming to Terms with the Past, Part II: On the Morality and Politics of Reparations for Slavery." *Political Theory* 32, no. 6 (2004): 750–72.

———. "Vergangenheitsbewäaltigung in the USA: On the Politics of the Memory of Slavery." *Political Theory* 30, no. 5 (2002): 623–48.

Médecins Sans Frontièères/Doctors Without Borders. *A Refugee Camp in the Heart of the City.* http://www.refugeecamp.org/home/.

Mercer, Philip. *Sympathy and Ethics: A Study of the Relationship Between Sympathy and Morality with Special Reference to Hume's Treatise.* Oxford: Clarendon, 1972.

Merwin, W. S. "Ogres." In *Poets Against the War,* edited by Sam Hamill with Sally Anderson and others, 137–38. New York: Thunder's Mouth Press/Nation Books, 2003.

Michnik, Adam. *The Church and the Left.* Translated by David Ost. Chicago: University of Chicago Press, 1993.

———. "Communism, the Church, and Witches: An Interview with Leszek Kołakowski." Originally published in *Gazeta Wyborcza,* November 21–22, 1992; translated by Marek Wilczynski in *Centennial Review* 37, no. 2 (1993): 13–38.

———. *Letters from Freedom: Post–Cold War Realities and Perspectives.* Translated by Jane Cave. Berkeley and Los Angeles: University of California Press, 1998.

———. *Letters from Prison, and Other Essays.* Translated by Maya Latynski. Berkeley and Los Angeles: University of California Press, 1985.

Michnik, Adam, and Vaclav Havel. "Confronting the Past: Justice or Revenge." *Journal of Democracy* 4, no. 1 (1993); reprinted in *Transitional Justice,* edited by Neil J. Kritz, 2:539–40. Washington, D.C.: U.S. Institute of Peace, 1995.

Miller, David. "Immigrants, Nations, and Citizenship," *Journal of Political Philosophy* 16, no. 4 (2008): 371–90.

———. *National Responsibility and Global Justice.* New York: Oxford University Press, 2007.

Miller, Judith. "Taking Two Bosnian Women's Case to the World." *New York Times,* February 23, 1997.

Miller, Richard W. *Globalizing Justice: The Ethics of Poverty and Power.* New York: Oxford University Press, 2010.

———. "Global Power and Economic Justice." In *Global Basic Rights,* edited by Charles R. Beitz and Robert E. Goodin, 156–80. New York: Oxford University Press, 2009.

———. "Moral Closeness and World Community." In *The Ethics of Assistance: Morality and the Distant Needy,* edited by Deen K. Chatterjee, 101–22. New York: Cambridge University Press, 2004.

Miłosz, Czesław. "A Poor Christian Looks at the Ghetto." In *The Collected Poems, 1931–1987.* New York: Ecco, 1988.

Minuteman Civil Defense Corp. "Chris Simcox Under Attack at Universities." MinutemanHQ.com, April 13, 2007. http://www.minutemanhq.com/hq/article.php?sid =253.

Mitchell, Katharyne. "Education for Democratic Citizenship: Transnationalism, Multiculturalism, and the Limits of Liberalism." *Harvard Educational Review* 71, no. 1 (2001): 51–78.

Morrison, Karl F. *"I Am You": The Hermeneutics of Empathy in Western Literature, Theology, and Art.* Princeton: Princeton University Press, 1988.

Morton, Christopher. Review of *Sahel: The End of the Road,* by Sebastião Salgado. *Anthropological Quarterly* 79, no. 1 (2006): 175–78.

Moseley, William G., and Leslie C. Gray, eds. *Hanging by a Thread: Cotton, Globalization, and Poverty in Africa.* Athens: Ohio University Press, 2008.

Mulisch, Harry. *The Assault.* Translated by Claire Nicholas White. New York: Pantheon, 1985.

———. *Criminal Case, 40/61, the Trial of Adolf Eichmann: An Eyewitness Account.* Translated by Robert Naborn, foreword by Debórah Dwork. Philadelphia: University of Pennsylvania Press, 2005.

Murphy, Liam B. *Moral Demands in Nonideal Theory.* New York: Oxford University Press, 2000.

My Neighbor, My Killer. Directed by Anne Aghion. Gacaca Productions, 2009. http://www.anneaghionfilms.com/.

Neill, Alex. "Empathy and (Film) Fiction." In *Post-theory: Reconstructing Film Studies,* edited by David Bordwell and Noëël Carroll, 179–80. Madison: University of Wisconsin Press, 1996.

Nesteruk, Jeffrey, and David T. Risser. "Conceptions of the Corporation and Ethical Decision Making in Business." *Business and Professional Ethics Journal* 12, no. 1 (1993): 73–90.

"Niger Leader Denies Hunger Claims." BBC News, August 9, 2005. http://news.bbc.co .uk/2/hi/africa/4133374.stm.

Nobles, Melissa. *The Politics of Official Apologies*. New York: Cambridge University Press, 2008.

Nuland, Sherwin B. *How We Die: Reflections on Life's Final Chapter*. New York: Vintage Books, 1993.

Nunca Más: The Report of the Argentine National Commission on the Disappeared. New York: Farrar, Straus and Giroux, 1986.

Nussbaum, Martha C. *Frontiers of Justice: Disability, Nationality, Species Membership*. Cambridge, Mass.: Belknap Press, 2006.

———. *Poetic Justice: The Literary Imagination and Public Life*. Boston: Beacon, 1995.

———. *Upheavals of Thought: The Intelligence of Emotions*. New York: Cambridge University Press, 2001.

———. *Women and Human Development: The Capabilities Approach*. New York: Cambridge University Press, 2000.

Nye, David E. *America as Second Creation: Technology and the Narratives of New Beginnings*. Cambridge, Mass.: MIT Press, 2003.

Oakeshott, Michael. "Education: The Engagement and Its Frustration." In *The Voice of Liberal Learning*, edited by Timothy Fuller, 54–55. New Haven: Yale University Press, 1989.

———. "The Voice of Poetry in the Conversation of Mankind." In *Rationalism in Politics, and Other Essays*, 197–247. London and New York: Methuen, 1962.

O'Byrne, Darren. "Citizenship." In *Cultural Geography: A Critical Dictionary of Concepts*, edited by David Atkinson, Peter Jackson, David Sibley, and Neil Washbourne. New York: I. B. Tauris, 2005.

O'Connor, Peg. *Oppression and Responsibility: A Wittgensteinian Approach to Social Practices and Moral Theory*. University Park: Pennsylvania State University Press, 2002.

Ó Gráda, Cormac. *Famine: A Short History*. Princeton: Princeton University Press, 2009.

O'Neill, Onora. "The Dark Side of Human Rights." *International Affairs* 81, no. 2 (2005): 427–39.

———. "Distant Strangers and Future Generations." In *Self and Future Generations: An Intercultural Conversation*, edited by Tae-Chang Kim and Ross Harrison, 62–69. Cambridge, UK: White Horse, 1999.

———. "Ending World Hunger." In *Matters of Life and Death*, edited by T. Regan, 264. 3rd ed. New York: McGraw-Hill, 1993.

———. "Global Justice: Whose Obligations?" In *The Ethics of Assistance: Morality and the Distant Needy*, edited by Deen K. Chatterjee, 242–59. New York: Cambridge University Press, 2004.

———. *Towards Justice and Virtue: A Constructive Account of Practical Reason*. New York: Cambridge University Press, 1996.

Ong, Aihwa. *Buddha Is Hiding: Refugees, Citizenship, the New America*. Berkeley and Los Angeles: University of California Press, 2003.

———. *Flexible Citizenship: The Cultural Logics of Transnationality*. Durham: Duke University Press, 1999.

———. "(Re)articulations of Citizenship." *PS: Political Science and Politics* 38, no. 4 (2005): 697–99.

Oren, Laura E. "Righting Child Custody Wrongs: The Children of the 'Disappeared' in Argentina." *Harvard Human Rights Journal* 14 (Spring 2001): 123–200.

Orsenna, Erik. *Voyage aux pays du coton: Petit précis de mondialisation.* Paris: Fayard, 2006.

Paine, Thomas. *Collected Writings.* Edited by Eric Foner. New York: Library of America, 1995.

Palmer, Parker J. *The Courage to Teach: Exploring the Inner Landscape of a Teacher's Life.* San Francisco: Jossey-Bass, 1998.

Phillips, Michael J. "Reappraising the Real Entity Theory of the Corporation." *Florida State University Law Review* 21, no. 4 (1994): 1061–1123.

"Photovoice: Social Change Through Photography." Institute for Photographic Empowerment, June 19, 2008. http://joinipe.org/welcome/archives/405.

Pieterse, Jan Nederveen. *Globalization or Empire?* New York: Routledge, 2004.

Planet Green Game. Starbucks Coffee Company and Global Green USA. http://www.planetgreengame.com/.

Plantinga, Carl. "Notes on Spectator Emotion and Ideological Film Criticism." In *Film Theory and Philosophy,* edited by Richard Allen and Murray Smith, 372–93. New York: Oxford University Press, 2003.

———. "The Scene of Empathy and the Human Face." In *Passionate Views: Film, Cognition, and Emotion,* edited by Carl Plantinga and Greg M. Smith, 239–55. Baltimore: Johns Hopkins University Press, 1999.

Pogge, Thomas. "'Assisting' the Global Poor." In *The Ethics of Assistance: Morality and the Distant Needy,* edited by Deen K. Chatterjee, 260–88. New York: Cambridge University Press, 2004.

———, ed. *Freedom from Poverty as a Human Right: Who Owes What to the Very Poor?* New York: Oxford University Press, 2002.

———. *World Poverty and Human Rights.* Cambridge, Mass.: Polity, 2002.

"Poles Start Receiving Payments for Slave Labor Under Nazis." *New York Times,* June 29, 2001.

Polgreen, Lydia. "Africa's Storied Colleges, Jammed and Crumbling." *New York Times,* May 20, 2007.

Poulton, Robin-Edward, and Ibrahim ag Youssouf. *A Peace of Timbuktu: Democratic Governance, Development, and African Peacemaking.* New York: United Nations, 1998.

Power, Samantha. *"A Problem from Hell": America and the Age of Genocide.* New York: Basic Books, 2002.

Presidential Advisory Commission on Holocaust Assets in the United States. *Plunder and Restitution.* Washington, D.C.: Presidential Advisory Commission on Holocaust Assets in the United States, 2000. http://www.pcha.gov/.

Presner, Todd Samuel. "What a Synoptic and Artificial View Reveals: Extreme History and the Modernism of W. G. Sebald's Realism." *Criticism* 46, no. 3 (2004): 341–60.

Promethean Fire. Paul Taylor Dance Company, video recording of Public Broadcasting Company broadcast. YouTube: part 1, http://www.youtube.com/watch?v=-6xLdZmOBM; part 2, http://www.youtube.com/watch?v=ChUWgScmb2A.

Prunier, Gérard. *Africa's World War: Congo, the Rwandan Genocide, and the Making of a Continental Catastrophe.* New York: Oxford University Press, 2009.

Quaid, Jennifer A. "The Assessment of Corporate Criminal Liability on the Basis of Corporate Identity: An Analysis." *McGill Law Journal* 43, no. 1 (1998): 67–114.

Raczymow, Henri. *Writing the Book of Esther: A Novel.* Translated by Dori Katz. New York: Holmes and Meier, 1995.

Reader, Soran. "Does a Basic Needs Approach Need Capabilities?" *Journal of Political Philosophy* 14, no. 3 (2006): 337–50.

Reich, Rob. *Bridging Liberalism and Multiculturalism in American Education.* Chicago: University of Chicago Press, 2002.

Rettig, Max. "Gacaca: Truth, Justice, and Reconciliation in Postconflict Rwanda?" *African Studies Review* 51, no. 3 (2008): 25–50.

Rivoli, Pietra. *The Travels of a T-Shirt in the Global Economy: An Economist Examines the Markets, Power, and Politics of World Trade*. Hoboken, N.J.: John Wiley, 2005.

Robben, Antonius C. G. M., and Marcelo M. Suarez-Orozco, eds. *Cultures Under Siege: Collective Violence and Trauma*. New York: Cambridge University Press, 2000.

Roberts, Richard L. *Two Worlds of Cotton: Colonialism and the Regional Economy in the French Soudan, 1800–1946*. Stanford: Stanford University Press, 1996.

Robinson, Fiona. *Globalizing Care: Ethics, Feminist Theory, and International Relations*. Boulder, Colo.: Westview, 1999.

———. "Human Rights and the Global Politics of Resistance: Feminist Perspectives." *Review of International Studies* 29 (December 2003): 161–80.

———. "NGOs and the Advancement of Economic and Social Rights: Philosophical and Practical Controversies." *International Relations* 17, no. 1 (2003): 79–96.

Rollin, Bernard E. *The Frankenstein Syndrome: Ethical and Social Issues in the Genetic Engineering of Animals*. New York: Cambridge University Press, 1995.

Rovane, Carol. *The Bounds of Agency: An Essay in Revisionary Metaphysics*. Princeton: Princeton University Press, 1998.

Rovine, Victoria L. *Bogolan: Shaping Culture Through Cloth in Contemporary Mali*. Washington, D.C.: Smithsonian Institution Press, 2001.

Rubenstein, Jennifer. "Distribution and Emergency." *Journal of Political Philosophy* 15, no. 3 (2007): 296–320.

Ruskin, John. *Modern Painters*. Vol. 2. 1846. Reprinted in *Selections from the Writings of John Ruskin*. N.p.: Obscure Press, 2007.

Sachs, Jeffrey D. *The End of Poverty: Economic Possibilities for Our Time*. New York: Penguin, 2005.

———. "The Millennium Village Project: A New Approach to Ending Poverty." Transcript of speech delivered at Center for Global Development. Washington, D.C., March 14, 2006.

Salgado, Sebastião. "Migrations: Humanity in Transition." *Photo District News*/Kodak "Legends" site featuring Salgado "Migrations" project. http://www.pdngallery.com /legends/legends10/.

Sanchez, Pedro, and others. "The African Millennium Villages." *PNAS* 104, no. 43 (2007): 16775–80.

Sanders, Mark. *Complicities: The Intellectual and Apartheid*. Durham: Duke University Press, 2002.

Saramago, José. *The Cave*. Translated by Margaret Jull Costa. New York: Harcourt, 2002.

Scanlon, T. M. "Symposium on Amartya Sen's Philosophy: 3 Sen and Consequentialism." *Economics and Philosophy* 17, no. 1 (2001): 39–50.

Schechner, Richard. *Performance Theory*. New York: Routledge, 1988.

Schlesinger, Philip. "W. G. Sebald and the Condition of Exile." *Theory, Culture, and Society* 21, no. 2 (2004): 43–67.

Schutte, Ofelia. "Dependency Work, Women, and the Global Economy." In *The Subject of Care: Feminist Perspectives on Dependency*, edited by Eva Feder Kittay and Ellen K. Feder, 138–58. Lanham, Md.: Rowman and Littlefield, 2002.

Schwarz, Daniel R. *Imagining the Holocaust*. New York: St. Martin's Press, 1999.

Sebald, W. G. *Austerlitz*. Translated by Anthea Bell. New York: Random House, 2001.

———. *The Emigrants.* Translated by Michael Hulse. New York: New Directions Books, 1996.

———. "The Last Word: Interview with Maya Jaggi." *Guardian,* December 21, 2001.

———. *On the Natural History of Destruction.* Translated by Anthea Bell. New York: Random House, 2003.

———. "Recovered Memories: Interview with Maya Jaggi." *Guardian,* September 22, 2001.

Segal, Lore. *Other People's Houses: A Novel.* 1964. Reprint, New York: The New Press, 1994.

Sells, Michael A. *The Bridge Betrayed: Religion and Genocide in Bosnia.* Berkeley and Los Angeles: University of California Press, 1998.

Sen, Amartya. "Consequential Evaluation and Practical Reason." *Journal of Philosophy* 97, no. 9 (2000): 477–502.

———. *Development as Freedom.* New York: Knopf, 1999.

———. "Elements of a Theory of Human Rights." *Philosophy and Public Affairs* 32, no. 4 (2004): 316–56.

———. *Poverty and Famines: An Essay on Poverty and Deprivation.* 1981. Reprinted in *The Amartya Sen and Jean Drèèze Omnibus,* 1–257. New York: Oxford University Press, 1999.

———. "Symposium on Amartya Sen's Philosophy: 4 Reply." *Economics and Philosophy* 17, no. 1 (2001): 51–66.

Sevenhuijsen, Selma. *Citizenship and the Ethics of Care: Feminist Considerations on Justice, Morality, and Politics.* New York: Routledge, 1998.

Sewall, Sarah. "Do the Right Thing: A Genocide Policy That Works." *Boston Review* 34, no. 5, (2009): 33–35.

Shapiro, Ian. *Political Criticism.* Berkeley and Los Angeles: University of California Press, 1990.

Shei, Ser-Min. "World Poverty and Moral Responsibility." In *Real World Justice: Grounds, Principles, Human Rights, and Social Institutions,* edited by Andreas Follesdal and Thomas Pogge, 139–56. Dordrecht, The Netherlands: Springer, 2005.

Shewey, Don. "Peter Sellars's CNN Euripides." *Village Voice,* January 23, 2003.

Shoah. Directed by Claude Lanzmann. New Yorker Films, 1985.

Shorris, Earl. *Riches for the Poor: The Clemente Course in the Humanities.* New York: Norton, 2000.

Shue, Henry. *Basic Rights: Subsistence, Affluence, and U.S. Foreign Policy.* 2nd ed. Princeton: Princeton University Press, 1980.

———. "Mediating Duties." *Ethics* 98, no. 4 (1988): 687–704.

Sidikou, Aïssata G. *Recreating Words, Reshaping Worlds: The Verbal Art of Women from Niger, Mali, and Senegal.* Trenton, N.J.: African World Press, 2001.

Simmons, A. John. *Justification and Legitimacy: Essays on Rights and Obligations.* New York: Cambridge University Press, 2001.

Singer, Peter. "Famine, Affluence, and Morality." *Philosophy and Public Affairs* 1, no. 1 (1972): 229–43.

———. *The Life You Can Save: Acting Now to End World Poverty.* New York: Random House, 2009.

Sliwinski, Sharon. "Camera War, Again." *Journal of Visual Culture* 5, no. 1 (2006): 89–93.

Slote, Michael. *The Ethics of Care and Empathy.* New York: Routledge, 2007.

Slovic, Paul. "'If I look at the mass I will never act': Psychic Numbing and Genocide." *Judgment and Decision Making* 2, no. 2 (2007): 1–17.

Smith, Leef. "Williamsburg Slave Auction Riles Virginia NAACP." *Washington Post,* October 8, 1994.

Smith, Murray. "The Logic and Legacy of Brechtianism." In *Post-theory: Reconstructing Film Studies,* edited by David Bordwell and Noëël Carroll, 130–48. Madison: University of Wisconsin Press, 1996.

Sontag, Susan. *Regarding the Pain of Others.* New York: Picador, 2003.

Spears, Ross, and Jude Cassidy, eds. *Agee: His Life Remembered.* With a narrative by Robert Coles. New York: Holt, Rinehart and Winston, 1985.

Spelman, Elizabeth V. *Fruits of Sorrow: Framing Our Attention to Suffering.* Boston: Beacon, 1997.

Spivak, Gayatri Chakravorty. "Can the Subaltern Speak?" In *Marxism and the Interpretation of Culture,* edited by Cary Nelson and Larry Grossberg, 271–313. Urbana: University of Illinois Press, 1988.

Staatz, John M., and Niama Nango Dembélé. "Agriculture for Development in Sub-Saharan Africa." Background paper for the *World Development Report, 2008,* World Bank, Washington, D.C. http://siteresources.worldbank.org /INTWDR2008 /Resources/2795087–1191427986785/StaatzJ&DembeleN_AgriForDevtInSSA_ve19.pdf.

Staatz, John M., Niama Nango Dembélé, Valerie Kelly, and Ramziath Adjao. "Agricultural Globalization in Reverse: The Impact of the Food Crisis in West Africa." Paper presented at the Geneva Trade and Development Forum, Crans-Monana, Switzerland, September 17–20, 2008.

Staples, Brent. "How Slavery Fueled Business in the North." Editorial, *New York Times,* July 24, 2000.

Strejilevich, Nora. "Testimony: Beyond the Language of Truth." *Human Rights Quarterly* 28, no. 3 (2006): 701–13.

Stueber, Karsten R. *Rediscovering Empathy: Agency, Folk Psychology, and the Human Sciences.* Cambridge, Mass.: MIT Press, 2006.

Suarez-Orozco, Marcelo M., ed. *Learning in the Global Era: International Perspectives on Globalization and Education.* Berkeley and Los Angeles: University of California Press, 2007.

"Symposium: The Jurisprudence of Slavery Reparations." *Boston University Law Review* 84 (April 2004): 1135–1466.

Szymborska, Wisława. "The End and the Beginning." In *View with a Grain of Sand,* translated by Stanisław Barańczak and Clare Cavanagh, 178–80. New York: Harcourt, Brace, 1995.

———. "Starvation Camp Near Jaslo." In *Poems, New and Collected, 1957–1997,* translated by Stanisław Barańczak and Clare Cavanagh, 38–39. New York: Harcourt, Brace, 1998.

Tan, Kok-Chor. "The Duty to Protect." In *Humanitarian Intervention,* edited by Terry Nardin and Melissa S. Williams, 84–116. Nomos 47. New York: New York University Press, 2006.

Taylor, Charles. "The Politics of Recognition." In *Multiculturalism,* edited by Amy Gutmann, 25–74. Exp. ed. Princeton: Princeton University Press, 1994.

Taylor, Jane. *Ubu and the Truth Commission.* Cape Town: University of Cape Town Press, 1998.

Tefft, James, Valerie Kelly, Victoria Wise, and John Staatz. "Linkages Between Child Nutrition and Agricultural Growth in Mali: A Summary of Preliminary Findings." *Policy Synthesis* 64 (April 2003). http://www.aec.msu.edu/agecon/fs2/polsyn /number64.pdf.

Teitel, Ruti G. *Transitional Justice.* New York: Oxford University Press, 2000.

Terry, Fiona. *Condemned to Repeat? The Paradox of Humanitarian Action.* Ithaca: Cornell University Press, 2002.

Thomson, Garrett. "Fundamental Needs." In *The Philosophy of Need,* edited by Soran Reader, 175–86. New York: Cambridge University Press, 2005.

Thomson, George. *Aeschylus and Athens: A Study in the Social Origins of Drama.* 1940. Reprint, New York: Haskell House, 1967.

Thurow, Roger, and Scott Kilman. *Enough: Why the World's Poorest Starve in an Age of Plenty.* New York: Public Affairs, 2009.

Tommasini, Anthony. "Making Music for Those Without a Voice." *New York Times,* January 24, 2007.

Tong, Rosemarie. "Feminist Perspectives on Empathy as an Epistemic Skill and Caring as a Moral Virtue." *Journal of Medical Humanities* 18, no. 3 (1997): 153–68.

Tooze, Adam. *The Wages of Destruction: The Making and Breaking of the Nazi Economy.* New York: Viking, 2007.

Tricycle Theatre. London. http://www.tricycle.co.uk/.

Tronto, Joan C. *Moral Boundaries: A Political Argument for an Ethic of Care.* New York: Routledge, 1993.

Turkle, Sherry. "Seeing Through Computers: Education in a Culture of Simulation." *American Prospect* 8, no. 31 (1997): 76–82.

———. "Virtuality and Its Discontents: Searching for Community in Cyberspace." *American Prospect* 7, no. 24 (1996): 50–57.

Turner, Victor. *The Anthropology of Performance.* New York: PAJ, 1986.

United Nations. *Human Development Report, 2007/2008: Fighting Climate Change: Human Solidarity in a Divided World.* New York: Palgrave Macmillan, United Nations Development Programme, 2007. http://hdr.undp.org/en/reports /global /hdr2007-2008/.

United Nations Development Programme. Women's Empowerment. http://www.undp .org/women/.

United Nations High Commissioner for Refugees. *The State of the World's Refugees: Human Displacement in the New Millennium.* New York: Oxford University Press, 2006.

United Nations Secretary-General. "Secretary-General's Report Lists Parties to Conflict Using Child Soldiers." Press Release SG/2082, HR/4635. http://www.un.org/News /Press/docs/2002/SG2082.doc.htm.

United States Senate Armed Services Committee. *Report of the U.S. Senate Armed Services Committee Inquiry into the Treatment of Detainees in U.S. Custody.* Washington, D.C.: United States Senate Armed Services Committee, 2009. http:// armed-services.senate.gov/Publications/Detainee%20Report%20Final _April%2022%202009.pdf.

University of North Carolina, Chapel Hill. "Slavery and the Making of the University." Manuscripts Department, UNC University Library, Chapel Hill, N.C. http://www.lib.unc.edu/mss/exhibits/slavery/index.html.

University Steering Committee on Slavery and Justice, Brown University, Providence, R.I. http://brown.edu/Research/Slavery_Justice/.

U.S. Congress. *Civil Liberties Act of 1988.* August 10, 1988. http://www.civics-online.org /library/formatted/texts/civilact1988.html.

U.S. Inspector General. *A Review of the FBI's Involvement in and Observations of Detainee Interrogations in Guantanamo Bay, Afghanistan, and Iraq.* Washington,

D.C.: Oversight and Review Division, Office of the Inspector General, U.S. Department of Justice, 2008. http://graphics8.nytimes.com/packages/pdf/washington/20080521_DETAIN_report.pdf.

Velasquez, Manuel. "Why Corporations Are Not Morally Responsible for Anything They Do." 1983. Reprinted in *Collective Responsibility: Five Decades of Debate in Theoretical and Applied Ethics,* edited by Larry May and Stacey Hoffman, 111–32. Savage, Md.: Rowman and Littlefield, 1991.

Vernon, Richard. "What Is Crime Against Humanity?" *Journal of Political Philosophy* 10, no. 3 (2002): 231–49.

Vollmann, William T. *Poor People.* New York: Ecco, 2007.

Wallace, John. "The Problem of Time: Enabling Students to Make Long-Term Commitments to Community-Based Learning." *Michigan Journal of Community Service-Learning* 7, no. 1 (2000): 133–41.

Walzer, Michael. *Interpretation and Social Criticism.* Cambridge: Harvard University Press, 1987.

———. *On Toleration.* New Haven: Yale University Press, 1997.

———. *Thick and Thin: Moral Argument at Home and Abroad.* Notre Dame: Notre Dame University Press, 1994.

Weidner, David. "JPMorgan Apologizes Over Slavery." MarketWatch, *Wall Street Journal* Digital Network, January 21, 2005. http://www.marketwatch.com/News/Story/Story.aspx?guid=%7BEB212AD8%2D4E10%2D4146%2D81CB%2DFE6022404198%7D&siteid=google&dist=google.

Weir, Allison. "The Global Universal Caregiver: Imagining Women's Liberation in the New Millennium." *Constellations* 12, no. 3 (2005): 308–30.

Weitz, Eric D. *A Century of Genocide: Utopias of Race and Nation.* Princeton: Princeton University Press, 2003.

Wenar, Leif. "Responsibility and Severe Poverty." In *Freedom from Poverty as a Human Right: Who Owes What to the Very Poor?* edited by Thomas Pogge, 255–74. New York: Oxford University Press, 2007.

Weschler, Lawrence. "The Velvet Purge: The Trials of Jan Kavan." *New Yorker,* October 19, 1992, 68–94.

West, Cornel. *Prophesy Deliverance! An Afro-American Revolutionary Christianity.* Louisville, Ky.: Westminster John Knox, 2002.

Westbrook, Jesyca. "JP Morgan Chase Creates 'Smart Start Louisiana.'" BlackCollege View.com, February 14, 2005. http://media.www.blackcollegeview.com/media/storage/paper928/news/2005/02/14/BusinessTechnology/Jp.Morgan.Chase.Creates.smart.Start.Louisiana-2472822.shtml.

Whipps, Judy D. "Jane Addams's Social Thought as a Model for a Pragmatist-Feminist Communitarianism." *Hypatia* 19, no. 2 (2004): 118–33.

Williams, Bernard. "A Critique of Utilitarianism." In *Utilitarianism: For and Against,* edited by J. J. C. Smart and Bernard Williams, 77–150. New York: Cambridge University Press, 1973.

———. *Shame and Necessity.* Berkeley and Los Angeles: University of California Press, 1993.

Williams, Melissa S. "Nonterritorial Boundaries of Citizenship." In *Identities, Affiliations, and Allegiances,* edited by Seyla Benhabib, Ian Shapiro, and Danilo Petranović, 226–56. New York: Cambridge University Press, 2007.

Williams, William Carlos. "Asphodel, That Greeny Flower." In *Journey to Love,* 41–87. New York: Random House, 1955.

Winter, Miriam. *Trains: A Memoir of a Hidden Childhood During and After World War II.* Jackson, Mich.: Kelton Press, 1997.

Wolin, Sheldon S. *Democracy Incorporated: Managed Democracy and the Specter of Inverted Totalitarianism.* Princeton: Princeton University Press, 2008.

———. *Politics and Vision: Continuity and Innovation in Western Political Thought.* Exp. ed. Princeton: Princeton University Press, 2004.

Wringe, Bill. "Needs, Rights, and Collective Obligations." In *The Philosophy of Need,* edited by Soran Reader, 187–207. New York: Cambridge University Press, 2005.

Young, James E. "Daniel Libeskind's Jewish Museum in Berlin: The Uncanny Arts of Memorial Architecture." *Jewish Social Studies* 6, no. 2 (2002): 1–23.

Youngs, Gillian. "Feminist International Relations: A Contradiction in Terms? Or: Why Women and Gender Are Essential to Understanding the World 'We' Live In." *International Affairs* 80, no. 1 (2004): 75–87.

INDEX

Credits